SRA Specific Skill Series
for Language Arts
Teacher's Manual

Leveled Books
in Nine Key
Language Arts Skill Areas

Grammar	Spelling	Paragraphs
Usage	Vocabulary	Writing Process
Mechanics	Sentences	Research

Columbus, OH

The **McGraw·Hill** Companies

Table of Contents

Cover: ©PhotoDisc/Getty Images, Inc.

SRAonline.com

 SRA

Copyright © 2005 by SRA/McGraw-Hill.

Send all inquiries to:
SRA/McGraw-Hill
4400 Easton Commons
Columbus, OH 43219

Printed in the United States of America.

ISBN 0-07-601746-X

7 8 9 WCE 12 11 10

A Skills Toolbox for Individualized Instruction in Writing and Language Arts

Specific Skill Series for Language Arts targets problem areas and provides intensive skills practice in these nine key language arts skill areas:

A supplement to any language arts program, this unique series gives students the opportunity to work at their own pace to reinforce their understanding and application of fundamental language arts skills—the skills they need to succeed in all other subject areas. Key features include

- **multiple-choice format** in each unit to effectively prepare students for standardized tests.
- **rule boxes** that explain language arts rules and include examples to illustrate the rules.
- exercises presented in **fact-based, real-world contexts.**
- **Language Activity Pages** (LAPs) in each book to **review, extend, and enrich skills.**
- **nonconsumable Student Editions** that make the program ideal for use in a resource room or independent study area.

Specific Skill Series for Language Arts is a companion to *Specific Skill Series,* a supplemental reading program that has been widely recognized for its effectiveness for over thirty years.

Leveled Books Meet Students' Individual Needs

The scope and sequence, complexity of skills, and readability in Levels A through H correspond to Grades 1 through 8. Students, however, may be placed in any level, depending on their individual instructional needs. *Placement Tests* help teachers place students in the correct level of each skill area.

Leveled books make ***Specific Skill Series for Language Arts*** appropriate for all ability levels—remedial, on-grade level, or enrichment.

● **Level A Starter Set (Grade 1)***

● **Level B Starter Set (Grade 2)**

● **Level C Starter Set (Grade 3)**

● **Level D Starter Set (Grade 4)**

● **Level E Starter Set (Grade 5)**

● **Level F Starter Set (Grade 6)**

● **Level G Starter Set (Grade 7)**

● **Level H Starter Set (Grade 8)**

*Each Starter Set also includes a *Teacher's Manual.*

Specific Skill Series for Language Arts
is available in the following boxed sets:

Primary Set (Levels A–D)

Grades 1-4

- 36 Student Editions
- 9 Placement Test books
- 1 Teacher's Manual

Middle Set (Levels C–F)

Grades 3-6

- 36 Student Editions
- 9 Placement Test books
- 1 Teacher's Manual

Upper Elementary Set (Levels E–H)

Grades 5-8

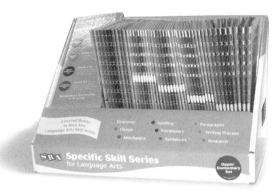

- 36 Student Editions
- 9 Placement Test books
- 1 Teacher's Manual

Complete Elementary Set (Levels A–F)

Grades 1-6

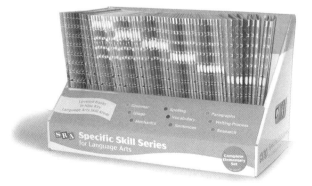

- 54 Student Editions
- 9 Placement Test books
- 1 Teacher's Manual

Using SRA Specific Skill Series
for Language Arts

Leveled books allow for differentiated instruction in any classroom setting.

● Independent Study
Students can work at their own pace during independent study time in a regular classroom, a resource room, or a Learning Activity Center. They can record their answers on the reproducible worksheets provided in the back of this *Teacher's Manual* and then submit their work for evaluation.

● Small Group
In small-group settings, teachers can lead students by first reviewing the language arts rules and examples provided in the rule boxes and then reading the exercise items aloud, having students record and discuss their answers.

● One-on-One/Tutorial
In one-on-one instructional settings, tutors can identify problem areas individual students may have in language arts and select units that target those areas. Tutors may also choose to work through whole books with students.

● Whole Class
Teachers can create overhead transparencies of the units in the skills books and lead the class in discussing the rule boxes and exercise items.

● After School
Specific Skill Series for Language Arts is ideal for students in after-school programs who need extra practice in language arts to catch up with other students. Students will learn new facts and read interesting stories as they work through the theme-based sets of exercises in each unit.

● Intervention Pull-Out Programs
Specific Skill Series for Language Arts includes the intensive skills practice that struggling students need to advance. All levels of the program can be used in pull-out programs to bring students up to grade level.

● Summer School
Students using the program in a summer-school setting will benefit from the intensive language arts remediation. For summer-school programs that focus on enrichment, students may be placed in upper levels.

Program Components

Student Editions

- 9 skill books in each level
- Leveled books span Grades 1–8 (Levels A–H)
- Standardized test format
- Nonconsumable

Placement Tests

- 1 *Placement Test* book for each skill area
- Contain pretests and posttests for diagnostic purposes
- Nonconsumable

Teacher's Manual

- 1 *Teacher's Manual* for the entire program
- Contains Answer Keys for Student Editions and Placement Tests
- Provides a step-by-step guide for using the program

Lesson Structure

The lessons in *Specific Skill Series for Language Arts* are presented in discrete units of skills practice. Each unit is two, four, or six pages long.

Rule boxes explain language arts skills clearly and concisely in terms appropriate for each level.

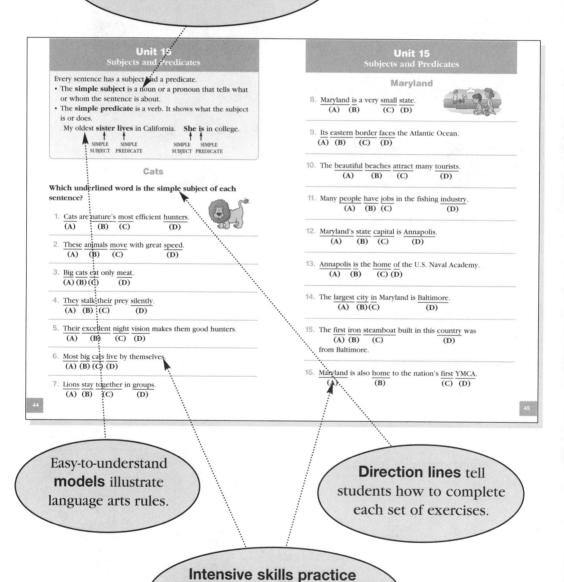

Unit 15
Subjects and Predicates

Every sentence has a subject and a predicate.
- The **simple subject** is a noun or a pronoun that tells what or whom the sentence is about.
- The **simple predicate** is a verb. It shows what the subject is or does.

My oldest **sister lives** in California. **She is** in college.

SIMPLE   SIMPLE   SIMPLE   SIMPLE
SUBJECT PREDICATE   SUBJECT PREDICATE

Cats

Which underlined word is the simple subject of each sentence?

1. Cats are nature's most efficient hunters.
   (A)   (B)   (C)   (D)

2. These animals move with great speed.
   (A)   (B)   (C)   (D)

3. Big cats eat only meat.
   (A)(B)(C)   (D)

4. They stalk their prey silently.
   (A)   (B) (C)   (D)

5. Their excellent night vision makes them good hunters.
   (A)   (B)   (C) (D)

6. Most big cats live by themselves.
   (A)(B)(C)(D)

7. Lions stay together in groups.
   (A)   (B)   (C)   (D)

44

Unit 15
Subjects and Predicates

Maryland

8. Maryland is a very small state.
   (A) (B)   (C) (D)

9. Its eastern border faces the Atlantic Ocean.
   (A) (B)   (C)   (D)

10. The beautiful beaches attract many tourists.
    (A)   (B)   (C)   (D)

11. Many people have jobs in the fishing industry.
    (A) (B) (C)   (D)

12. Maryland's state capital is Annapolis.
    (A)   (B)   (C)   (D)

13. Annapolis is the home of the U.S. Naval Academy.
    (A)   (B)   (C) (D)

14. The largest city in Maryland is Baltimore.
    (A)   (B)(C)   (D)

15. The first iron steamboat built in this country was
    (A) (B)   (C)   (D)
    from Baltimore.

16. Maryland is also home to the nation's first YMCA.
    (A).   (B)   (C) (D)

45

Easy-to-understand **models** illustrate language arts rules.

Direction lines tell students how to complete each set of exercises.

Intensive skills practice focuses on language arts rules presented in the unit.

Unit 12
Prepositions

A **preposition** is a word that tells about the position or direction of a noun or a pronoun.

That vase is **from** China.

Some Common Prepositions

about	across	after	against	around	at
between	by	during	for	from	in
into	near	of	off	on	out
over	through	to	under	up	with

Soap

Which underlined word is a preposition?

1. The first soap <u>was</u> a <u>blend</u> <u>of</u> two ingredients.
   (A) (B)   (C)   (D)

2. Animals' fat <u>was</u> mixed <u>with</u> <u>plant</u> <u>ash</u>.
            (A)   (B) (C) (D)

3. The ash <u>came</u> <u>from</u> the <u>soapwart</u> <u>plant</u>.
         (A)   (B)   (C)   (D)

4. Soap was <u>used</u> <u>not</u> <u>just</u> <u>for</u> cleaning.
          (A) (B) (C) (D)

5. It was <u>also</u> <u>sold</u> to sick <u>people</u> as <u>medicine</u>.
         (A) (B)(C)   (D)

6. Using soap was <u>not</u> <u>accepted</u> <u>by</u> all <u>cultures</u>.
           (A)   (B)   (C)   (D)

7. <u>During</u> the Middle Ages, people thought <u>that</u> bathing <u>could</u>
   (A)   (B)   (C)
   be dangerous!
   (D)

34

Unit 12
Prepositions

A **prepositional phrase** begins with a preposition and ends with a noun or a pronoun. A sentence can have more than one prepositional phrase or none at all.

The horse jumped **across the stream** and **over the fence**.

The horse was ridden **by me**.

The horse won a ribbon.

Teddy Bears

Is the underlined group of words in each sentence a prepositional phrase?

8. The idea of a teddy bear came <u>from a cartoon</u>.
   (A) Yes   (B) No

9. It was drawn in 1902 and showed a picture <u>of our twenty-sixth president</u>.
   (A) Yes   (B) No

10. Theodore Roosevelt was sometimes called Teddy <u>by his friends</u>.
    (A) Yes   (B) No

11. <u>On a camping trip</u>, the President saved a bear cub from being killed.
    (A) Yes   (B) No

12. The cartoon <u>showed the whole country</u> what happened.
    (A) Yes   (B) No

13. A toy maker put a little stuffed bear <u>in his window</u> with the cartoon, and the bears have sold well ever since.
    (A) Yes   (B) No

35

Language Activity Pages (LAPs)

Each book includes four Language Activity Pages (LAPs) to reinforce, apply, and extend the language arts skills students practiced in the units preceding each LAP.

Part A: Exercising Your Skill features a quiz-like review of key terms and concepts.

Part C: Exploring Language encourages application of skills to real-world contexts by featuring a form of writing: expository, narrative, personal, persuasive, descriptive, or poetry.

The Third LAP
Language Activity Pages

A. Exercising Your Skill

You have been learning about subjects and predicates. Answer these questions about what you have learned.

1. What is a complete subject?
   (A) the simple subject and all the words that describe it
   (B) the simple subject only
   (C) both the subject and the predicate

2. What is a compound predicate?
   (A) two or more simple predicates joined by a conjunction
   (B) two sentences joined by a conjunction
   (C) two or more simple subjects joined by a conjunction

B. Expanding Your Skill

Identify the underlined word or words in each sentence.

1. Volcanoes are a different kind of mountain.
   (A) simple predicate   (B) complete predicate
   (C) compound predicate   (D) simple subject

2. Inside the volcano, gas pressure forces the molten rock upward.
   (A) complete subject   (B) simple predicate
   (C) simple subject   (D) compound predicate

3. Cinder cones and lava domes are two kinds of volcanoes.
   (A) compound subject   (B) simple subject
   (C) compound predicate   (D) complete predicate

4. Lava may flow down the sides of the volcano or shoot into the air.
   (A) compound predicate   (B) simple predicate
   (C) complete predicate   (D) complete subject

54

The Third LAP
Language Activity Pages

C. Exploring Language

Expository Writing Read the paragraph below. Notice that it is missing some subjects and predicates. Number your paper from 1 to 5. Use the words from the box below to complete the paragraph.

poke	cats	like	balls and string	stalk and attack

Cats

(1)____ are curious animals. They (2)____ their noses into everything. They (3)____ anything that moves. (4)____ are usually their favorite toys. Most cats (5)____ catnip best of all.

D. Expressing Yourself

Choose one of these activities. When you are finished, give your paper to your teacher.

1. Draw a picture of yourself doing something that you like to do. Write a sentence at the bottom that tells about your picture. Make sure your sentence has a subject and a predicate. Underline the complete subject and circle the complete predicate in your sentence.

2. **WORK with a PARTNER** Choose a partner and think of a game that you both like to play. Write sentences that tell the rules for playing that game. Make sure that each sentence has a subject and a predicate. Underline the simple subject and simple predicate in each sentence. Circle any compound subjects or compound predicates.

55

Part B: Expanding Your Skill reviews and applies skills.

Part D: Expressing Yourself features two activities that encourage creativity and self-expression based on the language arts skills practiced in the units leading up to the LAP. One activity is always a Work-with-a-Partner activity to foster collaborative learning.

Scope and Sequence

The scope and sequence for *Specific Skill Series for Language Arts* reflects state curriculum guidelines in Grades 1 through 8, which include a wide variety of grammar, usage, mechanics, spelling, vocabulary, and writing skills. In addition, the scope and sequence was designed based on the language arts skills that appear most often on standardized tests.

The scope and sequence for **Grammar** is based on traditional grammar study and focuses on parts of speech and sentence structure.

The scope and sequence for **Usage** focuses on a variety of common usage problems including subject-verb agreement, proper use of verb tenses, pronoun-antecedent agreement, and misused words.

The scope and sequence for **Mechanics** focuses on the conventions of punctuation and capitalization.

The scope and sequence for **Spelling** focuses on spelling strategies rather than memorization of word lists.

The scope and sequence for **Vocabulary** focuses on word-learning skills and strategies rather than direct instruction on individual words.

The scope and sequence for **Sentences** focuses on the grammatical elements of a sentence, sentence combining, and common sentence problems.

The scope and sequence for **Paragraphs** focuses on the purposes, planning, and structure of paragraphs.

The scope and sequence for **Writing Process** focuses on the five stages of the writing process: planning, drafting, revising, editing/proofreading, and publishing.

The scope and sequence for **Research** focuses on research skills and processes.

GRAMMAR Scope and Sequence • Specific Skill Series for Language Arts

Unit/Level	Level A	Level B	Level C	Level D	Level E	Level F	Level G	Level H
Unit 1	Nouns	Nouns	Nouns	Nouns	Nouns	Nouns	Nouns	Nouns
Unit 2	Singular and Plural Nouns	Singular and Plural Nouns	Singular and Plural Nouns	Possessive Nouns	Possessive Nouns	Possessive Nouns	Possessive Nouns	Possessive Nouns
Unit 3	Possessive Nouns	Possessive Nouns	Possessive Nouns	Subject and Object Pronouns	Subject and Object Pronouns	Subject and Object Pronouns	Subject and Object Pronouns	Subject and Object Pronouns
Unit 4	Pronouns	Pronouns	Pronouns	Possessive Pronouns	Possessive Pronouns	Possessive Pronouns	Possessive Pronouns	Possessive Pronouns
Unit 5	Possessive Pronouns	Possessive Pronouns	Subject and Object Pronouns	Pronouns	Pronouns	Pronouns	Pronouns	Pronouns
Unit 6	Verbs	Interrogative Pronouns	Possessive Pronouns	Pronouns	Pronouns	Pronouns	Pronouns	Pronouns
Unit 7	Helping Verbs	Verbs	Interrogative Pronouns	Verbs	Verbs	Verbs	Verbs	Verbs
Unit 8	Adjectives	Helping Verbs	Verbs	Adjectives	Adjectives	Adjectives	Adjectives	Adjectives
Unit 9	Parts of a Sentence	Adjectives	Helping Verbs	Adverbs	Adverbs	Adverbs	Adverbs	Adverbs
Unit 10	Parts of a Sentence	Adverbs	Adjectives	Prepositions	Prepositions	Prepositions	Prepositions	Prepositions
Unit 11	Changing Sentences into Questions	Prepositions	Adverbs	Interjections and Conjunctions	Conjunctions	Conjunctions	Conjunctions	Conjunctions
Unit 12	Changing Sentences into Questions	Conjunctions	Prepositions	Subjects and Predicates	Subjects and Predicates	Subjects and Predicates	Subjects and Predicates	Subjects and Predicates
Unit 13		Interjections	Conjunctions	Direct Objects	Direct and Indirect Objects	Direct and Indirect Objects	Direct and Indirect Objects	Direct and Indirect Objects
Unit 14		Parts of a Sentence	Interjections	Clauses	Appositives	Appositives	Appositives	Appositives
Unit 15		Compound Subjects and Predicates	Subjects and Predicates	Clauses	Clauses	Gerunds	Gerunds	Gerunds
Unit 16		Changing Sentences into Questions	Compound Subjects and Predicates	Types of Sentences	Types of Sentences	Clauses	Infinitives	Infinitives
Unit 17		Changing Sentences into Questions	Complete Subjects and Predicates			Types of Sentences	Clauses	Clauses
Unit 18			Types of Sentences				Types of Sentences	Clauses
Unit 19			Changing Sentences into Questions					Types of Sentences

12

USAGE Scope and Sequence • Specific Skill Series for Language Arts

Unit/Level	Level A	Level B	Level C	Level D	Level E	Level F	Level G	Level H
Unit 1	Subject-Verb Agreement	Subject-Verb Agreement	Subject-Verb Agreement	Subject-Verb Agreement	Subject-Verb Agreement	Subject-Verb Agreement	Subject-Verb Agreement	Subject-Verb Agreement
Unit 2	Subject-Verb Agreement	Subject-Verb Agreement	The Verbs Be and Have	Subject-Verb Agreement	Subject-Verb Agreement	Subject-Verb Agreement	Subject-Verb Agreement	Subject-Verb Agreement
Unit 3	Subject-Verb Agreement	Subject-Verb Agreement	Subject-Verb Agreement	Adjective-Noun Agreement	Past-Tense Verbs	Subject-Verb Agreement	Past-Tense Verbs	Verb Tenses
Unit 4	Subject-Verb Agreement	Subject-Verb Agreement	Subject-Verb Agreement	Speaking of Yourself Last	Past-Tense Verbs	Past-Tense Verbs	Future Tense	Progressive Forms
Unit 5	The Verb Be	Subject-Verb Agreement	Subject-Verb Agreement	Past-Tense Verbs	Past Tense of Be	Future Tense	Perfect Tenses	Comparing with Adjectives and Adverbs
Unit 6	The Verb Have		Adjective-Noun Agreement	Past Tense of Be	Future Tense	Perfect Tenses	Comparing with Adjectives and Adverbs	Participles as Adjectives
Unit 7	Using This, That, These, and Those	The Verb Have	Speaking of Yourself Last	Comparing with Adjectives and Adverbs	Perfect Tenses	Comparing with Adjectives and Adverbs	Participles as Adjectives	Double Negatives
Unit 8	Past-Tense Verbs	Using This, That, These, and Those	Past-Tense Verbs	Future-Tense Verbs	Comparing with Adjectives and Adverbs	Participles as Adjectives	Double Negatives	Pronouns
Unit 9	Past Tense of Be	Adjective-Noun Agreement	Past Tense of Be	Perfect-Tense Verbs	Participles as Adjectives	Double Negatives	Pronouns	Avoiding Double Subjects
Unit 10	Comparing with Adjectives	Past-Tense Verbs	Comparing with Adjectives	Perfect-Tense Verbs	Double Negatives	Indefinite Pronouns	Active and Passive Voice	Active and Passive Voice
Unit 11	A and An	Past Tense of Be	Comparing with Adverbs	Verb Tenses	Indefinite Pronouns	Demonstrative Pronouns	Problem Verbs	Keeping Tenses Consistent
Unit 12	Agreement with Helping Verbs	Comparing with Adjectives	A and An	Double Negatives	Demonstrative Pronouns	Interrogative Pronouns	Misused Words	Problem Verbs
Unit 13		A and An	Agreement with Helping Verbs	Problem Verbs	Problem Verbs	Active and Passive Voice	Misused Phrases	Misused Words
Unit 14		Agreement with Helping Verbs	Future-Tense Verbs	Misused Words	Problem Verbs	Problem Verbs		Misused Phrases
Unit 15		Agreement with Helping Verbs	Present Perfect Tense		Misused Words	Misused Words		
Unit 16		Future-Tense Verbs	Verb Tenses			Misused Words		
Unit 17		Contractions	Contractions			Misused Phrases		
Unit 18			Double Negatives					
Unit 19			Problem Verbs					

MECHANICS Scope and Sequence • Specific Skill Series for Language Arts

Unit/Level	Level A	Level B	Level C	Level D	Level E	Level F	Level G	Level H
Unit 1	Capital Letters	Capital Letters	Capital Letters	Capital Letters	Capitalization	Capitalization	Capitalization	Capitalization
Unit 2	Capital Letters	Capital Letters	Capital Letters	Capital Letters	Capitalization	Capitalization	Capitalization	Capitalization
Unit 3	Capital Letters	Capital Letters	Capital Letters	Capital Letters	End Marks	Capitalization	Capitalization	Capitalization
Unit 4	Capital Letters	End Marks	End Marks	End Marks	Abbreviations	End Marks	End Marks	End Marks
Unit 5	End Marks	Capital Letters and End Marks	Abbreviations	Abbreviations	Commas	Abbreviations	Quotation Marks	Abbreviations
Unit 6	End Marks	Commas	Commas	Commas	Commas	Commas	Abbreviations	Commas
Unit 7	End Marks	Commas	Commas	Commas	Colons, Semicolons, and Hyphens	Commas	Commas	Commas
Unit 8	Capital Letters and End Marks	Commas	Colons	Commas	Quotation Marks and Underlining	Commas	Commas	Commas
Unit 9	Capital Letters and End Marks	Quotation Marks	Quotation Marks	Colons	Other Punctuation Marks	Colons, Semicolons, and Hyphens	Commas	Colons, Semicolons, and Hyphens
Unit 10	Contractions and Apostrophes	Contractions and Apostrophes	Underlining	Hyphens	Capitalization and Punctuation	Quotation Marks and Underlining	Colons and Semicolons	Quotation Marks and Underlining
Unit 11		Capitalization and Punctuation	Capitalization and Punctuation	Quotation Marks and Underlining		Other Punctuation Marks	Hyphens	Other Punctuation Marks
Unit 12			Capitalization and Punctuation	Capitalization and Punctuation		Capitalization and Punctuation	Underlining	Capitalization and Punctuation
Unit 13							Other Punctuation Marks	
Unit 14							Capitalization and Punctuation	

SPELLING Scope and Sequence • Specific Skill Series for Language Arts

Unit/Level	Level A	Level B	Level C	Level D	Level E	Level F	Level G	Level H
Unit 1	Pronunciation Strategy	Pronunciation Strategy	Pronunciation Strategy	Rhyming Strategy	Rhyming Strategy	Conventions Strategy	Conventions Strategy	Conventions Strategy
Unit 2	Pronunciation Strategy	Pronunciation Strategy	Pronunciation Strategy	Conventions Strategy	Conventions Strategy	Visualization Strategy	Visualization Strategy	Visualization Strategy
Unit 3	Pronunciation Strategy	Pronunciation Strategy	Pronunciation Strategy	Conventions Strategy	Visualization Strategy	Visualization Strategy	Visualization Strategy	Visualization Strategy
Unit 4	Visualization Strategy	Pronunciation Strategy	Rhyming Strategy	Visualization Strategy	Visualization Strategy	Meaning Strategy	Meaning Strategy	Meaning Strategy
Unit 5	Visualization Strategy	Vowel Substitution Strategy	Rhyming Strategy	Visualization Strategy	Compound Word Strategy	Dictionary Strategy	Dictionary Strategy	Dictionary Strategy
Unit 6	Visualization Strategy	Vowel Substitution Strategy	Conventions Strategy	Visualization Strategy	Meaning Strategy	Proofreading Strategy	Proofreading Strategy	Proofreading Strategy
Unit 7	Consonant Substitution Strategy	Consonant Substitution Strategy	Conventions Strategy	Compound Word Strategy	Dictionary Strategy	Family Strategy	Family Strategy	Family Strategy
Unit 8	Vowel Substitution Strategy	Rhyming Strategy	Visualization Strategy	Meaning Strategy	Proofreading Strategy	Foreign Language Strategy	Foreign Language Strategy	Foreign Language Strategy
Unit 9	Rhyming Strategy	Rhyming Strategy	Visualization Strategy	Dictionary Strategy	Family Strategy			
Unit 10	Rhyming Strategy	Conventions Strategy	Visualization Strategy	Proofreading Strategy	Foreign Language Strategy			
Unit 11	Conventions Strategy	Conventions Strategy	Compound Word Strategy	Family Strategy				
Unit 12	Conventions Strategy	Conventions Strategy	Meaning Strategy	Foreign Language Strategy				
Unit 13		Compound Word Strategy	Dictionary Strategy					
Unit 14		Meaning Strategy	Family Strategy					
Unit 15			Family Strategy					

15

VOCABULARY Scope and Sequence • Specific Skill Series for Language Arts

Unit/Level	Level A	Level B	Level C	Level D	Level E	Level F	Level G	Level H
Unit 1	Categories	Categories	Categories	Categorization	Categorization	Categorization	Categorization	Categorization
Unit 2	Categories	Synonyms	Synonyms	Synonyms and Antonyms	Synonyms and Antonyms	Synonyms and Antonyms	Synonyms and Antonyms	Synonyms and Antonyms
Unit 3	Synonyms	Antonyms	Antonyms	Idioms	Idioms	Figurative Language	Figurative Language	Figurative Language
Unit 4	Antonyms	Homographs	Idioms	Similes and Metaphors	Similes and Metaphors	Homonyms	Homonyms	Homonyms
Unit 5	Homographs	Homophones	Similes and Metaphors	Homonyms	Homonyms	Word Maps	Word Maps	Word Maps
Unit 6	Homophones	Word Maps	Homographs	Word Maps	Word Maps	Analogies	Analogies	Analogies
Unit 7	Compound Words	Linear Graphs	Homophones	Analogies	Analogies	Prefixes	Base Words and Affixes	Base Words and Affixes
Unit 8	Prefixes	Compound Words	Word Maps	Compound Words	Prefixes	Suffixes	Greek and Latin Roots and Affixes	Greek and Latin Roots and Affixes
Unit 9	Suffixes	Prefixes	Linear Graphs	Prefixes	Suffixes	Base Words	Anglo-Saxon Roots	Anglo-Saxon Roots
Unit 10	Guide Words	Suffixes	Compound Words	Suffixes	Base Words	Greek and Latin Roots	Context Clues	Context Clues
Unit 11	Definitions	Base Words	Prefixes	Base Words	Greek and Latin Roots	Context Clues	Context Clues	Context Clues
Unit 12		Context Clues	Suffixes	Greek and Latin Roots	Context Clues	Context Clues	Context Clues	Context Clues
Unit 13		Context Clues	Base Words	Context Clues	Context Clues	Context Clues	Connotation/Shades of Meaning	Connotation/Shades of Meaning
Unit 14		Guide Words	Context Clues	Context Clues	Context Clues	Context Clues	Syllables	Syllables
Unit 15		Syllables	Context Clues	Context Clues	Context Clues	Connotation/Shades of Meaning	Parts of a Dictionary Entry	Parts of a Dictionary Entry
Unit 16		Parts of a Dictionary Entry	Context Clues	Context Clues	Guide Words	Syllables	Multiple-Meaning Words	Multiple-Meaning Words
Unit 17		Multiple-Meaning Words	Guide Words	Guide Words	Syllables	Parts of a Dictionary Entry	Word Origins	Word Origins
Unit 18			Syllables	Syllables	Parts of a Dictionary Entry	Multiple-Meaning Words	Foreign Words and Phrases	Foreign Words and Phrases
Unit 19			Parts of a Dictionary Entry	Parts of a Dictionary Entry	Multiple-Meaning Words	Word Origins	Content-Area Words	Content-Area Words
Unit 20			Multiple-Meaning Words	Multiple-Meaning Words	Word Origins	Foreign Words and Phrases		
Unit 21				Word Origins	Content-Area Words	Content-Area Words		

SENTENCES Scope and Sequence • Specific Skill Series for Language Arts

Unit/Level	Level A	Level B	Level C	Level D	Level E	Level F	Level G	Level H
Unit 1	Building Sentences	Building Sentences	Building Sentences	Building Sentences	Building Sentences	Building Sentences	Building Sentences	Building Sentences
Unit 2	Building Sentences	Building Sentences	Building Sentences	Building Sentences	Building Sentences	Building Sentences	Combining Sentences	Combining Sentences
Unit 3	Building Sentences	Building Sentences	Building Sentences	Building Sentences	Building Sentences	Building Sentences	Combining Sentences	Combining Sentences
Unit 4	Building Sentences	Building Sentences	Building Sentences	Building Sentences	Building Sentences	Building Sentences	The Sound of Language	The Sound of Language
Unit 5	Building Sentences	Combining Sentences	Building Sentences	Building Sentences	Combining Sentences	Combining Sentences	Sentence Fluency	Sentence Fluency
Unit 6	Combining Sentences	Combining Sentences	Building Sentences	Building Sentences	Combining Sentences	Combining Sentences	Parallelism	Parallelism
Unit 7	Combining Sentences	Correct Word Order in a Sentence	Combining Sentences	Combining Sentences	Combining Sentences	The Sound of Language	Parallelism	Parallelism
Unit 8	Putting Words in the Correct Order	Parallelism	Combining Sentences	Combining Sentences	The Sound of Language	Sentence Fluency	Sentence Problems	Sentence Problems
Unit 9	Agreement with Verbs and Adjectives	Sentence Problems	Combining Sentences	Combining Sentences	Sentence Fluency	Parallelism	Sentence Problems	Sentence Problems
Unit 10	Sentence Problems	Sentence Problems	Combining Sentences	Correct Word Order	Parallelism	Sentence Problems	Expanding Sentences	Expanding Sentences
Unit 11	Adding Prepositional Phrases	Adding Prepositional Phrases	Combining Sentences	The Sound of Language	Sentence Problems	Expanding Sentences	Diagramming Sentences	Diagramming Sentences
Unit 12			Correct Word Order	Sentence Fluency	Expanding Sentences			
Unit 13			Parallelism	Parallelism				
Unit 14			Sentence Fluency	Sentence Problems				
Unit 15			Sentence Problems	Sentence Problems				
Unit 16			Sentence Problems	Sentence Problems				

17

PARAGRAPHS Scope and Sequence • Specific Skill Series for Language Arts

Unit/Level	Level A	Level B	Level C	Level D	Level E	Level F	Level G	Level H
Unit 1	Types of Paragraphs	Types of Paragraphs	Types of Paragraphs	Types of Paragraphs	Narrative Paragraphs	Narrative Paragraphs	Narrative Paragraphs	Narrative Paragraphs
Unit 2	Types of Paragraphs	Using a Web	Using a Web	Using a Web	Narrative Paragraphs	Narrative Paragraphs	Narrative Paragraphs	Narrative Paragraphs
Unit 3	Using a Web	Topic Sentences	Topic Sentences	Topic Sentences	Narrative Paragraphs	Narrative Paragraphs	Narrative Paragraphs	Narrative Paragraphs
Unit 4	Topic Sentences	Details	Details	Details	Narrative Paragraphs	Narrative Paragraphs	Narrative Paragraphs	Narrative Paragraphs
Unit 5	Topic Sentences	Closing Sentences	Closing Sentences	Closing Sentences	Persuasive Paragraphs	Persuasive Paragraphs	Persuasive Paragraphs	Persuasive Paragraphs
Unit 6	Details	Complete Paragraphs	Complete Paragraphs	Complete Paragraphs	Persuasive Paragraphs	Persuasive Paragraphs	Persuasive Paragraphs	Persuasive Paragraphs
Unit 7	Closing Sentences	Staying on Topic	Staying on Topic	Staying on Topic	Persuasive Paragraphs	Persuasive Paragraphs	Persuasive Paragraphs	Persuasive Paragraphs
Unit 8	Complete Paragraphs	Time and Order Words	Time and Order Words	Transition Words	Expository Paragraphs	Expository Paragraphs	Persuasive Paragraphs	Persuasive Paragraphs
Unit 9	Staying on Topic	Using Dialogue	Using Dialogue	Sentence Variety	Expository Paragraphs	Expository Paragraphs	Expository Paragraphs	Expository Paragraphs
Unit 10	Time and Order Words	Making Comparisons	Making Comparisons	Using Dialogue	Expository Paragraphs	Expository Paragraphs	Expository Paragraphs	Expository Paragraphs
Unit 11				Figurative Language	Writing Paragraphs	Writing Paragraphs	Expository Paragraphs	Expository Paragraphs
Unit 12						Writing Paragraphs	Writing Paragraphs	Writing Paragraphs
Unit 13					Writing Paragraphs	Writing Paragraphs	Writing Paragraphs	Writing Paragraphs
Unit 14						Writing Paragraphs	Writing Paragraphs	Writing Paragraphs
Unit 15					Writing Paragraphs	Writing Paragraphs	Writing Paragraphs	Writing Paragraphs
Unit 16							Writing Paragraphs	Writing Paragraphs

WRITING PROCESS Scope and Sequence • Specific Skill Series for Language Arts

Unit/Level	Level A	Level B	Level C	Level D	Level E	Level F	Level G	Level H
Unit 1	Getting Ideas	Getting Ideas	Getting Ideas	Getting Ideas	Getting Ideas	Getting Ideas	Getting Ideas	Getting Ideas
Unit 2	Planning	Planning	Planning	Planning	Planning	Planning	Planning	Planning
Unit 3	Planning	Planning	Planning	Drafting	Drafting	Drafting	Planning	Drafting
Unit 4	Writing	Writing	Drafting	Drafting	Drafting	Drafting	Drafting	Revising
Unit 5	Revising	Revising	Drafting	Revising	Revising	Revising	Drafting	Revising
Unit 6	Revising	Revising	Revising	Revising	Revising	Revising	Revising	Revising
Unit 7	Revising	Revising	Revising	Revising	Revising	Revising	Revising	Revising
Unit 8	Checking	Revising	Revising	Revising	Revising	Revising	Revising	Revising
Unit 9	Checking	Checking	Revising	Revising	Revising	Revising	Revising	Revising
Unit 10	Sharing	Checking	Editing/Proofreading	Editing/Proofreading	Editing/Proofreading	Editing/Proofreading	Editing/Proofreading	Editing/Proofreading
Unit 11		Sharing	Proofreading Marks	Proofreading Marks	Editing/Proofreading	Editing/Proofreading	Editing/Proofreading	Editing/Proofreading
Unit 12			Publishing	Publishing	Publishing	Publishing	Publishing	Publishing

19

RESEARCH Scope and Sequence • Specific Skill Series for Language Arts

Unit/Level	Level A	Level B	Level C	Level D	Level E	Level F	Level G	Level H
Unit 1	Parts of a Book	Using a Library	Using a Library	Using a Table of Contents	Using a Table of Contents and an Index	Getting Ideas and Narrowing a Topic	Getting Ideas and Narrowing a Topic	Getting Ideas and Narrowing a Topic
Unit 2	Using Books	Using a Table of Contents	Using a Table of Contents	Using an Index	Using an Encyclopedia	Formulating Questions	Formulating Questions	Formulating Questions
Unit 3	Using a Table of Contents	Using an Encyclopedia	Using an Index	Finding Magazine and Newspaper Articles	Finding Magazine and Newspaper Articles	Making a Research Statement	Making a Research Statement	Making a Research Statement
Unit 4	Using a Table of Contents	Key Word Searching	Using an Encyclopedia	Key Word Searching	Key Word Searching	Finding Information	Finding Information	Finding Information
Unit 5	Using an Encyclopedia	Evaluating a Web Site	Key Word Searching	Evaluating a Web Site	Evaluating a Web Site	Using a Table of Contents and an Index	Using an Atlas	Using an Atlas
Unit 6	Using an Encyclopedia	Reading a Chart	Evaluating a Web Site	Getting Ideas	Reading Graphs and Charts	Finding Newspaper and Magazine Articles	Finding Newspaper and Magazine Articles	Finding Newspaper and Magazine Articles
Unit 7	Reading a Chart	Taking a Survey	Reading a Chart	Asking Questions	Getting Ideas and Narrowing Your Topic	Key Word Searching	Key Word Searching	Key Word Searching
Unit 8	Taking a Survey	Reading a Diagram	Taking a Survey	Making a Research Statement	Formulating Questions	Evaluating Web Sites	Evaluating Web Sites	Evaluating Web Sites
Unit 9	Finding Information	Getting Ideas	Reading a Diagram	Finding Information	Making a Research Statement	Reading Graphs and Charts	Reading Graphs and Charts	Reading Graphs and Charts
Unit 10	Taking Notes	Asking Questions	Getting Ideas	Comparing Information across Sources	Identifying Sources	Comparing Information across Sources	Comparing Sources	Comparing Sources
Unit 11		Making a Research Statement	Asking Questions	Evaluating Information	Comparing Information across Sources	Taking Notes	Taking Notes	Taking Notes
Unit 12		Finding Information	Making a Research Statement	Taking Notes	Taking Notes	Summarizing	Summarizing	Summarizing
Unit 13		Taking Notes	Finding Information	Summarizing	Summarizing	Writing an Outline	Writing an Outline	Writing an Outline
Unit 14			Evaluating Information	Writing an Outline	Writing an Outline	Writing Introductory Paragraphs	Writing Introductory Paragraphs	Writing Introductory Paragraphs
Unit 15				Writing Paragraphs	Writing Introductory Paragraphs	Writing Supporting Paragraphs	Writing Supporting Paragraphs	Writing Supporting Paragraphs
Unit 16				Writing a Bibliography	Writing Supporting Paragraphs	In-Text Citations	In-Text Citations	In-Text Citations
Unit 17					Writing Concluding Paragraphs	Writing Concluding Paragraphs	Writing Concluding Paragraphs	Writing Concluding Paragraphs
Unit 18					Writing a Bibliography	Writing a Bibliography	Writing a Bibliography	Writing a Bibliography

Placement Tests

The purpose of the Placement Tests is to help teachers place students in the correct level of the program for each skill area. There are three levels of Placement Tests—Primary, Intermediate, and Advanced. The tests consist of representative pages selected from the Student Editions.

Each level has two forms—Form X and Form Y. Either form may be used as a pretest for student placement or a posttest to measure student progress.

A complete explanation of how to administer and evaluate the Placement Tests is located on the "To the Teacher" page of each *Placement Test* book.

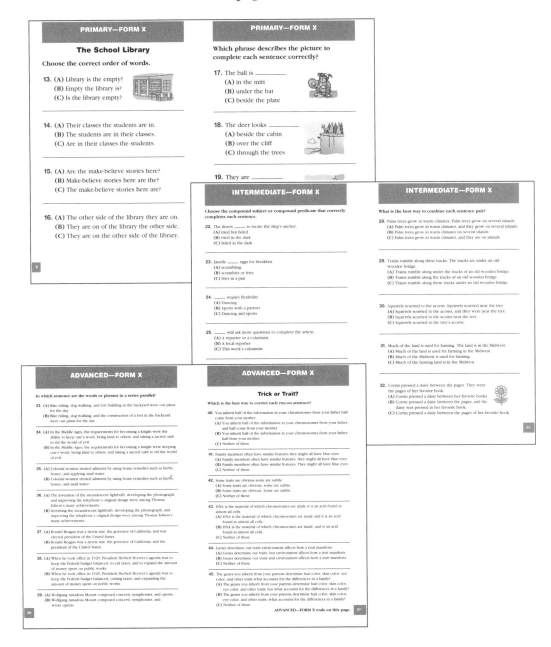

Test-Taking Strategies

The multiple-choice format of *Specific Skill Series for Language Arts* provides students with excellent standardized test-taking practice. Teachers may wish to discuss the following test-taking strategies with students before students begin working in the skill books.

● Read Carefully

The first rule of taking a test is to read each question carefully. If you don't read the questions carefully, you will probably make a mistake. For multiple-choice questions, keep in mind that the word *not* could be part of the question, which affects your answer choice. It is just as important to read each answer choice carefully.

● Process of Elimination

Sometimes you will know when an answer choice isn't right. When this happens, you can eliminate, or cross out, the answer choice. When you eliminate an answer choice, it is easier to find the correct answer because you have fewer answers to choose from.

● Skipping Difficult Questions

Not all of the items on a test are equally difficult. Some are easier than others. It is important that you answer as many questions as you can. The best way to do this is to skip questions that are difficult and come back to them later. By doing this, you will be more likely to try all of the questions. Remember, some of the questions at the end of a test might be easy, so it is important to try them before you run out of time.

● Staying with the First Answer

On a test, the first answer you choose is usually correct. Even if you aren't sure which answer is correct, your first answer is correct more often than it is wrong.

● Taking the Best Guess

Guessing is something we do every day. For example, when you look outside and see that it is cloudy, you might guess that it is going to rain. When you take a test, you may also find it useful to guess. You should not guess the answer to every question, but if you aren't sure which answer is correct, you should guess rather than not answer.

● Skimming a Passage

A mistake that many students make when taking tests is taking too long to read a passage. On a test, you should skim the passage. This means you should read it quickly without trying to remember all of the information. You can always look back at the passage when you have to answer questions. When you skim a passage, all you want to do is get an idea of what it is about. This is different from the kind of reading you do for fun or when studying.

SRA Specific Skill Series
for Language Arts

Specific Skill Series for Language Arts...

✔ provides **targeted, skills-intensive practice** to reinforce **fundamental language arts skills** for students at all ability levels.

✔ allows each student to work at his or her own pace to gain proficiency in **nine key language arts skill areas**—grammar, usage, mechanics, spelling, vocabulary, sentences, paragraphs, writing process, and research.

✔ features **multiple-choice formats** throughout each book to effectively prepare students for **standardized testing situations.**

✔ expands instructional options to include **any classroom setting**, such as one-on-one, small-group, whole-class, after-school, intervention, and summer-school environments.

✔ **complements any reading/language arts curriculum** in Grades 1 through 8.

✔ joins *SRA Specific Skill Series,* a widely recognized supplemental reading program, to form a family of **skills-intensive programs** that target problem areas in reading and language arts.

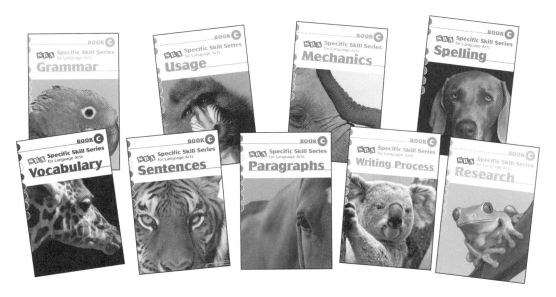

Specific Skill Series
for Language Arts

ANSWER KEYS

for Student Editions
Levels A–H

Unit 1
Nouns
pp. 6–9

1.C 2.B 3.D 4.A 5.C
6.A 7.E 8.F 9.B 10.D
11.B 12.A 13.B 14.B 15.A
16.B 17.A 18.B 19.B 20.A

Unit 2
Singular and Plural Nouns
pp. 10–13

1.A 2.A 3.B 4.A 5.B
6.B 7.B 8.A 9.B 10.A
11.B 12.A 13.A 14.B 15.B
16.A 17.B 18.B 19.A 20.B
21.A 22.B 23.A 24.B

Unit 3
Possessive Nouns
pp. 14–17

1.B 2.A 3.A 4.A 5.B
6.A 7.B 8.B 9.A 10.B
11.C 12.A 13.C 14.A 15.B
16.A 17.C 18.C 19.B 20.A

The First LAP
Language Activity Pages
pp. 18–19

A: 1. noun 2. proper
3. possessive 4. plural; **B:** 1. car
2. man 3. frogs 4. nails
5. bushes 6. foxes; **C:** 1. zoo
2. bears 3. elephants 4. blanket
5. lunch; **D:** 1. Answers will
vary. 2. Answers will vary.

Unit 4
Pronouns
pp. 20–23

1.D 2.C 3.A 4.B 5.E
6.F 7.D 8.A 9.B 10.C
11.B 12.A 13.B 14.A 15.B
16.B 17.C 18.C 19.A 20.B

Unit 5
Possessive Pronouns
pp. 24–27

1.A 2.C 3.B 4.C 5.B
6.C 7.A 8.A 9.A 10.B
11.B 12.A 13.B 14.A 15.B
16.B 17.A 18.B

Unit 6
Verbs
pp. 28–31

1.B 2.A 3.B 4.A 5.A
6.A 7.B 8.A 9.A 10.B
11.A 12.B 13.A 14.A 15.B
16.A 17.A 18.B 19.A 20.A

Unit 7
Helping Verbs
pp. 32–35

1.B 2.A 3.B 4.A 5.A
6.B 7.A 8.B 9.A 10.B
11.A 12.A 13.B 14.A 15.A
16.B 17.A 18.B 19.B 20.A

The Second LAP
Language Activity Pages
pp. 36–37

A: 1. pronoun 2. possessive
3. verbs 4. helping; **B:** 1. she
2. they 3. mine 4. his
5. throws 6. ask; **C:** 1.H 2.M
3.P 4.H 5.P 6.M 7.H 8.M 9.P
10.P; **D:** 1. Answers will vary.
2. Answers will vary.

Unit 8
Adjectives
pp. 38–43

1.A 2.B 3.A 4.A 5.B
6.A 7.A 8.A 9.A 10.B
11.A 12.B 13.B 14.A 15.B
16.A 17.B 18.B 19.B 20.B
21.A 22.A 23.B 24.A 25.B
26.B 27.A 28.B 29.A 30.A
31.A 32.B

Unit 9
Parts of a Sentence
pp. 44–45

1.C 2.B 3.A 4.C 5.A
6.C 7.A 8.C 9.A 10.B
11.C 12.B

Unit 10
Parts of a Sentence
pp. 46–51

1.C 2.B 3.B 4.C 5.A
6.C 7.B 8.A 9.C 10.A
11.C 12.B 13.C 14.C 15.A
16.B 17.B 18.C 19.A 20.A
21.C 22.B 23.B 24.A 25.C
26.B 27.C 28.A 29.A 30.C
31.B 32.A 33.C 34.A

The Third LAP
Language Activity Pages
pp. 52–53

A: 1. Adjectives 2. Sentences
3. noun 4. verb; **B:** 1. big
2. red 3. ten 4. five 5. that
6. these; **C:** 1.V 2.A 3.A 4.A
5.V 6.N 7.N 8.A 9.V 10.V;
D: 1. Answers will vary.
2. Answers will vary.

Unit 11
Changing Sentences
into Questions
pp. 54–57

1.B 2.A 3.C 4.A 5.A
6.C 7.B 8.B 9.A 10.B
11.C 12.A 13.C 14.C 15.B
16.A

Unit 12
Changing Sentences
into Questions
pp. 58–61

1.A 2.C 3.A 4.B 5.B
6.C 7.A 8.C 9.C 10.B
11.A 12.C 13.A 14.A 15.C
16.B

The Last LAP
Language Activity Pages
pp. 62–63

A: 1. sentence 2. question
3. verb 4. helping; **B:** 1. Is
snow white? 2. Are some
leaves green? 3. Will leaves
change color? 4. Is a ball
round? 5. Has Beth gone?
6. Can water freeze?; **C:** 2. Are
there many types of rocks?
3. Will plants grow without
light? 5. Can clouds be
different?; **D:** 1. Answers will
vary. 2. Answers will vary.

Unit 1
Nouns
pp. 6–9

1.B	2.B	3.A	4.B	5.A
6.A	7.A	8.A	9.B	10.B
11.A	12.B	13.A	14.B	15.A
16.B	17.B	18.B	19.A	20.B
21.A	22.B	23.A	24.B	25.A

Unit 2
Singular and Plural Nouns
pp. 10–11

1.B	2.A	3.B	4.B	5.A
6.B	7.A	8.B	9.B	10.A

Unit 3
Possessive Nouns
pp. 12–13

1.B	2.A	3.B	4.B	5.B
6.A	7.B	8.B	9.A	10.B

Unit 4
Pronouns
pp. 14–17

1.A	2.A	3.B	4.B	5.C
6.A	7.B	8.B	9.A	10.A
11.C	12.A	13.C	14.B	15.C
16.A	17.A	18.B	19.C	20.A
21.B	22.A	23.A	24.C	25.A

Unit 5
Possessive Pronouns
pp. 18–21

1.B	2.C	3.A	4.A	5.B
6.B	7.C	8.A	9.A	10.A
11.B	12.C	13.A	14.C	15.C
16.A	17.C	18.C	19.B	20.B
21.A	22.B	23.B	24.C	25.B
26.A				

Unit 6
Interrogative Pronouns
pp. 22–23

1.A	2.B	3.B	4.A	5.B
6.B	7.A	8.A	9.A	10.B
11.B	12.A	13.B	14.A	

The First LAP
Language Activity Pages
pp. 24–25
A: 1.A 2.B 3.B; **B:** 1.A 2.B 3.C
4.B; **C:** 1. zoo 2. Patrick
3. manatee 4. lion 5. Museum
of Modern Art; **D:** 1. Answers
will vary. 2. Lima, Peru;
Kampala, Uganda; Stockholm,
Sweden

Unit 7
Verbs
pp. 26–27

1.B	2.B	3.A	4.B	5.A
6.A	7.B	8.B	9.A	10.A
11.A	12.B			

Unit 8
Helping Verbs
pp. 28–29

1.B	2.A	3.A	4.B	5.B
6.A	7.A	8.B	9.A	10.A
11.B	12.B			

Unit 9
Adjectives
pp. 30–31

1.B	2.A	3.A	4.B	5.A
6.A	7.A	8.B	9.B	10.A
11.B	12.B			

Unit 10
Adverbs
pp. 32–35

1.A	2.B	3.B	4.A	5.A
6.A	7.B	8.B	9.B	10.B
11.A	12.A	13.B	14.A	15.B
16.A	17.A	18.B	19.B	20.B
21.A	22.A	23.B	24.B	25.B
26.B	27.A	28.B		

The Second LAP
Language Activity Pages
pp. 36–37
A: 1.C 2.B; **B:** 1.B 2.A 3.A
4.B 5.B; **C:** 1. fly 2. swim
3. crawl 4. hop 5. has;
D: 1. Answers will vary.
2. Answers will vary.

Unit 11
Prepositions
pp. 38–39

1.B	2.B	3.A	4.A	5.B
6.B	7.A	8.B	9.A	10.B
11.A	12.A			

Unit 12
Conjunctions
pp. 40–41

1.B	2.A	3.A	4.B	5.B
6.A	7.A	8.B	9.B	10.A
11.A	12.A			

Unit 13
Interjections
pp. 42–43

1.B	2.A	3.A	4.A	5.A
6.B	7.A	8.A	9.A	10.A
11.B	12.A			

Unit 14
Parts of a Sentence
pp. 44–49

1.A	2.A	3.B	4.B	5.A
6.B	7.A	8.B	9.A	10.B
11.A	12.B	13.B	14.C	15.A
16.C	17.B	18.A	19.B	20.C
21.C	22.A	23.B	24.B	25.D
26.A	27.D	28.C	29.B	30.C

Unit 15
**Compound Subjects
and Predicates**
pp. 50–51

1.A	2.B	3.B	4.A	5.A
6.A	7.B	8.A		

The Third LAP
Language Activity Pages
pp. 52–53
A: 1.B 2.C; **B:** 1.A 2.B 3.B
4.B; **C:** 1.I 2.P 3.C 4.P 5.C
6.I 7.P; **D:** 1. Answers will
vary. 2. Answers will vary.

Unit 16
**Changing Sentences
into Questions**
pp. 54–57

1.C	2.A	3.A	4.B	5.C
6.C	7.A	8.A	9.B	10.B
11.C	12.C	13.A	14.B	15.A
16.B	17.C	18.C		

Unit 17
**Changing Sentences
into Questions**
pp. 58–61

1.B	2.A	3.B	4.B	5.C
6.A	7.A	8.C	9.A	10.C
11.B	12.B	13.A	14.C	15.A
16.B	17.C	18.B		

The Last LAP
Language Activity Pages
pp. 62–63
A: 1.B 2.B; **B:** 1. Are zebras
related to horses and donkeys?
2. Can a zebra run very fast?
3. Are these animals hunted by
lions? 4. Are zebras covered
with stripes? 5. Can families
recognize each other by their
stripes? **C:** 1. Is basketball your
favorite sport? 2. Is it hard to
play in front of a big crowd?
3. Will your team win the
championship? **D:** 1. Answers
will vary. 2. Answers will vary.

Unit 1
Nouns
pp. 6–9

1.A 2.A 3.C 4.C 5.B
6.A 7.C 8.C 9.B 10.C
11.A 12.C 13.B 14.A 15.C
16.A 17.B 18.A 19.C 20.C
21.A 22.B 23.C 24.A 25.D
26.D 27.A 28.D 29.A 30.B
31.C 32.C

Unit 2
Singular and Plural Nouns
pp. 10–13

1.B 2.A 3.A 4.B 5.B
6.A 7.A 8.A 9.A 10.A
11.B 12.B 13.B 14.A 15.B
16.A 17.B 18.A 19.B 20.B
21.A 22.A 23.B 24.B 25.B
26.A 27.A 28.A 29.B 30.A
31.A 32.B 33.B 34.A

Unit 3
Possessive Nouns
pp. 14–15

1.A 2.B 3.A 4.A 5.B
6.B 7.A 8.A 9.A 10.B
11.A 12.B 13.B 14.A 15.B
16.A

Unit 4
Pronouns
pp. 16–17

1.B 2.B 3.A 4.A 5.C
6.B 7.C 8.A 9.B 10.B
11.B 12.A 13.B 14.C 15.B
16.A

Unit 5
Subject and Object Pronouns
pp. 18–19

1.A 2.A 3.B 4.B 5.B
6.A 7.A 8.B 9.B 10.A
11.B 12.A 13.B 14.A

Unit 6
Possessive Pronouns
pp. 20–21

1.B 2.B 3.A 4.A 5.C
6.C 7.B 8.B 9.A 10.B
11.A 12.C

Unit 7
Interrogative Pronouns
pp. 22–23

1.A 2.A 3.B 4.A 5.B
6.A 7.A 8.A 9.B 10.A
11.A 12.B 13.A 14.B 15.A
16.A 17.B 18.B

The First LAP
Language Activity Pages
pp. 24–25

A: 1.C 2.B 3. subject pronoun-B, object pronoun-C, possessive pronoun-A; **B:** 1.B 2.A 3.A 4.C; **C:** 1.B 2.F 3.C 4.D 5.A 6.E; **D:** 1. Answers will vary. 2. Answers will vary.

Unit 8
Verbs
pp. 26–27

1.B 2.B 3.C 4.A 5.D
6.B 7.A 8.A 9.B 10.A
11.B 12.C 13.B 14.A 15.B
16.C

Unit 9
Helping Verbs
pp. 28–29

1.A 2.C 3.B 4.B 5.C
6.A 7.B 8.C 9.D 10.B
11.A 12.B 13.C 14.C 15.B

Unit 10
Adjectives
pp. 30–31

1.C 2.A 3.C 4.D 5.C
6.A 7.B 8.A 9.B 10.A
11.C 12.A 13.D 14.C 15.B
16.A

Unit 11
Adverbs
pp. 32–33

1.B 2.C 3.C 4.D 5.D
6.B 7.A 8.B 9.B 10.A
11.A 12.B

Unit 12
Prepositions
pp. 34–37

1.D 2.B 3.B 4.D 5.C
6.C 7.A 8.A 9.A 10.A
11.A 12.B 13.A 14.A 15.B
16.C 17.C 18.B 19.C 20.C
21.C 22.B 23.A 24.A 25.A
26.C 27.C 28.C

Unit 13
Conjunctions
pp. 38–39

1.C 2.C 3.D 4.A 5.B
6.B 7.A 8.C 9.D 10.D
11.A 12.D 13.A 14.C

Unit 14
Interjections
pp. 40–41

1.A 2.A 3.D 4.A 5.A
6.A 7.A 8.D 9.A 10.A
11.D 12.A 13.D 14.A 15.A
16.A

The Second LAP
Language Activity Pages
pp. 42–43

A: 1.B 2.C 3.A; **B:** 1.B 2.A 3.C 4.A; **C:** 1. in 2. to 3. and 4. with 5. at 6. of 7. but; **D:** 1. Answers will vary. 2. Answers will vary.

Unit 15
Subjects and Predicates
pp. 44–47

1.A 2.B 3.B 4.A 5.D
6.C 7.A 8.A 9.C 10.B
11.A 12.C 13.A 14.B 15.C
16.A 17.B 18.C 19.D 20.C
21.C 22.A 23.B 24.A 25.B
26.B 27.A 28.C 29.B 30.A
31.B 32.C

Unit 16
Compound Subjects and Predicates
pp. 48–51

1.A 2.B 3.B 4.A 5.B
6.B 7.A 8.A 9.A 10.B
11.A 12.A 13.B 14.A 15.A
16.A 17.B 18.A 19.B 20.A
21.A 22.A 23.B 24.A 25.B
26.A

Unit 17
Complete Subjects and Predicates
pp. 52–53

1.A 2.A 3.B 4.A 5.B
6.A 7.B 8.A 9.B 10.A
11.A 12.B

The Third LAP
Language Activity Pages
pp. 54–55

A: 1.A 2.A; **B:** 1.B 2.C 3.A 4.A; **C:** 1. cats 2. poke 3. stalk and attack 4. balls and string 5. like; **D:** 1. Answers will vary. 2. Answers will vary.

(continued on next page)

■■■■■ **Unit 18** ■■■■■
Types of Sentences
pp. 56–59

1.A	2.B	3.A	4.A	5.B
6.A	7.B	8.B	9.A	10.B
11.B	12.A	13.A	14.B	15.B
16.A	17.B	18.D	19.A	20.A
21.C	22.D	23.B	24.C	25.D

■■■■■ **Unit 19** ■■■■■
Changing Sentences
into Questions
pp. 60–61

1.A	2.B	3.A	4.C	5.B
6.A	7.B	8.B	9.C	10.B

■■■■ **The Last LAP** ■■■■
Language Activity Pages
pp. 62–63

A: 1.B 2.B; **B:** 1.B 2.A 3.B
4.A 5.B; **C:** 1. You get out
everything you need, and you
put it on the table. CP 2. You
spread ketchup and mustard on
both slices of bread. SS 3. You
put two slices of lunch meat
on one slice of bread, and then
you put the two slices of bread
together. CP
4. You cut the sandwich in
half. SS; **D:** 1. Answers will
vary. 2. Answers will vary.

Unit 1
Nouns
pp. 6–9

1.A	2.D	3.C	4.D	5.B
6.D	7.D	8.A	9.D	10.C
11.B	12.D	13.A	14.D	15.A
16.C	17.C	18.D	19.B	20.A
21.A	22.D	23.C	24.C	25.A
26.C	27.B	28.D		

Unit 2
Possessive Nouns
pp. 10–11

1.B	2.A	3.A	4.A	5.B
6.B	7.A	8.A	9.A	10.A
11.B	12.A	13.A	14.B	15.B
16.A				

Unit 3
Subject and Object Pronouns
pp. 12–17

1.C	2.A	3.C	4.C	5.A
6.A	7.D	8.B	9.C	10.C
11.D	12.D	13.A	14.B	15.B
16.A	17.A	18.B	19.C	20.D
21.C	22.A	23.D	24.D	25.A
26.C	27.B	28.C	29.A	30.D
31.A	32.B	33.A	34.D	35.C

Unit 4
Possessive Pronouns
pp. 18–19

1.A	2.B	3.A	4.B	5.B
6.A	7.C	8.B	9.A	10.D
11.B	12.C			

Unit 5
Pronouns
pp. 20–21

1.B	2.B	3.A	4.A	5.A
6.B	7.B	8.A	9.A	10.A
11.A	12.B	13.B	14.A	15.A

Unit 6
Pronouns
pp. 22–23

1.A	2.A	3.B	4.B	5.A
6.B	7.A	8.A	9.B	10.A
11.A	12.B	13.B	14.A	15.B

The First LAP
Language Activity Pages
pp. 24–25

A: 1. interrogative 2. possessive
3. intensive 4. object 5. proper
6. compound 7. reflexive
8. demonstrative; **B:** 1. My 2. I
3. we 4. That 5. him 6. they
7. them 8. himself; **C:** 1. Barton
Elementary School 2. carnival
3. success 4. activities 5. adults

6. children 7. money
8. playground 9. Ms. Han
10. principal 11. school
12. students 13. teachers
14. parents 15. event 16. night;
D: 1. Answers will vary.
2. Answers will vary.

Unit 7
Verbs
pp. 26–27

1.B	2.B	3.A	4.B	5.A
6.A	7.A	8.A	9.B	10.B
11.B	12.A			

Unit 8
Adjectives
pp. 28–29

1.D	2.A	3.C	4.A	5.A
6.B	7.C	8.B	9.A	10.B
11.A	12.C	13.A	14.C	15.C

Unit 9
Adverbs
pp. 30–31

1.D	2.C	3.B	4.A	5.A
6.B	7.A	8.B	9.A	10.B
11.A	12.B	13.B	14.B	

Unit 10
Prepositions
pp. 32–33

1.B	2.A	3.B	4.B	5.A
6.B	7.A	8.B	9.A	10.A
11.B	12.B	13.A	14.A	

Unit 11
Interjections and Conjunctions
pp. 34–35

1.A	2.B	3.A	4.B	5.B
6.A	7.A	8.B	9.A	10.B
11.B	12.A	13.A	14.A	

The Second LAP
Language Activity Pages
pp. 36–37

A: 1. proper 2. preposition
3. object 4. action 5. adverb
6. coordinating 7. subordinating
8. interjection; **B:** 1. adj. 2. adj.
3. verb 4. adj. 5. verb 6. adv.
7. adj. 8. verb 9. verb 10. adv.;
C: 1. prep. 2. prep. 3. conj.
4. prep. 5. prep. 6. conj.
7. conj. 8. prep. 9. conj.
10. prep.; **D:** 1. Answers will
vary. 2. Answers will vary.

Unit 12
Subjects and Predicates
pp. 38–43

1.C	2.B	3.B	4.C	5.A
6.B	7.C	8.B	9.C	10.B
11.A	12.B	13.B	14.D	15.C
16.A	17.B	18.A	19.B	20.B
21.A	22.B	23.A	24.B	25.B
26.A	27.A	28.B	29.A	30.A
31.B	32.A	33.A	34.B	35.B
36.A	37.B	38.B	39.A	40.A
41.A	42.B			

Unit 13
Direct Objects
pp. 44–47

1.A	2.A	3.A	4.B	5.B
6.A	7.B	8.B	9.A	10.A
11.B	12.A	13.A	14.B	15.A
16.B	17.B	18.A	19.B	20.B
21.A	22.A	23.B	24.A	25.A
26.A	27.B	28.B	29.B	30.A
31.B	32.A	33.B	34.A	35.A
36.A	37.A	38.B	39.A	40.B

The Third LAP
Language Activity Pages
pp. 48–49

A: 1. complete 2. direct
3. predicate 4. compound
5. complete; **B:** 1.SS 2.CP
3.DO 4.CS 5.DO 6.SP;
C: 1. No 2. Yes 3. No 4. Yes
5. Yes; **D:** 1. Answers will vary.
2. Answers will vary.

Unit 14
Clauses
pp. 50–55

1.A	2.B	3.B	4.A	5.B
6.A	7.B	8.A	9.A	10.B
11.A	12.A	13.B	14.A	15.A
16.B	17.B	18.A	19.A	20.A
21.A	22.B	23.B	24.B	25.A
26.B	27.A	28.B	29.B	30.A
31.B	32.B	33.A	34.B	35.A
36.A	37.B	38.A	39.B	40.A
41.B	42.A			

Unit 15
Clauses
pp. 56–57

1.A	2.B	3.B	4.B	5.A
6.A	7.A	8.A	9.B	10.B
11.A	12.A	13.A	14.B	15.B
16.A				

(continued on next page)

■■■■ **Unit 16** ■■■■
Types of Sentences
pp. 58–61

1.B	2.A	3.B	4.A	5.A
6.B	7.A	8.B	9.A	10.A
11.A	12.B	13.A	14.B	15.A
16.B	17.C	18.B	19.C	20.B
21.B	22.C	23.C	24.A	25.A
26.B	27.C	28.A	29.B	30.C

■■■■ **The Last LAP** ■■■■
Language Activity Pages
pp. 62–63
A: 1.A 2.D 3.C 4.E 5.B; **B:** 1.D
2.D 3.D 4.I 5.I; **C:** 1.S 2.CP
3.CX 4.S; **D:** 1. Answers will
vary. 2. Answers will vary.

Unit 1
Nouns
pp. 6–9

1.D	2.A	3.C	4.D	5.C
6.B	7.A	8.C	9.D	10.B
11.C	12.D	13.D	14.A	15.B
16.C	17.A	18.D	19.B	20.A
21.D	22.B	23.C	24.C	25.D
26.A	27.B	28.B	29.A	30.C
31.A	32.D	33.D	34.B	35.A
36.D	37.B	38.B		

Unit 2
Possessive Nouns
pp. 10–11

1.A	2.B	3.A	4.A	5.A
6.B	7.A	8.B	9.B	10.A
11.B	12.A	13.A	14.B	15.A
16.A	17.B	18.A		

Unit 3
Subject and Object Pronouns
pp. 12–15

1.B	2.A	3.A	4.B	5.B
6.A	7.A	8.A	9.B	10.B
11.A	12.B	13.B	14.A	15.A
16.B	17.A	18.B	19.C	20.D
21.B	22.D	23.C	24.A	25.C
26.C	27.A	28.C	29.B	30.D

Unit 4
Possessive Pronouns
pp. 16–17

1.A	2.B	3.A	4.B	5.B
6.A	7.B	8.C	9.B	10.A
11.A	12.C	13.C	14.B	15.A

Unit 5
Pronouns
pp. 18–19

1.B	2.B	3.A	4.B	5.B
6.A	7.B	8.A	9.B	10.A
11.B	12.A	13.B	14.B	15.B

Unit 6
Pronouns
pp. 20–21

1.B	2.C	3.A	4.B	5.A
6.B	7.D	8.B	9.A	10.A
11.B	12.A	13.A	14.B	

The First LAP
Language Activity Pages
pp. 22–23
A: 1. pronoun 2. possessive 3. singular 4. plural 5. indefinite 6. interrogative 7. reflexive 8. compound 9. object 10. subject; **B:** 1. our 2. We 3. others 4. Nobody 5. us 6. She 7. them 8. It;

C: 1. editor 2. city's 3. plan 4. Parker Park 5. mall 6. Spring Avenue 7. park 8. plants 9. neighbors 10. children 11. places 12. stores 13. cars 14. traffic 15. pollution 16. space; **D:** 1. Answers will vary. 2. Answers will vary.

Unit 7
Verbs
pp. 24–25

1.B	2.A	3.A	4.A	5.B
6.B	7.A	8.A	9.A	10.A
11.B	12.C	13.B	14.C	

Unit 8
Adjectives
pp. 26–27

1.A	2.A	3.A	4.A	5.B
6.A	7.B	8.C	9.A	10.B
11.C	12.A	13.B	14.A	15.D

Unit 9
Adverbs
pp. 28–29

1.A	2.A	3.B	4.A	5.B
6.A	7.B	8.B	9.A	10.B
11.D	12.C	13.D	14.C	15.B

Unit 10
Prepositions
pp. 30–31

1.B	2.A	3.B	4.A	5.A
6.B	7.B	8.B	9.B	10.A
11.B	12.B	13.B	14.A	15.A
16.A	17.B	18.A		

Unit 11
Conjunctions
pp. 32–33

1.A	2.A	3.B	4.A	5.A
6.B	7.A	8.C	9.A	10.C
11.B	12.C	13.C	14.A	15.B

The Second LAP
Language Activity Pages
pp. 34–35
A: 1. adjective 2. adverb 3. proper 4. demonstrative 5. helping 6. preposition 7. conjunction 8. subordinating 9. Correlative 10. coordinating; **B:** 1. prep 2. prep 3. conj 4. prep 5. conj 6. prep 7. prep 8. conj 9. conj 10. conj; **C:** 1.V 2.V 3.ADV 4.ADJ 5.ADJ 6.ADJ 7.V 8.ADJ 9.V 10.ADV; **D:** 1. Answers will vary. 2. Answers will vary.

Unit 12
Subjects and Predicates
pp. 36–39

1.B	2.A	3.A	4.A	5.B
6.A	7.B	8.B	9.A	10.B
11.A	12.A	13.B	14.A	15.B
16.B	17.B	18.A	19.A	20.B
21.A	22.A	23.B	24.A	25.A
26.B	27.B	28.A	29.B	30.A
31.B	32.A	33.A	34.B	35.A
36.B				

Unit 13
Direct and Indirect Objects
pp. 40–43

1.A	2.A	3.B	4.B	5.A
6.B	7.A	8.B	9.C	10.C
11.B	12.D	13.C	14.B	15.D
16.A	17.B	18.C	19.A	20.A
21.B	22.A	23.A	24.B	25.B
26.B	27.A	28.A	29.B	30.B
31.A	32.B	33.A	34.A	35.B
36.A	37.B	38.A		

Unit 14
Appositives pp. 44–47

1.A	2.B	3.A	4.B	5.B
6.A	7.B	8.A	9.A	10.B
11.A	12.A	13.B	14.A	15.B
16.A	17.B	18.B	19.A	20.A
21.B	22.B	23.B	24.A	25.B
26.A	27.B	28.B	29.A	30.A
31.A	32.B	33.A	34.B	

The Third LAP
Language Activity Pages
pp. 48–49
A: 1. sentence 2. complete 3. appositive 4. participial 5. indirect 6. direct 7. subject 8. predicate; **B:** 1.AP 2.PP 3.PP 4.AP 5.PP 6.AP 7.AP 8.AP; **C:** 1.S 2.P 3.DO 4.P 5.DO 6.S 7.DO 8.P 9.IO 10.DO; **D:** 1. Answers will vary. 2. Answers will vary.

Unit 15
Clauses pp. 50–55

1.A	2.B	3.B	4.A	5.A
6.B	7.B	8.A	9.B	10.A
11.B	12.A	13.A	14.A	15.A
16.B	17.A	18.A	19.B	20.A
21.A	22.A	23.B	24.A	25.A
26.A	27.B	28.B	29.A	30.A
31.B	32.A	33.A	34.A	35.B
36.A	37.A	38.A	39.B	40.A
41.A	42.B	43.A	44.A	45.A

(continued on next page)

Unit 16
Types of Sentences
pp. 56–61

1.A	2.A	3.B	4.B	5.A
6.B	7.B	8.A	9.B	10.A
11.A	12.A	13.B	14.A	15.B
16.A	17.B	18.A	19.B	20.B
21.A	22.A	23.A	24.B	25.C
26.C	27.A	28.B	29.B	30.A
31.C	32.C	33.A	34.A	35.B
36.B	37.A	38.B	39.A	40.A
41.A	42.D	43.C	44.C	45.C
46.D	47.B	48.B	49.C	50.D

The Last LAP
Language Activity Pages
pp. 62–63

A: 1. adjective 2. adverb
3. Dependent 4. Independent
5. compound-complex
6. simple 7. complex
8. compound; **B:** 1.I 2.D 3.D
4.I 5.I 6.D; **C:** 1.S 2.CPCX
3.S 4.CX 5.CP 6.CX;
D: 1. Answers will vary.
2. Answers will vary.

Unit 1
Nouns
pp. 6–9

1.A 2.A 3.B 4.B 5.B
6.C 7.D 8.A 9.C 10.D
11.A 12.B 13.C 14.B 15.C
16.C 17.B 18.D 19.C 20.D
21.C 22.A 23.B 24.B 25.D
26.B 27.C 28.D 29.B 30.A
31.D 32.D 33.A 34.C 35.B.
36.D 37.A 38.B 39.A 40.B
41.C 42.B

Unit 2
Possessive Nouns
pp. 10–11

1.B 2.C 3.C 4.B 5.C
6.A 7.C 8.C 9.A 10.C
11.C 12.B 13.C 14.A 15.B
16.A 17.C 18.B

Unit 3
Subject and Object Pronouns
pp. 12–15

1.A 2.A 3.A 4.B 5.A
6.B 7.A 8.B 9.B 10.B
11.A 12.B 13.B 14.B 15.B
16.A 17.B 18.B 19.A 20.B
21.B 22.A 23.C 24.A 25.D
26.C

Unit 4
Possessive Pronouns
pp. 16–17

1.B 2.A 3.A 4.B 5.D
6.C 7.C 8.B

Unit 5
Pronouns
pp. 18–19

1.A 2.B 3.D 4.A 5.B
6.D 7.B 8.A 9.B 10.B
11.B 12.A 13.B 14.B 15.B

Unit 6
Pronouns
pp. 20–21

1.A 2.A 3.B 4.B 5.A
6.B 7.B 8.A 9.B 10.A
11.B 12.B 13.A 14.B

The First LAP
Language Activity Pages
pp. 22–23

A: 1.C 2.C 3.B 4.C;
B: 1. savings 2. town 3. kinds
4. shoes 5. member 6. family
7. needs 8. boots 9. slippers
10. quality 11. products
12. staff 13. employees
14. hours 15. sale 16. effect

17. Friday 18. Saturday;
C: 1. My, possessive 2. I,
subject 3. We, subject 4. some,
indefinite 5. that, relative
6. me, object 7. Everyone,
indefinite 8. All, indefinite
9. himself, intensive 10. Our,
possessive; **D:** 1. Answers will
vary. 2. Answers will vary.

Unit 7
Verbs
pp. 24–25

1.B 2.B 3.A 4.A 5.A
6.B 7.B 8.A 9.B 10.B
11.A 12.C

Unit 8
Adjectives
pp. 26–27

1.B 2.A 3.C 4.A 5.D
6.B 7.A 8.C 9.D 10.D
11.B 12.C 13.A 14.B

Unit 9
Adverbs
pp. 28–29

1.B 2.C 3.B 4.C 5.D
6.A 7.B 8.A 9.B 10.C
11.A 12.C 13.D 14.A 15.B
16.B

Unit 10
Prepositions
pp. 30–31

1.B 2.D 3.D 4.A 5.B
6.C 7.D 8.B 9.D 10.C
11.D 12.D 13.B 14.D 15.B

Unit 11
Conjunctions
pp. 32–33

1.B 2.A 3.A 4.B 5.A
6.B 7.A 8.A 9.C 10.B
11.B 12.B 13.C 14.C

The Second LAP
Language Activity Pages
pp. 34–35

A: 1.B 2.C 3.A; **B:** 1.B 2.C
3.A 4.D 5.A; **C:** 1.PP 2.CC
3.P 4.PP 5.SC 6.CC 7.SC 8.P
9.SC 10.PP;
D: 1. Answers will vary.
2. Answers will vary.

Unit 12
Subjects and Predicates
pp. 36–39

1.A 2.B 3.C 4.B 5.B
6.D 7.A 8.C 9.C 10.A
11.A 12.A 13.B 14.A 15.B
16.A 17.A 18.B 19.B 20.C
21.C 22.B 23.C 24.B 25.A
26.D 27.A 28.A 29.B 30.A
31.A 32.B 33.A 34.B

Unit 13
Direct and Indirect Objects
pp. 40–43

1.C 2.B 3.C 4.A 5.D
6.B 7.B 8.C 9.D 10.A
11.B 12.C 13.A 14.D 15.A
16.C 17.A 18.D 19.B 20.A
21.A 22.B 23.A 24.A 25.A
26.B 27.B 28.B 29.B 30.A
31.A 32.A 33.B 34.B 35.A
36.A 37.B 38.A 39.B 40.A

Unit 14
Appositives pp. 44–45

1.B 2.A 3.C 4.B 5.D
6.B 7.B 8.D 9.A 10.B
11.A 12.A 13.B 14.A 15.B

Unit 15
Gerunds pp. 46–47

1.B 2.A 3.A 4.B 5.A
6.B 7.B 8.B 9.A 10.B
11.A 12.A 13.B 14.A 15.A

The Third LAP
Language Activity Pages
pp. 48–49

A: 1.B 2.B 3.B 4.A; **B:** 1.AP
2.GP 3.A 4.AP 5.G; **C:** 1.C
2.E 3.B 4.F 5.A 6.D;
D: 1. Answers will vary.
2. Answers will vary.

Unit 16
Clauses
pp. 50–55

1.A 2.A 3.B 4.A 5.B
6.B 7.A 8.B 9.B 10.B
11.A 12.A 13.B 14.B 15.B
16.B 17.A 18.A 19.B 20.A
21.B 22.A 23.B 24.A 25.B
26.B 27.A 28.A 29.B 30.B
31.B 32.B 33.A 34.B 35.A
36.A 37.B 38.A 39.A 40.B
41.A 42.B 43.A 44.A 45.B
46.A 47.A 48.B 49.B 50.A

(continued on next page)

━━━━ **Unit 17** ━━━━
Types of Sentences
pp. 56–61

1.A	2.B	3.B	4.B	5.A
6.A	7.A	8.B	9.C	10.C
11.A	12.C	13.C	14.A	15.B
16.B	17.B	18.A	19.B	20.A
21.A	22.A	23.A	24.D	25.C
26.A	27.B	28.D	29.A	30.B
31.A	32.D	33.D	34.B	35.B
36.A	37.C	38.C	39.A	40.C
41.C	42.D	43.A	44.B	45.A
46.B	47.A	48.D		

━━━━ **The Last LAP** ━━━━
Language Activity Pages
pp. 62–63

A: 1.B 2.C 3.B 4.A; **B:** 1.S
2.CX 3.S 4.CP 5.CPCX; **C:** 1.I
2.D 3.I 4.D 5.I 6.I 7.D 8.D;
D: 1. Answers will vary.
2. Answers will vary.

Unit 1
Nouns
pp. 6–9

1.B 2.A 3.D 4.D 5.E
6.C 7.D 8.E 9.D 10.A
11.E 12.D 13.E 14.E 15.C
16.E 17.C 18.D 19.B 20.A
21.A 22.B 23.A 24.A 25.B

Unit 2
Possessive Nouns
pp. 10–11

1.B 2.A 3.C 4.C 5.A
6.B 7.A 8.C 9.B 10.A
11.B 12.C 13.A 14.B 15.A
16.C

Unit 3
Subject and Object Pronouns
pp. 12–15

1.A 2.B 3.A 4.A 5.A
6.A 7.B 8.A 9.A 10.B
11.A 12.A 13.A 14.A 15.B
16.A 17.B 18.A 19.B 20.C
21.B 22.A 23.C 24.C 25.B
26.A 27.C 28.D 29.A 30.D

Unit 4
Possessive Pronouns
pp. 16–17

1.A 2.A 3.B 4.A 5.B
6.B 7.A 8.B 9.B 10.A
11.B 12.A 13.B 14.A 15.B
16.B 17.B 18.B 19.B 20.A

Unit 5
Pronouns
pp. 18–19

1.A 2.A 3.B 4.B 5.A
6.A 7.A 8.B 9.B 10.B
11.A 12.A

Unit 6
Pronouns
pp. 20–21

1.A 2.B 3.C 4.A 5.B
6.D 7.C 8.C 9.A 10.A
11.B 12.A 13.B 14.A 15.A
16.B

The First LAP
Language Activity Pages
pp. 22–23

A: 1.B 2.D 3.C 4.B; **B:** 1. aunts
2. uncles 3. in-laws 4. town
5. Pella 6. Iowa 7. Tulip
Festival 8. celebration 9. spring
10. time 11. community
12. heritage 13. parade
14. men 15. women
16. children 17. costumes
18. flowers 19. tulips
20. mealtime 21. plenty
22. food 23. festivities 24. days
25. fun; **C:** 1. It 2. myself 3. I
4. their 5. Our 6. me 7. all
8. those; **D:** 1. Answers will
vary. 2. Answers will vary.

Unit 7
Verbs
pp. 24–25

1.A 2.B 3.C 4.A 5.C
6.B 7.C 8.A 9.B 10.A
11.A 12.C 13.A 14.C 15.B
16.A 17.B 18.C

Unit 8
Adjectives
pp. 26–27

1.A 2.B 3.D 4.E 5.A
6.B 7.E 8.A 9.C 10.D
11.D 12.A

Unit 9
Adverbs
pp. 28–29

1.B 2.A 3.C 4.E 5.D
6.A 7.C 8.C 9.B 10.E
11.C 12.E

Unit 10
Prepositions
pp. 30–31

1.B 2.A 3.B 4.B 5.B
6.A 7.B 8.A 9.B 10.B
11.A 12.A

Unit 11
Conjunctions
pp. 32–33

1.A 2.B 3.A 4.C 5.B
6.B 7.C 8.B 9.C 10.A
11.B 12.B 13.C 14.B 15.C
16.A

The Second LAP
Language Activity Pages
pp. 34–35

A: 1.B 2.C 3.A 4.D;
B: 1. adjective 2. verb
3. adjective 4. adjective
5. verb 6. adverb
7. preposition 8. conjunction
9. adjective 10. adjective
11. adjective 12. verb
13. adjective 14. adjective
15. adverb 16. verb 17. verb
18. adverb 19. conjunction
20. adjective 21. conjunction
22. adjective; **C:** 1. conjunction
2. adverb 3. preposition
4. preposition 5. verb
6. adverb 7. conjunction
8. preposition 9. conjunction
10. adverb 11. adverb
12. preposition 13. conjunction
14. adverb; **D:** 1. Answers will
vary. 2. Answers will vary.

Unit 12
Subjects and Predicates
pp. 36–39

1.A 2.B 3.B 4.A 5.B
6.B 7.B 8.A 9.B 10.A
11.B 12.B 13.A 14.A 15.A
16.B 17.A 18.B 19.B 20.B
21.A 22.A 23.B 24.A 25.B
26.B 27.B 28.B 29.A 30.B

Unit 13
Direct and Indirect Objects
pp. 40–43

1.B 2.E 3.C 4.E 5.C
6.E 7.E 8.C 9.D 10.C
11.A 12.E 13.C 14.D 15.A
16.A 17.B 18.A 19.B 20.A
21.B 22.A 23.A 24.B 25.B
26.A 27.A 28.A 29.B 30.A
31.B 32.A 33.B 34.A

Unit 14
Appositives
pp. 44–45

1.C 2.D 3.B 4.B 5.A
6.B 7.B 8.A 9.B 10.A
11.A 12.B 13.B 14.A 15.A

Unit 15
Gerunds
pp. 46–47

1.B 2.B 3.A 4.A 5.A
6.B 7.A 8.A 9.A 10.B
11.A 12.C 13.B 14.B 15.A
16.C

Unit 16
Infinitives
pp. 48–49

1.A 2.B 3.B 4.A 5.A
6.B 7.A 8.A 9.B 10.A
11.A 12.A 13.A 14.B 15.B
16.B

(continued on next page)

The Third LAP

Language Activity Pages
pp. 50–51

A: 1. sentence 2. subject
3. predicate 4. direct object
5. indirect object; **B:** 1.IP 2.AP
3.GP 4.AP 5.GP 6.IP 7.GP
8.IP; **C:** 1.SS 2.DO 3.SP 4.PP
5.SS 6.PP 7.SP 8.DO 9.DO
10.PP 11.SP 12.SS 13.DO
14. PP; **D:** 1. Answers will vary.
2. Answers will vary.

Unit 17

Clauses
pp. 52–57

1.B	2.A	3.A	4.A	5.B
6.B	7.B	8.A	9.B	10.A
11.A	12.B	13.B	14.B	15.B
16.A	17.B	18.B	19.B	20.A
21.A	22.B	23.B	24.A	25.A
26.B	27.B	28.A	29.A	30.A
31.C	32.A	33.A	34.A	35.B
36.C	37.A	38.B	39.A	40.A
41.B	42.C	43.C	44.A	45.C
46.A	47.A	48.B	49.B	50.A

Unit 18

Types of Sentences
pp. 58–61

1.B	2.A	3.A	4.B	5.A
6.B	7.A	8.B	9.A	10.C
11.C	12.C	13.B	14.B	15.A
16.B	17.A	18.A	19.C	20.A
21.D	22.A	23.B	24.D	25.A
26.D				

The Last LAP

Language Activity Pages
pp. 62–63

A: 1.C 2.A 3.C 4.A; **B:** 1.A
2.A 3.B 4.B; **C:** 1.S 2.CX
3.CPCX 4.CX 5. CP;
D: 1. Answers will vary.
2. Answers will vary.

Unit 1
Nouns
pp. 6–9

1.A 2.C 3.D 4.D 5.B
6.B 7.D 8.C 9.D 10.C
11.B 12.A 13.A 14.A 15.B
16.B 17.A 18.B 19.A 20.B
21.B 22.A 23.B 24.A 25.B
26.A 27.B 28.A

Unit 2
Possessive Nouns
pp. 10–11

1.C 2.B 3.B 4.A 5.A
6.B 7.A 8.B 9.C 10.A
11.C 12.A 13.A 14.A

Unit 3
Subject and Object Pronouns
pp. 12–15

1.A 2.B 3.A 4.A 5.B
6.A 7.A 8.B 9.A 10.A
11.A 12.A 13.B 14.C 15.A
16.D 17.A 18.D 19.C 20.A
21.A 22.B 23.B 24.A 25.B
26.A 27.A 28.B

Unit 4
Possessive Pronouns
pp. 16–17

1.A 2.B 3.A 4.B 5.B
6.A 7.B 8.A 9.A 10.B
11.A 12.B 13.A 14.B

Unit 5
Pronouns pp. 18–19

1.B 2.B 3.B 4.B 5.A
6.A 7.A 8.B 9.A 10.A
11.B 12.B

Unit 6
Pronouns pp. 20–21

1.B 2.C 3.D 4.B 5.A
6.C 7.B 8.B 9.B 10.A
11.B 12.B 13.B 14.B 15.A

The First LAP
Language Activity Pages
pp. 22–23

A: 1.C 2.D 3.A 4.C; **B:** 1. Jess
2. week 3. farm 4. family
5. "city slicker" 6. experience
7. work 8. barn 9. job
10. animals 11. highlight
12. trip 13. Iowa State Fair
14. brother 15. events
16. pressure 17. judges
18. prize 19. time 20. Monica;
C: 1. I 2. us 3. she 4. myself
5. my 6. hers 7. we 8. all
9. me 10. her; **D:** 1. Answers
will vary. 2. Answers will vary.

Unit 7
Verbs
pp. 24–25

1.C 2.B 3.C 4.A 5.C
6.B 7.C 8.A 9.B 10.A
11.B 12.A 13.C 14.B 15.C

Unit 8
Adjectives
pp. 26–27

1.A 2.B 3.B 4.A 5.A
6.A 7.A 8.D 9.B 10.B
11.D 12.C

Unit 9
Adverbs
pp. 28–29

1.B 2.E 3.D 4.E 5.D
6.D 7.D 8.A 9.B 10.B

Unit 10
Prepositions
pp. 30–31

1.B 2.B 3.A 4.B 5.A
6.A 7.A 8.B 9.A 10.B
11.B 12.B

Unit 11
Conjunctions
pp. 32–33

1.B 2.A 3.B 4.B 5.A
6.C 7.C 8.B 9.A 10.C
11.A 12.A 13.B 14.C

The Second LAP
Language Activity Pages
pp. 34–35

A: 1.B 2.A 3.D 4.A; **B:**
1. adjective 2. verb 3. adjective
4. adjective 5. adjective 6. verb
7. adjective 8. verb 9. adverb
10. adjective 11. adverb
12. adjective 13. adjective
14. verb 15. adjective;
C: 1. adjective 2. verb
3. preposition 4. verb
5. preposition 6. preposition
7. adjective 8. conjunction
9. conjunction 10. preposition
11. adverb 12. conjunction
13. preposition 14. verb
15. conjunction; **D:** 1. Answers
will vary. 2. Answers will vary.

Unit 12
Subjects and Predicates
pp. 36–39

1.B 2.A 3.A 4.A 5.B
6.A 7.B 8.A 9.B 10.A
11.A 12.B 13.B 14.A 15.A
16.B 17.A 18.B 19.A 20.A
21.B 22.A 23.A 24.B 25.A
26.B 27.A 28.B 29.A 30.B
31.B 32.A

Unit 13
Direct and Indirect Objects
pp. 40–41

1.A 2.C 3.B 4.C 5.A
6.A 7.B 8.C 9.A 10.A
11.A 12.C 13.B 14.B 15.B
16.A 17.A 18.B

Unit 14
Appositives
pp. 42–43

1.A 2.E 3.C 4.A 5.D
6.B 7.A 8.B 9.A 10.A
11.B 12.B

Unit 15
Gerunds
pp. 44–45

1.A 2.B 3.A 4.B 5.A
6.A 7.A 8.B 9.A 10.A
11.B 12.C 13.B 14.B 15.A

Unit 16
Infinitives
pp. 46–47

1.A 2.B 3.A 4.B 5.B
6.A 7.B 8.A 9.A 10.A
11.A 12.A 13.B 14.B 15.A
16.B

The Third LAP
Language Activity Pages
pp. 48–49

A: 1. gerund 2. indirect object
3. infinitive 4. predicate
5. appositive; **B:** 1.AP 2.A
3.G 4.GP 5.I 6.IP; **C:** 1.SS
2.SS 3.DO 4.IP 5.PP 6.IP
7.SP 8.PP 9.SP 10.DO 11.PP
12.SP 13.DO 14.PP 15.SS
16.SP 17.SS 18.IO 19.DO
20.AP; **D:** 1. Answers will vary.
2. Answers will vary.

(continued on next page)

Unit 17
Clauses
pp. 50–55

1.A	2.A	3.B	4.A	5.B
6.B	7.B	8.A	9.B	10.B
11.B	12.A	13.A	14.A	15.B
16.A	17.A	18.B	19.A	20.A
21.A	22.B	23.B	24.A	25.B
26.A	27.B	28.A	29.B	30.A
31.C	32.A	33.A	34.C	35.B
36.A	37.C	38.A	39.A	40.A
41.C	42.B	43.C	44.A	45.A
46.A	47.C	48.C		

Unit 18
Clauses
pp. 56–57

1.B	2.B	3.B	4.A	5.B
6.A	7.A	8.B	9.A	10.B
11.A	12.B	13.A	14.B	15.B
16.B	17.A	18.A	19.B	20.A

Unit 19
Types of Sentences
pp. 58–61

1.A	2.B	3.A	4.B	5.A
6.A	7.A	8.B	9.C	10.C
11.A	12.C	13.A	14.B	15.B
16.C	17.A	18.B	19.B	20.B
21.A	22.B	23.C	24.C	25.B
26.A	27.B	28.A	29.B	30.D
31.D	32.B			

The Last LAP
Language Activity Pages
pp. 62–63

A: 1.A 2.B 3.E 4.D 5.F 6.C;
B: 1.D 2.D 3.D 4.I 5.I;
C: 1.SS 2.CP 3.CP 4.SS
5.CPCX 6.SCX; **D:** 1. Answers
will vary. 2. Answers will vary.

Unit 1
Subject-Verb Agreement
pp. 6–9

1.B 2.A 3.B 4.B 5.A
6.B 7.A 8.A 9.B 10.B
11.B 12.B 13.A 14.A 15.B
16.A 17.B 18.B 19.A 20.A
21.B 22.B

Unit 2
Subject-Verb Agreement
pp. 10–13

1.B 2.A 3.A 4.B 5.A
6.A 7.B 8.B 9.A 10.A
11.B 12.B 13.A 14.A 15.A
16.B 17.A 18.B 19.B 20.A

Unit 3
Subject-Verb Agreement
pp. 14–17

1.A 2.A 3.B 4.A 5.B
6.B 7.A 8.B 9.B 10.A
11.A 12.B 13.A 14.A 15.B
16.B 17.A 18.A 19.B 20.A

Unit 4
Subject-Verb Agreement
pp. 18–21

1.A 2.B 3.A 4.A 5.B
6.B 7.A 8.A 9.B 10.B
11.A 12.A 13.A 14.B 15.A
16.B 17.A 18.A 19.B 20.B
21.A 22.A

The First LAP
Language Activity Pages
pp. 22–23

A: 1. singular 2. plural 3. verb;
B: 1. writes 2. write 3. coach
4. coaches 5. build 6. build
7. draws 8. watch 9. watch;
C: 1. climb 2. waves 3. likes
4. play 5. watches;
D: 1. Answers will vary.
2. Answers will vary.

Unit 5
The Verb *Be*
pp. 24–29

1.A 2.B 3.B 4.A 5.B
6.A 7.B 8.B 9.A 10.B
11.A 12.B 13.A 14.B 15.B
16.B 17.B 18.A 19.B 20.A
21.B 22.B 23.A 24.B 25.B
26.A 27.A 28.B 29.A 30.B
31.A 32.B

Unit 6
The Verb *Have*
pp. 30–35

1.B 2.B 3.A 4.B 5.A
6.B 7.A 8.B 9.A 10.B
11.A 12.A 13.B 14.B 15.A
16.A 17.A 18.A 19.A 20.A
21.A 22.B 23.B 24.B 25.A
26.A 27.A 28.B 29.A 30.B
31.A 32.A 33.A 34.B

The Second LAP
Language Activity Pages
pp. 36–37

A: 1. verbs 2. be 3. have;
B: 1. are 2. is 3. are 4. have
5. has 6. have 7. has 8. is
9. has; **C:** 1. has 2. am 3. have
4. are; **D:** 1. Answers will vary.
2. Answers will vary.

Unit 7
**Using *This, That, These,*
and *Those***
pp. 38–41

1.A 2.A 3.B 4.B 5.A
6.B 7.A 8.B 9.B 10.A
11.B 12.A 13.B 14.A 15.B
16.B 17.A 18.A 19.B 20.A
21.B 22.A

Unit 8
Past-Tense Verbs
pp. 42–43

1.B 2.A 3.A 4.B 5.A
6.A 7.B 8.A 9.B 10.A

Unit 9
Past Tense of *Be*
pp. 44–47

1.A 2.B 3.A 4.A 5.B
6.A 7.B 8.B 9.B 10.A
11.B 12.A 13.B 14.B 15.A
16.A 17.A 18.B 19.B 20.B

The Third LAP
Language Activity Pages
pp. 48–49

A: 1. adjectives 2. singular
3. plural 4. verbs; **B:** 1. that
2. these 3. that 4. lasted
5. ended 6. cheered; **C:** 1. This
2. lasted 3. Those 4. moved
5. crashed 6. That;
D: 1. Answers will vary.
2. Answers will vary.

Unit 10
Comparing with Adjectives
pp. 50–53

1.B 2.A 3.A 4.B 5.A
6.A 7.A 8.B 9.B 10.A
11.B 12.A 13.B 14.A 15.A
16.B 17.A 18.A 19.A 20.B

Unit 11
A* and *An
pp. 54–57

1.A 2.B 3.A 4.A 5.A
6.B 7.A 8.B 9.A 10.A
11.B 12.A 13.A 14.B 15.A
16.B 17.A 18.B 19.B 20.A
21.B 22.A

Unit 12
**Agreement with
Helping Verbs**
pp. 58–61

1.A 2.B 3.B 4.A 5.A
6.B 7.A 8.B 9.A 10.B
11.B 12.A 13.A 14.B 15.A
16.A 17.A 18.B 19.B 20.A
21.A 22.B

The Last LAP
Language Activity Pages
pp. 62–63

A: 1. adjective 2. articles
3. consonant 4. vowel;
B: 1. smaller 2. were 3. was
4. cleaner 5. am 6. fastest;
C: 1. a 2. a 3. quicker
4. fastest 5. an; **D:** 1. Answers
will vary. 2. Answers will vary.

Unit 1
Subject-Verb Agreement
pp. 6–7

1.B 2.B 3.B 4.A 5.B
6.A 7.A 8.A 9.B 10.B

Unit 2
Subject-Verb Agreement
pp. 8–9

1.A 2.A 3.B 4.B 5.B
6.B 7.A 8.A 9.B 10.B

Unit 3
Subject-Verb Agreement
pp. 10–11

1.A 2.B 3.B 4.A 5.B
6.A 7.A 8.A 9.B 10.B
11.B 12.B

Unit 4
Subject-Verb Agreement
pp. 12–15

1.A 2.B 3.B 4.A 5.B
6.A 7.B 8.A 9.A 10.B
11.A 12.A 13.A 14.B 15.A
16.A 17.A 18.A 19.B 20.A
21.A 22.B 23.A 24.B 25.A

Unit 5
Subject-Verb Agreement
pp. 16–19

1.B 2.B 3.A 4.A 5.B
6.A 7.A 8.A 9.B 10.B
11.B 12.B 13.B 14.B 15.A
16.B 17.B 18.A 19.A 20.B
21.A 22.A 23.B 24.B 25.A
26.A 27.B 28.A

The First LAP
Language Activity Pages
pp. 20–21

A: 1.A 2.A 3.A; **B:** 1. run
2. pretends 3. float 4. float
5. agrees 6. agrees 7. toss
8. tosses; **C:** 1. dentist keeps
2. She and her assistant take
3. tools clean 4. they make
5. dentist tells; **D:** 1. Answers
will vary. 2. Answers will vary.

Unit 6
The Verb *Be*
pp. 22–23

1.B 2.B 3.A 4.A 5.B
6.B 7.A 8.A 9.A 10.A

Unit 7
The Verb *Have*
pp. 24–25

1.A 2.A 3.A 4.B 5.A
6.A 7.A 8.B 9.A 10.B
11.B 12.A

Unit 8
**Using *This, That, These,*
and *Those***
pp. 26–27

1.A 2.B 3.A 4.B 5.B
6.B 7.A 8.B 9.B 10.A
11.A 12.A

Unit 9
Adjective-Noun Agreement
pp. 28–29

1.A 2.B 3.A 4.B 5.B
6.B 7.A 8.B 9.A 10.B
11.A 12.A 13.A 14.B

The Second LAP
Language Activity Pages
pp. 30–31

A: 1.A 2.C 3.D 4.B; **B:** 1. go
2. likes 3. are 4. have 5. swim;
C: 1. are 2. go 3. love
4. laughs; **D:** 1. Answers will
vary. 2. Answers will vary.

Unit 10
Past-Tense Verbs
pp. 32–37

1.B 2.A 3.B 4.B 5.A
6.B 7.B 8.A 9.B 10.A
11.B 12.A 13.A 14.A 15.B
16.B 17.A 18.B 19.B 20.A
21.B 22.B 23.A 24.A 25.B
26.A 27.A 28.A 29.A 30.B
31.B 32.A 33.B 34.A 35.A
36.A 37.B 38.A

Unit 11
Past Tense of *Be*
pp. 38–41

1.A 2.B 3.B 4.A 5.B
6.A 7.A 8.B 9.A 10.A
11.B 12.B 13.A 14.A 15.A
16.B 17.B 18.A 19.B 20.B
21.A 22.B 23.B 24.A

Unit 12
Comparing with Adjectives
pp. 42–43

1.A 2.B 3.A 4.B 5.A
6.A 7.B 8.A 9.B 10.A

Unit 13
A* and *An
pp. 44–45

1.B 2.B 3.A 4.B 5.A
6.B 7.A 8.B 9.A 10.B

The Third LAP
Language Activity Pages
pp. 46–47

A: 1.B 2.A 3.B 4.B;
B: 1. go/went 2. comes/came
3. see/saw 4. like/liked;
C: 1. biggest 2. smaller
3. noisier; **D:** 1. Answers will
vary. 2. Answers will vary.

Unit 14
**Agreement with
Helping Verbs**
pp. 48–51

1.B 2.B 3.A 4.B 5.A
6.B 7.A 8.A 9.A 10.B
11.A 12.A 13.B 14.A 15.B
16.A 17.A 18.B 19.B 20.A
21.B 22.B 23.B 24.A 25.A

Unit 15
**Agreement with
Helping Verbs**
pp. 52–53

1.B 2.A 3.A 4.A 5.B
6.A 7.A 8.B 9.A 10.B
11.A 12.A 13.B 14.A

Unit 16
Future-Tense Verbs
pp. 54–57

1.A 2.C 3.B 4.D 5.B
6.C 7.A 8.A 9.C 10.B
11.B 12.C 13.A 14.C 15.B
16.A 17.B 18.C 19.A 20.A
21.C 22.B

Unit 17
Contractions
pp. 58–61

1.B 2.B 3.A 4.B 5.A
6.B 7.A 8.B 9.A 10.B
11.B 12.B 13.B 14.A 15.C
16.C 17.B 18.B 19.A 20.C
21.C 22.C 23.B 24.A

The Last LAP
Language Activity Pages
pp. 62–63

A: 1.D 2.A 3.B; **B:** 1. present
2. past 3. future 4. present;
C: 1. They're 2. It's 3. I'm
4. We're; **D:** 1. Answers will
vary. 2. Answers will vary.

Unit 1
Subject-Verb Agreement
pp. 6–7

1.B	2.B	3.B	4.A	5.A
6.B	7.B	8.A	9.A	10.B
11.B	12.B	13.B	14.A	15.B

Unit 2
The Verbs *Be* and *Have*
pp. 8–9

1.A	2.B	3.A	4.B	5.B
6.A	7.A	8.B	9.A	10.A
11.B	12.B	13.A	14.B	15.A
16.B				

Unit 3
Subject-Verb Agreement
pp. 10–13

1.B	2.B	3.A	4.A	5.B
6.A	7.B	8.A	9.B	10.A
11.B	12.B	13.A	14.A	15.B
16.B	17.A	18.A	19.B	20.A
21.B	22.B	23.A	24.B	25.B
26.B	27.C	28.B	29.A	30.C

Unit 4
Subject-Verb Agreement
pp. 14–17

1.A	2.A	3.B	4.B	5.A
6.B	7.A	8.A	9.B	10.A
11.A	12.A	13.B	14.A	15.B
16.B	17.A	18.B	19.A	20.A
21.A	22.A	23.B	24.A	25.B
26.B	27.A	28.A	29.B	30.A

The First LAP
Language Activity Pages
pp. 18–19

A: 1.B 2.B; **B:** 1.B 2.A 3.B 4.A
5.A; **C:** 1.B 2.F 3.C 4.D 5.E
6.A; **D:** 1. Answers will vary.
2. Answers will vary.

Unit 5
Subject-Verb Agreement
pp. 20–21

1.B	2.A	3.A	4.B	5.A
6.B	7.A	8.B	9.A	10.A
11.B	12.A	13.A	14.B	15.B

Unit 6
Adjective-Noun Agreement
pp. 22–23

1.A	2.A	3.B	4.B	5.A
6.A	7.A	8.B	9.A	10.B
11.B	12.B	13.B	14.A	

Unit 7
Speaking of Yourself Last
pp. 24–25

1.A	2.B	3.B	4.C	5.A
6.A	7.B	8.A	9.C	10.C
11.C	12.B	13.C	14.A	

Unit 8
Past-Tense Verbs
pp. 26–29

1.B	2.B	3.A	4.A	5.B
6.A	7.B	8.A	9.A	10.B
11.B	12.A	13.A	14.A	15.B
16.A	17.A	18.B	19.B	20.A
21.B	22.A	23.B	24.B	25.B
26.B	27.A	28.A	29.B	30.B
31.A	32.B	33.A	34.B	

Unit 9
Past Tense of *Be*
pp. 30–31

1.B	2.B	3.B	4.B	5.A
6.B	7.A	8.B	9.A	10.A
11.B	12.B			

Unit 10
Comparing with Adjectives
pp. 32–35

1.C	2.B	3.C	4.A	5.C
6.B	7.C	8.B	9.A	10.A
11.C	12.C	13.A	14.A	15.B
16.C	17.B	18.C	19.A	20.A
21.C	22.B	23.A	24.C	25.A
26.C				

Unit 11
Comparing with Adverbs
pp. 36–37

1.B	2.B	3.A	4.B	5.A
6.B	7.A	8.B	9.A	10.B
11.B	12.A	13.B	14.A	

The Second LAP
Language Activity Pages
pp. 38–39

A: 1.C 2.A 3.B; **B:** 1.B 2.B
3.A 4.B; **C:** 1. is 2. reasons
3. endangers 4. people
5. depend; **D:** 1. Answers will
vary. 2. Answers will vary.

Unit 12
A* and *An
pp. 40–41

1.A	2.B	3.A	4.B	5.A
6.A	7.A	8.B	9.B	10.A
11.B	12.A	13.B	14.A	15.B
16.B				

Unit 13
Agreement with Helping Verbs
pp. 42–43

1.A	2.C	3.B	4.B	5.A
6.B	7.A	8.A	9.C	10.A
11.C	12.B	13.A	14.A	15.B
16.C	17.B	18.C		

Unit 14
Future-Tense Verbs
pp. 44–45

1.B	2.C	3.B	4.A	5.C
6.C	7.A	8.A	9.C	10.B
11.B	12.C	13.A	14.B	

Unit 15
Perfect-Tense Verbs
pp. 46–47

1.C	2.B	3.A	4.A	5.B
6.A	7.C	8.B	9.A	10.C
11.B	12.C	13.A	14.B	

Unit 16
Verb Tenses
pp. 48–49

1.B	2.C	3.A	4.B	5.A
6.C	7.B	8.A	9.D	10.C
11.D	12.A	13.B	14.C	

The Third LAP
Language Activity Pages
pp. 50–51

A: 1.A 2.C 3.B; **B:** 1. picked
2. will start 3. fed 4. travels
5. talked; **C:** 1. are moving
2. are looking 3. have 4. will
make; **D:** 1. Answers will vary.
2. Answers will vary.

Unit 17
Contractions
pp. 52–55

1.B	2.A	3.A	4.B	5.B
6.B	7.A	8.B	9.A	10.A
11.A	12.B	13.A	14.B	15.C
16.C	17.B	18.A	19.A	20.B
21.B	22.A	23.B	24.C	25.A
26.B	27.B	28.A	29.C	30.A
31.A	32.C			

Unit 18
Double Negatives
pp. 56–59

1.A	2.A	3.B	4.B	5.A
6.B	7.B	8.A	9.A	10.B
11.A	12.A	13.A	14.B	15.A
16.B	17.B	18.B	19.A	20.B
21.A	22.A	23.A	24.B	25.A
26.B	27.B	28.B	29.A	30.A

(continued on next page)   **41**

▬▬▬ Unit 19 ▬▬▬
Problem Verbs
pp. 60–61

1.B 2.A 3.B 4.B 5.A
6.A 7.A 8.B 9.A 10.B
11.A 12.B 13.A 14.A

▬▬ The Last LAP ▬▬
Language Activity Pages
pp. 62–63

A: 1.A 2.B 3.A; **B:** 1. They
will 2. We are 3. He is 4. will
not 5. I have; **C:** 1. it's
2. We're 3. haven't ever *or*
have never 4. sets 5. I'm;
D: 1. Answers will vary.
2. Answers will vary.

Unit 1
Subject-Verb Agreement
pp. 6–9

1.A	2.A	3.A	4.B	5.B
6.A	7.A	8.B	9.B	10.B
11.B	12.A	13.A	14.B	15.B
16.B	17.A	18.A	19.B	20.B
21.B	22.A	23.A	24.A	25.B
26.B	27.A	28.B	29.B	30.A

Unit 2
Subject-Verb Agreement
pp. 10–13

1.A	2.A	3.A	4.B	5.A
6.B	7.B	8.C	9.C	10.B
11.A	12.C	13.B	14.A	15.C
16.B	17.B	18.A	19.B	20.A
21.A	22.B	23.A	24.A	25.B
26.B	27.A	28.B	29.A	30.B
31.A	32.B	33.A	34.A	

Unit 3
Adjective-Noun Agreement
pp. 14–15

1.A	2.A	3.B	4.B	5.A
6.A	7.B	8.B	9.A	10.B
11.B	12.A	13.B	14.A	15.A
16.B				

The First LAP
Language Activity Pages
pp. 16–17

A: 1.C 2.A 3.B; **B:** 1.A 2.A 3.B
4.B 5.B; **C:** 1. We are 2. troop
screeches 3. Aardvarks and
gazelles live 4. Bands roam
5. I plan 6. we stand 7. Ngan
photographs 8. trip is;
D: 1. Answers will vary.
2. Answers will vary.

Unit 4
Speaking of Yourself Last
pp. 18–19

1.A	2.B	3.B	4.C	5.C
6.C	7.B	8.B	9.A	10.A
11.B	12.C	13.A	14.C	

Unit 5
Past-Tense Verbs
pp. 20–23

1.A	2.B	3.C	4.C	5.A
6.B	7.A	8.B	9.A	10.C
11.C	12.C	13.A	14.B	15.A
16.B	17.A	18.B	19.A	20.A
21.B	22.B	23.B	24.A	25.A
26.B	27.A	28.B	29.A	30.B
31.B	32.A	33.B	34.B	

Unit 6
Past Tense of *Be*
pp. 24–25

1.A	2.B	3.B	4.A	5.A
6.B	7.B	8.B	9.A	10.B
11.B	12.A	13.B	14.A	

Unit 7
Comparing with Adjectives and Adverbs
pp. 26–29

1.A	2.A	3.B	4.B	5.B
6.B	7.A	8.B	9.B	10.A
11.B	12.B	13.B	14.B	15.A
16.A	17.A	18.A	19.B	20.A
21.B	22.A	23.B	24.A	25.B
26.A	27.B	28.A		

The Second LAP
Language Activity Pages
pp. 30–31

A: 1.C 2.B 3.A; **B:** 1.A 2.B 3.B
4.B 5.A; **C:** 1. smaller
2. strongest 3. faster
4. quickest 5. faster;
D: 1. Answers will vary.
2. Answers will vary.

Unit 8
Future-Tense Verbs
pp. 32–35

1.C	2.C	3.B	4.C	5.C
6.B	7.A	8.C	9.B	10.A
11.C	12.B	13.B	14.A	15.A
16.A	17.C	18.B	19.C	20.A
21.B	22.C	23.C	24.B	25.A
26.B	27.A	28.A	29.C	30.C
31.B	32.C			

Unit 9
Perfect-Tense Verbs
pp. 36–39

1.A	2.C	3.C	4.A	5.B
6.A	7.C	8.C	9.B	10.A
11.C	12.B	13.B	14.A	15.A
16.A	17.A	18.B	19.B	20.A
21.A	22.B	23.B	24.A	25.B
26.A	27.A	28.B	29.B	30.A
31.A	32.B			

Unit 10
Perfect-Tense Verbs
pp. 40–41

1.C	2.B	3.A	4.C	5.A
6.B	7.C	8.C	9.A	10.B
11.B	12.A	13.C	14.A	15.B
16.A				

Unit 11
Verb Tenses
pp. 42–45

1.C	2.A	3.B	4.B	5.C
6.A	7.D	8.A	9.C	10.B
11.C	12.B	13.A	14.D	15.D
16.C	17.B	18.A	19.B	20.A
21.C	22.D	23.C	24.B	25.D
26.A	27.A	28.B	29.D	30.C

The Third LAP
Language Activity Pages
pp. 46–47

A: 1.A 2.C 3.A; **B:** 1. will
freeze 2. played 3. drawn
4. will hang 5. left; **C:** 1. past
2. past perfect 3. past
4. present 5. present perfect
6. future; **D:** 1. Answers will
vary. 2. Answers will vary.

Unit 12
Double Negatives
pp. 48–51

1.A	2.B	3.B	4.C	5.B
6.C	7.A	8.B	9.A	10.A
11.B	12.C	13.B	14.A	15.B
16.C	17.B	18.A	19.B	20.A
21.C	22.C	23.A	24.B	25.A
26.C	27.A	28.B	29.B	30.C
31.A	32.B			

Unit 13
Problem Verbs
pp. 52–55

1.B	2.B	3.A	4.A	5.B
6.A	7.B	8.A	9.A	10.B
11.B	12.A	13.B	14.B	15.A
16.B	17.B	18.A	19.B	20.B
21.B	22.A	23.B	24.B	25.B
26.B	27.A	28.B	29.B	30.A
31.B	32.B	33.B	34.B	35.B
36.A	37.B	38.B		

Unit 14
Misused Words
pp. 56–61

1.A	2.B	3.A	4.B	5.B
6.A	7.B	8.A	9.B	10.B
11.A	12.B	13.A	14.B	15.A
16.A	17.B	18.A	19.A	20.B
21.B	22.B	23.A	24.B	25.A
26.B	27.A	28.A	29.B	30.B
31.B	32.B	33.B	34.B	35.A
36.B	37.B	38.A	39.B	40.A
41.B	42.A	43.B	44.A	45.B
46.A	47.A	48.B	49.B	50.A
51.B	52.A			

(continued on next page)

▰▰ The Last LAP ▰▰
Language Activity Pages
pp. 62–63

A: 1.B 2.A 3.A; **B:** 1. Correct
2. "A hamster won't be any
trouble," she told her parents.
3. "They don't need walking,"
Alicia argued. 4. Correct 5. It
wasn't a surprise when she
picked up her birthday present
the next day, and something
inside was moving. **C:** 1. have
ever seen 2. can feed 3. fewer
chores 4. less time 5. have
gone 6. Between you and me;
D: 1. Answers will vary.
2. Answers will vary.

Unit 1
Subject-Verb Agreement
pp. 6–9

1.B 2.A 3.A 4.B 5.B
6.B 7.A 8.A 9.A 10.B
11.A 12.A 13.B 14.A 15.B
16.B 17.A 18.B 19.B 20.A
21.C 22.A 23.A 24.B 25.C
26.A 27.C 28.B 29.A 30.C
31.C 32.A 33.B 34.B

Unit 2
Subject-Verb Agreement
pp. 10–13

1.A 2.C 3.B 4.B 5.C
6.B 7.A 8.A 9.C 10.A
11.B 12.C 13.A 14.A 15.B
16.B 17.A 18.B 19.B 20.A
21.B 22.A 23.A 24.B 25.A
26.B 27.A 28.B

Unit 3
Past-Tense Verbs
pp. 14–17

1.A 2.C 3.B 4.B 5.A
6.B 7.C 8.C 9.B 10.A
11.B 12.A 13.C 14.A 15.A
16.C 17.A 18.C 19.A 20.C
21.B 22.A 23.A 24.C 25.A
26.B 27.B 28.A 29.B 30.C
31.C 32.A 33.B 34.C 35.A

Unit 4
Past-Tense Verbs
pp. 18–21

1.A 2.A 3.B 4.A 5.B
6.B 7.B 8.A 9.B 10.A
11.A 12.A 13.B 14.A 15.B
16.A 17.A 18.B 19.B 20.B
21.A 22.B 23.A 24.A 25.B
26.A 27.B 28.A 29.B 30.A
31.B 32.B 33.A 34.A 35.B

Unit 5
Past Tense of _Be_
pp. 22–23

1.B 2.B 3.A 4.B 5.A
6.A 7.A 8.B 9.A 10.A
11.B 12.A 13.B 14.B 15.B
16.A 17.B 18.A

The First LAP
Language Activity Pages
pp. 24–25

A: 1. present 2. past
3. irregular 4. inverted 5. two
6. prepositional 7. Singular
8. Plural; **B:** 1.S, for my class
2.P, in my class 3.S, near the
city 4.P, of the zoo 5.P,
throughout the day 6.P, like

people 7.S, with the zoo guides
8.P, during lunch; **C:** 1. went
2. were 3. bought 4. chose
5. ate 6. met 7. took 8. begun
9. sang 10. was; **D:** 1. Answers
will vary. 2. Answers will vary.

Unit 6
Future Tense
pp. 26–27

1.C 2.C 3.B 4.A 5.C
6.A 7.C 8.C 9.B 10.A
11.C 12.B 13.C 14.A 15.C
16.B

Unit 7
Perfect Tenses
pp. 28–31

1.C 2.A 3.A 4.B 5.C
6.B 7.A 8.C 9.B 10.A
11.B 12.A 13.C 14.A 15.C
16.C 17.B 18.C 19.A 20.B
21.A 22.B 23.C 24.A 25.B
26.C 27.A 28.C 29.B 30.C
31.A 32.B 33.A 34.B 35.C
36.B 37.A 38.C

Unit 8
Comparing with Adjectives and Adverbs
pp. 32–35

1.B 2.B 3.A 4.B 5.A
6.A 7.A 8.B 9.A 10.B
11.A 12.A 13.B 14.B 15.A
16.B 17.A 18.A 19.B 20.A
21.B 22.B 23.A 24.A 25.A
26.A 27.B 28.A 29.A 30.B
31.A 32.B 33.A 34.B 35.B
36.A

Unit 9
Participles as Adjectives
pp. 36–37

1.B 2.A 3.B 4.A 5.A
6.B 7.A 8.B 9.B 10.B
11.A 12.A 13.B 14.A 15.B
16.B 17.B 18.A 19.B 20.A

The Second LAP
Language Activity Pages
pp. 38–39

A: 1. present 2. past 3. future
4. comparative 5. superlative
6. participle; **B:** 1. present
2. past 3. present 4. future
5. present 6. past 7. present
8. future; **C:** 1. smaller 2. more
3. best 4. farther 5. less
6. nicest 7. bigger;
D: 1. Answers will vary.
2. Answers will vary.

Unit 10
Double Negatives
pp. 40–41

1.C 2.C 3.A 4.B 5.A
6.A 7.C 8.B 9.C 10.A
11.C 12.B

Unit 11
Indefinite Pronouns
pp. 42–45

1.B 2.A 3.B 4.B 5.A
6.B 7.A 8.A 9.A 10.B
11.A 12.B 13.A 14.B 15.B
16.A 17.B 18.A 19.A 20.B
21.A 22.A 23.B 24.B 25.A
26.B 27.B 28.A 29.B 30.A
31.B 32.B 33.A 34.A 35.B
36.A 37.B 38.A

Unit 12
Demonstrative Pronouns
pp. 46–47

1.A 2.A 3.A 4.B 5.A
6.B 7.B 8.A 9.B 10.B
11.A 12.A 13.A 14.B 15.B
16.B 17.A 18.B 19.B 20.A

The Third LAP
Language Activity Pages
pp. 48–49

A: 1. negative 2. affirmative
3. double 4. indefinite
5. phrase 6. demonstrative; **B:**
1.N 2.N 3.A 4.A 5.A 6.N 7.A
8.N 9.A 10.A 11.N 12.N; **C:**
1.S 2.S 3.P 4.S 5.P 6.P 7.P
8.P 9.S 10.S; **D:** 1. Answers
will vary. 2. Answers will vary.

Unit 13
Problem Verbs
pp. 50–51

1.A 2.B 3.A 4.A 5.A
6.B 7.B 8.A 9.B 10.B
11.A 12.B 13.B 14.A 15.B
16.A 17.A 18.A 19.B 20.A

Unit 14
Problem Verbs
pp. 52–55

1.B 2.A 3.B 4.B 5.A
6.B 7.A 8.A 9.A 10.B
11.A 12.B 13.A 14.B 15.B
16.B 17.A 18.B 19.A 20.A
21.B 22.A 23.B 24.B 25.B
26.A 27.B 28.A 29.A 30.B
31.A 32.B 33.B 34.A 35.A
36.A 37.B 38.A

(continued on next page)   45

Unit 15
Misused Words
pp. 56–61

1.B	2.A	3.A	4.A	5.B
6.B	7.B	8.B	9.A	10.A
11.B	12.A	13.A	14.A	15.B
16.B	17.A	18.B	19.A	20.A
21.B	22.B	23.A	24.A	25.B
26.A	27.B	28.B	29.A	30.A
31.A	32.B	33.A	34.B	35.A
36.B	37.B	38.A	39.A	40.B
41.A	42.B	43.B	44.B	45.A
46.A	47.B	48.B	49.B	50.A

The Last LAP
Language Activity Pages
pp. 62–63

A: 1.F 2.T 3.T 4.T 5.F 6.T 7.F 8.F; **B:** 1.I 2.C 3.C 4.I 5.I 6.C 7.I 8.C 9.I 10.C 11.I 12.C; **C:** 1. than 2. past 3. can 4. Between 5. well 6. fewer 7. may 8. good 9. seen 10. say; **D:** 1. Answers will vary. 2. Answers will vary.

Unit 1
Subject-Verb Agreement
pp. 6–7

1.A	2.A	3.B	4.A	5.B
6.A	7.A	8.B	9.A	10.B
11.B	12.B	13.B	14.A	15.B
16.A	17.A	18.B		

Unit 2
Subject-Verb Agreement
pp. 8–9

1.B	2.A	3.A	4.B	5.A
6.B	7.B	8.A	9.B	10.A
11.B	12.A	13.B	14.A	15.B
16.A	17.B	18.B	19.A	20.B

Unit 3
Subject-Verb Agreement
pp. 10–13

1.B	2.A	3.B	4.B	5.A
6.B	7.B	8.A	9.A	10.B
11.B	12.A	13.A	14.A	15.B
16.A	17.A	18.B	19.A	20.B
21.B	22.B	23.A	24.A	25.A
26.A	27.B	28.A	29.B	30.B
31.B	32.A	33.A	34.B	35.B
36.B				

Unit 4
Past-Tense Verbs
pp. 14–19

1.A	2.B	3.A	4.C	5.C
6.B	7.A	8.B	9.B	10.C
11.A	12.B	13.C	14.A	15.A
16.C	17.B	18.A	19.A	20.C
21.C	22.A	23.B	24.A	25.B
26.B	27.B	28.A	29.A	30.B
31.A	32.B	33.A	34.B	35.B
36.B	37.B	38.A	39.B	40.B
41.B	42.A	43.A	44.B	45.A
46.A	47.A	48.B	49.A	50.B

The First LAP
Language Activity Pages
pp. 20–21
A: 1.A 2.B 3.A 4.C; **B:** 1.A 2.B
3.B 4.B 5.B; **C:** 1. faced 2. fall
3. had 4. were 5. thought
6. was 7. was 8. sought 9. was
10. hit 11. measured 12. have
13. Do; **D:** 1. Answers will
vary. 2. Answers will vary.

Unit 5
Future Tense
pp. 22–23

1.C	2.A	3.B	4.A	5.B
6.C	7.A	8.A	9.C	10.A
11.B	12.A	13.B	14.C	15.B
16.A				

Unit 6
Perfect Tenses
pp. 24–27

1.A	2.B	3.C	4.A	5.C
6.C	7.A	8.C	9.B	10.A
11.B	12.C	13.A	14.B	15.B
16.C	17.C	18.B	19.A	20.C
21.C	22.A	23.B	24.C	25.A
26.B	27.A	28.C	29.B	30.B
31.C	32.A	33.A	34.B	35.C
36.C	37.A	38.B		

Unit 7
Comparing with Adjectives and Adverbs
pp. 28–31

1.A	2.A	3.B	4.B	5.A
6.A	7.A	8.A	9.B	10.B
11.B	12.A	13.A	14.B	15.B
16.B	17.B	18.A	19.B	20.A
21.B	22.B	23.B	24.B	25.B
26.A	27.A	28.B	29.A	30.B
31.B	32.A	33.B	34.A	35.B
36.B	37.A	38.A		

Unit 8
Participles as Adjectives
pp. 32–33

1.A	2.C	3.B	4.C	5.B
6.A	7.A	8.C	9.B	10.B
11.C	12.B	13.A	14.C	15.C
16.C	17.B	18.A	19.A	20.C

The Second LAP
Language Activity Pages
pp. 34–35
A: 1. superlative
2. future-perfect
3. present-perfect
4. comparative 5. participle
6. past-perfect; **B:** 1.B 2.A
3.A 4.B 5.A 6.B; **C:** 1. bigger
2. more 3. more 4. further
5. highest 6. hungrier;
D: 1. Answers will vary.
2. Answers will vary.

Unit 9
Double Negatives
pp. 36–37

1.A	2.C	3.B	4.C	5.B
6.C	7.B	8.B	9.A	10.B
11.A	12.C	13.C	14.A	15.B

Unit 10
Indefinite Pronouns
pp. 38–41

1.B	2.A	3.A	4.B	5.B
6.B	7.B	8.B	9.A	10.B
11.B	12.B	13.A	14.B	15.B
16.A	17.A	18.A	19.B	20.B
21.B	22.A	23.B	24.A	25.A
26.B	27.B	28.A	29.B	30.A
31.B	32.A	33.B	34.B	35.A
36.A	37.A	38.B	39.B	40.B
41.A	42.A	43.B	44.B	45.B
46.B				

Unit 11
Demonstrative Pronouns
pp. 42–43

1.A	2.A	3.A	4.A	5.B
6.A	7.B	8.B	9.B	10.A
11.A	12.B	13.B	14.B	15.B
16.A	17.A	18.B	19.B	20.B

Unit 12
Interrogative Pronouns
pp. 44–45

1.B	2.A	3.A	4.C	5.B
6.C	7.A	8.B	9.C	10.B
11.C	12.A	13.C	14.B	15.C
16.A	17.B	18.A	19.B	20.B
21.A	22.A	23.C	24.A	

The Third LAP
Language Activity Pages
pp. 46–47
A: 1.A 2.A 3.A; **B:** 1.C 2.A
3.A 4.B 5.C 6.B; **C:** 1. I didn't
think I'd ever find the book I
was looking for. 2. My uncle
took me to three different
stores today and none of them
had it. 3. Nobody anywhere
had even heard of the title.
4. It won't take any longer
than a week for the store to
get it, I was told. 5. There is
nothing more frustrating than
waiting for a book I want to
read right now! **D:** 1. Answers
will vary. 2. Answers will vary.

Unit 13
Active and Passive Voice
pp. 48–49

1.A.	2.B	3.A	4.B	5.A
6.A	7.B	8.A	9.B	10.B
11.A	12.A	13.A	14.A	15.B

(continued on next page)

■■■■ Unit 14 ■■■■
Problem Verbs
pp. 50–53

1.A	2.A	3.B	4.B	5.B
6.A	7.B	8.A	9.B	10.A
11.A	12.A	13.A	14.A	15.A
16.A	17.B	18.A	19.B	20.A
21.A	22.B	23.A	24.B	25.B
26.A	27.A	28.A	29.B	30.A
31.B	32.A	33.B	34.B	35.B
36.B	37.B	38.B		

■■■■ Unit 15 ■■■■
Misused Words
pp. 54–57

1.A	2.B	3.A	4.B	5.B
6.B	7.A	8.A	9.B	10.B
11.B	12.A	13.B	14.B	15.A
16.A	17.B	18.A	19.B	20.B
21.B	22.B	23.B	24.B	25.B
26.B	27.B	28.B	29.A	30.A
31.A	32.B	33.B	34.B	35.B
36.A	37.B	38.A		

■■■■ Unit 16 ■■■■
Misused Words
pp. 58–59

1.A	2.A	3.A	4.B	5.B
6.A	7.B	8.B	9.B	10.A
11.B	12.B	13.B	14.B	15.B
16.B				

■■■■ Unit 17 ■■■■
Misused Phrases
pp. 60–61

1.A	2.B	3.A	4.A	5.B
6.A	7.B	8.A	9.B	10.B
11.A	12.B	13.A	14.B	15.B
16.A	17.A	18.A	19.A	20.A
21.A	22.B			

■■■■ The Last LAP ■■■■
Language Activity Pages
pp. 62–63

A: 1.A 2.B 3.A; **B:** 1.P 2.A
3.A 4.A 5.P 6.P 7.P 8.A;
C: 1. Anyone 2. who 3. lies
4. inside 5. Everyone 6. then
7. who 8. kind of 9. had lived
10. have gone; **D:** 1. Answers
will vary. 2. Answers will vary.

Unit 1
Subject-Verb Agreement
pp. 6–9

1.A	2.A	3.C	4.B	5.B
6.B	7.C	8.A	9.B	10.A
11.C	12.C	13.A	14.B	15.C
16.A	17.A	18.B	19.B	20.B
21.A	22.B	23.A	24.A	25.A
26.A	27.B	28.B	29.B	30.A
31.B	32.B			

Unit 2
Subject-Verb Agreement
pp. 10–13

1.A	2.B	3.A	4.A	5.B
6.B	7.B	8.B	9.A	10.A
11.B	12.A	13.C	14.C	15.B
16.B	17.C	18.A	19.C	20.B
21.A	22.A	23.B	24.A	25.B
26.B	27.B	28.B	29.A	30.B
31.A	32.B	33.B	34.A	35.B

Unit 3
Past-Tense Verbs
pp. 14–19

1.A	2.B	3.B	4.A	5.B
6.B	7.B	8.A	9.C	10.A
11.A	12.C	13.B	14.A	15.B
16.A	17.B	18.A	19.C	20.A
21.A	22.C	23.C	24.B	25.B
26.A	27.B	28.A	29.A	30.C
31.C	32.B	33.A	34.C	35.B
36.A	37.B	38.C	39.B	40.A
41.A	42.B			

The First LAP
Language Activity Pages
pp. 20–21

A: 1.D 2.F 3.E 4.C 5.A 6.B;
B: 1. wrote 2. ridden 3. told
4. sold 5. swim 6. tore 7. done
8. feel 9. found 10. flown;
C: 1. signed 2. needed 3. was
4. stayed 5. chose 6. donated
7. was 8. were 9. set 10. grew
11. were 12. continued
13. were 14. is 15. Have;
D: 1. Answers will vary.
2. Answers will vary.

Unit 4
Future Tense
pp. 22–23

1.C	2.A	3.C	4.B	5.A
6.B	7.C	8.C	9.A	10.A
11.B	12.A	13.B	14.C	15.A

Unit 5
Perfect Tenses
pp. 24–27

1.A	2.C	3.A	4.B	5.B
6.A	7.C	8.B	9.C	10.C
11.A	12.B	13.C	14.A	15.C
16.B	17.A	18.B	19.C	20.A
21.A	22.C	23.B	24.C	25.A
26.B	27.A	28.C	29.A	30.B
31.C	32.C			

Unit 6
Comparing with Adjectives and Adverbs
pp. 28–29

1.C	2.A	3.A	4.C	5.C
6.B	7.C	8.A	9.A	10.C
11.A	12.B			

The Second LAP
Language Activity Pages
pp. 30–31

A: 1. Present-perfect tense
2. Future tense
3. Future-perfect tense
4. Superlative form
5. Future-progressive tense
6. Past-perfect tense
7. Comparative form
8. Adjective base form;
B: 1. easier 2. more
mountainous 3. wealthiest
4. more neatly
5. less powerfully 6. more
successful 7. short 8. shortest
9. most slowly 10. least rapid;
C: 1. will be getting 2. scariest
3. have prepared 4. had
completed 5. will be
continuing 6. have studied
7. will escape 8. will create
9. will launch 10. most
amazing; **D:** 1. Answers will
vary. 2. Answers will vary.

Unit 7
Participles as Adjectives
pp. 32–37

1.A	2.A	3.B	4.A	5.B
6.A	7.B	8.D	9.B	10.C
11.A	12.C	13.B	14.C	15.A
16.C	17.A	18.A	19.B	20.B
21.A	22.B	23.A	24.A	25.A
26.B	27.B	28.A	29.B	30.A
31.B	32.A	33.A	34.B	35.B
36.A	37.A	38.B	39.B	40.A
41.B	42.B			

Unit 8
Double Negatives
pp. 38–39

1.A	2.C	3.B	4.C	5.B
6.A	7.C	8.B	9.C	10.A
11.A	12.B	13.C	14.B	

Unit 9
Pronouns pp. 40–45

1.A	2.A	3.B	4.C	5.B
6.A	7.B	8.C	9.C	10.A
11.B	12.C	13.A	14.A	15.C
16.A	17.C	18.A	19.A	20.A
21.B	22.A	23.B	24.B	25.A
26.A	27.A	28.B	29.C	30.C
31.A	32.A	33.C	34.B	35.B
36.A	37.B	38.A	39.C	40.A
41.B	42.C	43.B	44.A	45.C
46.C	47.B	48.A	49.A	50.B
51.C	52.B			

The Third LAP
Language Activity Pages
pp. 46–47

A: 1.B 2.A 3.I 4.C 5.D 6.E
7.G 8.F 9.J 10.H; **B:** 1.A 2.B
3.A 4.A; **C:** 1. is 2. delete
hardly 3. leaves 4. consider
5. has 6. this; **D:** 1. Answers
will vary. 2. Answers will vary.

Unit 10
Active and Passive Voice
pp. 48–49

1.A	2.B	3.A	4.A	5.B
6.A	7.B	8.B	9.A	10.A
11.A	12.A	13.B	14.A	15.A
16.A				

Unit 11
Problem Verbs pp. 50–53

1.A	2.A	3.A	4.B	5.B
6.A	7.B	8.A	9.B	10.C
11.A	12.B	13.C	14.B	15.B
16.A	17.A	18.B	19.B	20.B
21.A	22.B	23.B	24.B	25.B
26.B	27.A	28.A	29.A	30.B
31.A	32.B			

Unit 12
Misused Words pp. 54–59

1.B	2.A	3.A	4.B	5.A
6.B	7.A	8.A	9.B	10.A
11.B	12.B	13.A	14.B	15.B
16.B	17.A	18.A	19.B	20.A
21.A	22.B	23.B	24.A	25.A
26.B	27.B	28.A	29.A	30.B
31.A	32.B	33.A	34.A	35.B
36.B	37.B	38.A	39.A	40.B
41.B	42.A	43.B	44.A	45.A

(continued on next page)

▬▬▬▬ **Unit 13** ▬▬▬▬

Misused Phrases

pp. 60–61

1.B　2.B　3.A　4.A　5.A

6.B　7.A　8.B　9.B　10.A

11.B　12.B　13.A　14.A　15.B

16.B　17.A　18.B

▬▬▬▬ **The Last LAP** ▬▬▬▬

Language Activity Pages

pp. 62–63

A: 1.F　2.T　3.F　4.T　5.T　6.F

7.F　8.F　9.T　10.T; **B:** 1.C　2.I

3.I　4.I　5.C　6.C　7.I　8.C　9.C

10.I; **C:** 1. Every day　2. were

3. affected　4. was done　5. led

6. passed　7. set　8. unique

9. lose　10. preceded;

D: 1. Answers will vary.

2. Answers will vary.

Unit 1
Subject-Verb Agreement
pp. 6–9

1.C 2.A 3.C 4.A 5.C
6.C 7.B 8.B 9.B 10.A
11.A 12.B 13.C 14.B 15.A
16.C 17.C 18.B 19.B 20.A
21.A 22.B 23.A 24.A 25.B
26.B 27.B 28.A 29.A 30.A
31.A 32.B 33.A 34.A 35.B
36.B 37.B 38.A

Unit 2
Subject-Verb Agreement
pp. 10–13

1.A 2.B 3.B 4.A 5.A
6.A 7.A 8.B 9.A 10.B
11.B 12.A 13.A 14.B 15.C
16.A 17.B 18.C 19.A 20.B
21.A 22.A 23.A 24.A 25.B
26.B 27.A 28.B 29.B 30.A
31.A 32.A 33.A 34.A 35.A
36.A

Unit 3
Verb Tenses
pp. 14–19

1.A 2.B 3.C 4.C 5.A
6.B 7.B 8.A 9.C 10.A
11.B 12.B 13.B 14.A 15.A
16.A 17.B 18.C 19.C 20.B
21.A 22.A 23.A 24.B 25.B
26.B 27.C 28.C 29.A 30.B
31.C 32.B 33.A 34.A 35.C
36.A 37.B 38.B 39.A 40.A
41.A 42.A 43.B 44.C 45.B
46.A 47.B 48.A

The First LAP
Language Activity Pages
pp. 20–21

A: 1.A 2.C 3.A 4.B; **B:** 1. built
2. flew 3. freeze 4. held
5. kept 6. ring 7. sank
8. become 9. hurt 10. jumped;
C: 1. carries 2. are 3. passes
4. directs 5. is called 6. have
learned 7. has 8. have
9. begun 10. will require;
D: 1. Answers will vary.
2. Answers will vary.

Unit 4
Progressive Forms
pp. 22–27

1.A 2.B 3.B 4.C 5.C
6.A 7.A 8.B 9.B 10.C
11.B 12.A 13.C 14.B 15.B
16.C 17.C 18.A 19.C 20.B
21.A 22.A 23.C 24.B 25.A

26.C 27.A 28.A 29.C 30.B
31.C 32.C 33.B 34.A 35.A
36.B 37.C 38.C 39.B 40.A
41.A 42.C 43.B 44.A 45.B
46.A 47.A 48.B 49.A 50.C
51.C 52.C 53.A 54.B 55.C
56.C 57.C 58.B 59.C 60.A
61.B 62.C 63.A 64.B

Unit 5
Comparing with Adjectives
and Adverbs
pp. 28–29

1.C 2.B 3.A 4.A 5.A
6.C 7.A 8.A 9.A 10.A
11.B 12.C 13.B 14.B 15.A
16.A

Unit 6
Participles as Adjectives
pp. 30–33

1.C 2.A 3.A 4.C 5.A
6.B 7.C 8.C 9.C 10.A
11.C 12.C 13.B 14.B 15.C
16.A 17.B 18.C 19.B 20.A
21.B 22.A 23.B 24.B 25.A
26.B 27.A 28.A 29.B 30.B
31.A 32.B

The Second LAP
Language Activity Pages
pp. 34–35

A: 1.A 2.B 3.A 4.B;
B: 1. luckier 2. more colorful
3. least likely 4. most difficult
5. sandier 6. more strenuous
7. most slowly 8. beautifully
9. earliest 10. most deeply;
C: 1. is 2. are developing
3. more productive 4. be
feeding 5. has been going
6. had been growing 7. have
helped 8. will be continuing;
D: 1. Answers will vary.
2. Answers will vary.

Unit 7
Double Negatives
pp. 36–37

1.B 2.C 3.A 4.C 5.B
6.A 7.A 8.C 9.B 10.A
11.C 12.A 13.A 14.B 15.A
16.B

Unit 8
Pronouns
pp. 38–43

1.B 2.A 3.A 4.B 5.A
6.B 7.A 8.A 9.A 10.A
11.B 12.B 13.A 14.B 15.A
16.A 17.B 18.B 19.A 20.A

21.B 22.A 23.B 24.A 25.B
26.A 27.B 28.A 29.B 30.B
31.B 32.B 33.A 34.A 35.B
36.A 37.B 38.B 39.A 40.A
41.B 42.A 43.A 44.C 45.B
46.A 47.C 48.B 49.A 50.B

Unit 9
Avoiding Double Subjects
pp. 44–45

1.A 2.C 3.B 4.C 5.A
6.B 7.B 8.C 9.A 10.B
11.C 12.A 13.C 14.C 15.A

The Third LAP
Language Activity Pages
pp. 46–47

A: 1.J 2.I 3.E 4.C 5.D 6.F 7.G
8.H 9.B 10.A; **B:** 1.A 2.A 3.B
4.B 5.A; **C:** 1. The goal of dog
training is to make your dog
into a pleasant, obedient
companion. 2. The first
objective is to housebreak your
puppy and teach it to answer
to its name. 3. People don't...,
4....like dogs jumping up on
them or taking their food.
5. When it is fully grown, the
dog could knock down a child.
6. Well-trained dogs would
never do this. 7. Simple
commands your dog needs to
learn include sitting, heeling,
staying down, and coming
when called. 8. Proper dog
training has as its goal for you:
to form a team in which the
dog happily and willingly obeys
its pack leader, which is you!
D: 1. Answers will vary.
2. Answers will vary.

Unit 10
Active and Passive Voice
pp. 48–49

1.A 2.B 3.A 4.B 5.A
6.A 7.B 8.B 9.A 10.A
11.B 12.B 13.A 14.B 15.B
16.A 17.B 18.B 19.A 20.B

Unit 11
Keeping Tenses Consistent
pp. 50–51

1.B 2.A 3.C 4.C 5.C
6.C 7.A 8.C 9.B 10.A
11.B 12.B 13.B 14.A 15.A
16.A 17.B 18.A 19.A 20.B

(continued on next page)

Unit 12
Problem Verbs
pp. 52–53

1.A	2.B	3.A	4.B	5.A
6.A	7.B	8.B	9.A	10.B
11.B	12.A	13.A	14.A	15.B
16.A				

Unit 13
Misused Words
pp. 54–57

1.A	2.A	3.B	4.B	5.A
6.A	7.A	8.A	9.B	10.A
11.B	12.A	13.A	14.B	15.A
16.B	17.A	18.A	19.B	20.A
21.A	22.B	23.B	24.B	25.A
26.A	27.B	28.A	29.A	30.A
31.B	32.A	33.B	34.B	35.A
36.B	37.B	38.B		

Unit 14
Misused Phrases
pp. 58–61

1.A	2.B	3.A	4.B	5.B
6.B	7.A	8.B	9.A	10.B
11.B	12.B	13.A	14.A	15.B
16.B	17.B	18.A	19.B	20.B
21.B	22.A	23.B	24.B	25.A
26.B	27.B	28.B	29.B	30.B
31.A	32.B	33.B	34.A	

The Last LAP
Language Activity Pages
pp. 62–63

A: 1.A 2.B 3.A 4.C; **B:** 1.C
2. laid 3.C 4.C 5. A lot 6.C
7. altogether 8. Besides 9.C
10. unique; **C:** 1. affects 2. he
3. Besides 4. highly valued
5. unique 6. Altogether
7. these 8. a lot; **D:** 1. Answers
will vary. 2. Answers will vary.

Unit 1
Capital Letters
pp. 6–9

1.A	2.A	3.C	4.B	5.C
6.A	7.C	8.B	9.A	10.C
11.A	12.B	13.C	14.B	15.B
16.A	17.C	18.B	19.A	20.B

Unit 2
Capital Letters
pp. 10–13

1.B	2.A	3.A	4.B	5.A
6.A	7.A	8.B	9.B	10.A
11.A	12.B	13.A	14.B	15.A
16.A	17.A	18.B	19.A	20.B
21.A	22.A			

The First LAP
Language Activity Pages
pp. 14–15

A: 1. capital 2. name 3. Words 4. Sentences; **B:** 1. Our 2. Becker 3. Jason 4. I 5. We 6. Drake; **C:** 1. Grandpa 2. Please 3. I 4. Sharon; **D:** 1. Answers will vary. 2. Answers will vary.

Unit 3
Capital Letters
pp. 16–21

1.C	2.A	3.B	4.C	5.B
6.D	7.A	8.D	9.B	10.C
11.A	12.C	13.A	14.D	15.B
16.B	17.D	18.B	19.C	20.C
21.D	22.A	23.A	24.B	25.B
26.B	27.A	28.B	29.B	30.A
31.B	32.A	33.A	34.A	35.B

Unit 4
Capital Letters
pp. 22–25

1.A	2.B	3.C	4.A	5.A
6.B	7.B	8.C	9.A	10.B
11.A	12.A	13.B	14.B	15.B
16.B	17.B	18.A	19.A	20.B
21.A	22.B			

The Second LAP
Language Activity Pages
pp. 26–27

A: 1. word 2. day 3. name; **B:** 1. Friday 2. Sparky 3. March 4. I 5. Sparky; **C:** 1. Correct 2. He 3. Monday 4. May 5. Correct 6. September 7. I 8. Mom; **D:** 1. Answers will vary. 2. Answers will vary.

Unit 5
End Marks
pp. 28–33

1.B	2.B	3.A	4.A	5.A
6.A	7.A	8.B	9.A	10.A
11.A	12.A	13.B	14.A	15.B
16.A	17.B	18.A	19.A	20.B
21.A	22.A	23.B	24.A	25.B
26.A	27.B	28.B	29.B	30.A
31.B	32.B	33.B	34.A	35.B

Unit 6
End Marks
pp. 34–39

1.A	2.B	3.A	4.A	5.B
6.A	7.A	8.B	9.B	10.A
11.A	12.B	13.A	14.B	15.B
16.B	17.B	18.A	19.A	20.B
21.A	22.B	23.B	24.A	25.B
26.B	27.A	28.B	29.B	30.A
31.B	32.A	33.A	34.A	35.B
36.B	37.A	38.A		

Unit 7
End Marks
pp. 40–41

1.B	2.A	3.A	4.B	5.A
6.A	7.B	8.B	9.A	10.A
11.A	12.A			

The Third LAP
Language Activity Pages
pp. 42–43

A: 1. end marks 2. period 3. question 4. point; **B:** 1. ? 2. ? 3. ! 4. .; **C:** 1. . 2. . 3. ? 4. ! 5. ? 6. .; **D:** 1. Answers will vary. 2. Answers will vary.

Unit 8
Capital Letters and End Marks
pp. 44–49

1.B	2.A	3.C	4.B	5.A
6.C	7.A	8.B	9.C	10.C
11.B	12.B	13.A	14.C	15.A
16.B	17.C	18.A	19.A	20.B
21.C	22.A	23.D	24.B	25.D
26.C	27.D	28.A	29.C	30.B

Unit 9
Capital Letters and End Marks
pp. 50–55

1.C	2.D	3.A	4.B	5.B
6.D	7.A	8.B	9.C	10.B
11.D	12.A	13.A	14.C	15.B
16.D	17.A	18.C	19.C	20.B
21.D	22.A	23.C	24.C	25.B
26.B	27.A	28.C	29.B	30.B
31.A	32.C	33.B	34.C	35.A

Unit 10
Contractions and Apostrophes
pp. 56–61

1.A	2.B	3.B	4.B	5.A
6.B	7.A	8.A	9.B	10.A
11.B	12.A	13.A	14.B	15.A
16.A	17.B	18.B	19.A	20.A
21.B	22.B	23.A	24.A	25.B
26.B	27.A	28.B	29.A	30.B

The Last LAP
Language Activity Pages
pp. 62–63

A: 1. capital 2. end 3. contraction 4. apostrophe; **B:** 1. aren't 2. won't 3. weren't 4. didn't; **C:** 1. I've 2. I'm 3. won't 4. can't 5. isn't 6. she's; **D:** 1. Answers will vary. 2. Answers will vary.

Unit 1
Capital Letters
pp. 6–9

1.A 2.A 3.A 4.A 5.A
6.B 7.A 8.A 9.B 10.C
11.A 12.A 13.B 14.A 15.B
16.A 17.A 18.A 19.B 20.B
21.B 22.B 23.A 24.A

Unit 2
Capital Letters
pp. 10–13

1.B 2.C 3.B 4.A 5.D
6.C 7.C 8.B 9.A 10.B
11.B 12.A 13.A 14.A 15.B
16.B 17.B 18.B 19.A 20.A
21.B 22.A 23.B 24.A

Unit 3
Capital Letters
pp. 14–17

1.A 2.B 3.C 4.A 5.B
6.D 7.B 8.A

The First LAP
Language Activity Pages
pp. 18–19

A: 1.A 2.B; **B:** 1. Friday, July 16, 2004 2. Dear Sarah, 3. It is beautiful. 4. Nevada 5. Your friend,; **C:** 1. Maine 2. August 3. Thursday 4. Jim;
D: 1. Answers will vary.
2. Answers will vary.

Unit 4
End Marks
pp. 20–23

1.A 2.A 3.B 4.B 5.B
6.B 7.B 8.B 9.A 10.B
11.A 12.B 13.A 14.B 15.A
16.B 17.B 18.A 19.B 20.B
21.A 22.A 23.B 24.B

Unit 5
Capital Letters and End Marks
pp. 24–29

1.C 2.A 3.C 4.C 5.D
6.C 7.C 8.B 9.B 10.C
11.A 12.C 13.B 14.D 15.A
16.C 17.C 18.D 19.A 20.C
21.C 22.C 23.D 24.C 25.A
26.D 27.C 28.A

The Second LAP
Language Activity Pages
pp. 30–31

A: 1.B 2.B 3.C 4.A; **B:** 1. . 2. ? 3. . . 4. !; **C:** Sunday, October 10, 2004 Dear Gloria, Tomorrow our class is going to a special garden in Richmond. Mr. Torrez said we might even get to taste some apples! I will write another letter and tell you all about it. Your cousin, Eva; **D:** 1. Answers will vary. 2. Answers will vary.

Unit 6
Commas
pp. 32–35

1.B 2.A 3.A 4.A 5.B
6.B 7.B 8.A 9.B 10.B
11.B 12.A 13.A 14.A 15.B
16.A 17.B 18.B

Unit 7
Commas
pp. 36–37

1.A 2.B 3.A 4.D 5.B

Unit 8
Commas
pp. 38–43

1.B 2.B 3.B 4.A 5.A
6.A 7.A 8.A 9.B 10.A
11.B 12.B 13.B 14.A 15.B
16.B 17.B 18.B 19.B 20.B
21.B 22.C 23.B 24.A 25.C
26.A 27.C 28.C 29.B 30.B

The Third LAP
Language Activity Pages
pp. 44–45

A: 1.B 2.A; **B:** 1. September 6, 1620 2. Miles Standish, William Bradford, and Edward Winslow 3. November 9, but had to 4. said, "was harsh." 5. corn, wheat, and peas.; **C:** 1. I have three dogs named Paws, Max, and Buddy. 2. My parents brought them home from Athens, Ohio. 3. The dogs were all born on May 26, 2003. 4. We all live at 34 Fox Road, Westerville, Ohio.
D: 1. Answers will vary.
2. Answers will vary.

Unit 9
Quotation Marks
pp. 46–51

1.A 2.C 3.C 4.B 5.D
6.A 7.A 8.C 9.C 10.D
11.B 12.B 13.C 14.B 15.B
16.C 17.A 18.B 19.C 20.B
21.C 22.C 23.B 24.B 25.B
26.B 27.C 28.B

Unit 10
Contractions and Apostrophes
pp. 52–55

1.A 2.A 3.A 4.A 5.A
6.B 7.B 8.A 9.A 10.A
11.B 12.A 13.B 14.B 15.A
16.A 17.A 18.B

Unit 11
Capitalization and Punctuation
pp. 56–61

1.C 2.A 3.A 4.C 5.A
6.B 7.A 8.C 9.C 10.A
11.C 12.C 13.A 14.C 15.B
16.A 17.C 18.A 19.B 20.B
21.B 22.D 23.C 24.B 25.C

The Last LAP
Language Activity Pages
pp. 62–63

A: 1.C 2.A; **B:** 1. Jim asked, "Did you know that wolves are related to dogs?" 2. "Yes," answered Scott, "they also travel in groups called packs." 3. "How many wolves travel in a pack?" 4. "It depends," said Scott, "but each pack always has a leader." **C:** 1. I'm 2. You're 3. We're 4. I've;
D: 1. Answers will vary.
2. Answers will vary.

Unit 1
Capital Letters
pp. 6–9

1.A	2.B	3.D	4.B	5.B
6.A	7.C	8.B	9.D	10.B
11.D	12.B	13.A	14.D	15.D
16.B	17.A	18.C	19.B	20.A
21.D	22.B	23.B	24.D	25.C
26.A	27.C	28.D		

Unit 2
Capital Letters
pp. 10–13

1.B	2.A	3.B	4.C	5.D
6.A	7.B	8.A	9.D	10.C
11.B	12.B	13.C	14.A	15.D
16.C	17.A	18.A	19.B	20.A
21.C	22.D	23.A	24.D	25.B
26.D	27.A	28.B	29.C	30.C

Unit 3
Capital Letters
pp. 14–17

1.C	2.B	3.B	4.A	5.A
6.B	7.A	8.C	9.A	10.B
11.C	12.A	13.C	14.B	15.C
16.D	17.B	18.A		

The First LAP
Language Activity Pages
pp. 18–19

A: 1.B 2.A 3.C; **B:** 1.C 2.A 3.A; **C:** 1. March 2. Dear 3. Saturday 4. We 5. Day 6. Your; **D:** 1. Answers will vary. 2. Answers will vary.

Unit 4
End Marks
pp. 20–23

1.A	2.A	3.B	4.A	5.B
6.B	7.A	8.B	9.A	10.B
11.A	12.A	13.A	14.B	15.A
16.B	17.A	18.B	19.B	20.B
21.B	22.A	23.B	24.B	25.A
26.B	27.B	28.A	29.B	30.B
31.A	32.B	33.A	34.A	35.B

Unit 5
Abbreviations
pp. 24–29

1.A	2.C	3.B	4.A	5.C
6.D	7.C	8.B	9.C	10.A
11.D	12.A	13.B	14.C	15.B
16.C	17.A	18.B	19.C	20.C
21.C	22.A	23.B	24.C	25.B
26.A	27.B	28.A		

The Second LAP
Language Activity Pages
pp. 30–31

A: 1.C 2.B 3.A; **B:** 1.B 2.B 3.A 4.B; **C:** 1. Mr. 2. M. V. 3. Pl. 4. Dr. 5. Rd.; **D:** 1. Answers will vary. 2. Answers will vary.

Unit 6
Commas
pp. 32–35

1.B	2.A	3.A	4.B	5.A
6.A	7.B	8.B	9.C	10.A
11.B	12.A	13.D	14.B	15.B

Unit 7
Commas
pp. 36–41

1.C	2.B	3.A	4.A	5.B
6.B	7.C	8.A	9.A	10.B
11.A	12.A	13.B	14.A	15.B
16.C	17.A	18.C	19.B	20.A
21.C	22.B	23.A	24.C	25.B
26.A	27.C	28.B		

The Third LAP
Language Activity Pages
pp. 42–43

A: 1.A 2.B 3.C; **B:** 1.B 2.A 3.A; **C:** 1. Do you enjoy camping, swimming, or canoeing? 2. Oh, I know what you are thinking. 3. You need the new, improved Row-Bot 3000 Deluxe! 4. Order by August 5, 2005, and you will get a free Row-Bot T-shirt for even more fun! 5. Write to 1343 Ridge Road, Memphis, Tennessee 38152 for more information. **D:** 1. Answers will vary. 2. Answers will vary.

Unit 8
Colons
pp. 44–47

1.B	2.A	3.A	4.B	5.A
6.B	7.A	8.B	9.B	10.A
11.B	12.A	13.B	14.B	15.A
16.B	17.C	18.A	19.B	20.B
21.A	22.B	23.C	24.B	

Unit 9
Quotation Marks
pp. 48–53

1.B	2.A	3.C	4.C	5.A
6.B	7.B	8.C	9.A	10.B
11.B	12.C	13.B	14.A	15.C
16.C	17.B	18.B	19.A	20.C
21.B	22.A	23.B	24.C	25.B
26.A	27.C	28.A	29.B	30.C

Unit 10
Underlining
pp. 54–55

1.A	2.B	3.B	4.B	5.A
6.A	7.A	8.B	9.A	10.A
11.B	12.A	13.A	14.B	

Unit 11
Capitalization and Punctuation
pp. 56–59

1.B	2.A	3.D	4.C	5.D
6.A	7.C	8.B	9.C	10.D
11.A	12.C	13.B	14.A	15.D
16.D	17.B	18.A	19.C	20.A
21.A	22.D	23.B	24.D	25.A
26.A				

Unit 12
Capitalization and Punctuation
pp. 60–61

1.A	2.C	3.B	4.C	5.B
6.B				

The Last LAP
Language Activity Pages
pp. 62–63

A: 1.B 2.A 3.C; **B:** 1.B 2.A 3.B; **C:** 1. Dear Mr. Barbados: 2. <u>Toy Story</u> 3. When I bought the movie, a salesperson at your store told me, "All of the products we sell are guaranteed to work, or we will replace them for free." 4. If you are out of stock, you may send me one of the following movies instead: <u>Shrek</u>, <u>A Bug's Life</u>, or <u>Spy Kids</u>. 5. <u>Shrek</u>, <u>A Bug's Life</u>, or <u>Spy Kids</u>.; **D:** 1. Answers will vary. 2. Answers will vary.

Unit 1
Capital Letters
pp. 6–9

1.B	2.A	3.B	4.B	5.B
6.D	7.B	8.D	9.B	10.A
11.D	12.D	13.B	14.B	15.B
16.D	17.B	18.B	19.B	20.A
21.D	22.C	23.B	24.B	25.D
26.A	27.C	28.D		

Unit 2
Capital Letters
pp. 10–13

1.B	2.D	3.A	4.B	5.C
6.D	7.A	8.D	9.C	10.B
11.C	12.D	13.C	14.D	15.C
16.B	17.A	18.B	19.C	20.D
21.A	22.A	23.C	24.B	25.C
26.C	27.D	28.C	29.C	30.C
31.A	32.D			

Unit 3
Capital Letters
pp. 14–17

1.A	2.C	3.C	4.D	5.B
6.D	7.C	8.D	9.A	10.C
11.A	12.D	13.B	14.B	15.A
16.D	17.C	18.B	19.D	20.C
21.C	22.A			

The First LAP
Language Activity Pages
pp. 18–19

A: 1.B 2.B 3.C; **B:** 1.C 2.A
3.A 4.C 5.B; **C:** 1. July
2. Allen 3. Mammoth 4. I
5. Aunt 6. Your; **D:** 1. Answers
will vary. 2. Answers will vary.

Unit 4
End Marks
pp. 20–21

1.B	2.A	3.A	4.A	5.C
6.A	7.A	8.A	9.B	10.B
11.A	12.C	13.B	14.A	15.A
16.A				

Unit 5
Abbreviations
pp. 22–27

1.B	2.C	3.C	4.C	5.B
6.C	7.A	8.A	9.B	10.B
11.A	12.A	13.A	14.B	15.A
16.A	17.B	18.A	19.A	20.B
21.A	22.A	23.B	24.A	25.B
26.A	27.A	28.B	29.A	30.A
31.B	32.D	33.C	34.B	35.C
36.A	37.D	38.B		

The Second LAP
Language Activity Pages
pp. 28–29

A: 1.A 2.B 3.A; **B:** 1.B 2.A 3.A
4.C; **C:** in., min., L, m, Tues.,
Mon., Thurs., Sun.;
D: 1. Answers will vary.
2. Answers will vary.

Unit 6
Commas pp. 30–33

1.B	2.A	3.B	4.A	5.A
6.B	7.A	8.A	9.B	10.A
11.A	12.B	13.B	14.B	15.C
16.B	17.B	18.D	19.A	20.D
21.B	22.B			

Unit 7
Commas pp. 34–37

1.B	2.C	3.A	4.B	5.C
6.B	7.A	8.C	9.A	10.A
11.B	12.C	13.A	14.B	15.C
16.A	17.B	18.A	19.B	20.B
21.A	22.C			

Unit 8
Commas pp. 38–43

1.A	2.B	3.B	4.C	5.C
6.B	7.A	8.B	9.C	10.A
11.C	12.B	13.A	14.B	15.C
16.B	17.A	18.B	19.A	20.B
21.C	22.C	23.B	24.A	25.C
26.A	27.B	28.A	29.B	30.B
31.C	32.A	33.C	34.B	35.B
36.C	37.A	38.A		

The Third LAP
Language Activity Pages
pp. 44–45

A: 1.C 2.A 3.A; **B:** 1.B 2.B
3.A; **C:** 1. Whenever I go on a
hike, I always follow the same
routine. 2. First, I put on my
most comfortable clothes and
my hiking boots. 3. Next, I
enter the woods behind my
house. 4. Finally, I spin around
with my eyes closed. 5. My
favorite seasons to hike are
summer, fall, and winter.
6. I used to hike in the spring
as well, but in the past few
years it has been too muddy.
D: 1. Answers will vary.
2. Answers will vary.

Unit 9
Colons pp. 46–47

1.A	2.C	3.B	4.B	5.B
6.C	7.A	8.D		

Unit 10
Hyphens
pp. 48–49

1.A	2.B	3.B	4.C	5.D
6.C	7.B	8.D		

Unit 11
Quotation Marks
and Underlining
pp. 50–55

1.A	2.C	3.A	4.B	5.B
6.B	7.A	8.B	9.C	10.A
11.B	12.C	13.A	14.A	15.A
16.B	17.C	18.B	19.C	20.B
21.A	22.A	23.A	24.A	25.A
26.B	27.A	28.B	29.B	30.A
31.B	32.A	33.A	34.B	35.A
36.B	37.B	38.B	39.A	40.B
41.A	42.B			

Unit 12
Capitalization and
Punctuation
pp. 56–61

1.C	2.B	3.D	4.A	5.C
6.B	7.C	8.B	9.D	10.B
11.B	12.A	13.A	14.C	15.C
16.C	17.B	18.C	19.A	20.B
21.A	22.B	23.C	24.A	25.A
26.B	27.A	28.C	29.C	30.A
31.B	32.D	33.B	34.B	35.C
36.A				

The Last LAP
Language Activity Pages
pp. 62–63

A: 1.C 2.B 3.A; **B:** 1.B 2.A
3.A 4.B; **C:** 1. Dear Mr. Roper:
2. You told me, "If I can be of
help next year, please let me
know." 3. Would you be
willing to donate advertising
space in the Circleville Journal?
4. We need the space to ask
for the donation of fifty-four
saplings to plant on Arbor Day.
5. If you cannot donate the
advertising space, you can help
us in one of the following
ways: donate trees, ask your
staff to donate trees, or help
plant trees on Arbor Day.
6. The mayor said, "I will
mention every member of the
business community who
contributes to the Arbor Day
celebration." **D:** 1. Answers
will vary. 2. Answers will vary.

Unit 1
Capitalization
pp. 6–11

1.C	2.B	3.B	4.A	5.A
6.D	7.C	8.B	9.A	10.B
11.C	12.D	13.B	14.A	15.D
16.C	17.A	18.C	19.D	20.C
21.A	22.B	23.C	24.D	25.C
26.A	27.D	28.C	29.C	30.B
31.A	32.C	33.D	34.B	35.B
36.A	37.B	38.B	39.A	40.C
41.C	42.A	43.C	44.B	45.A
46.A	47.B	48.C		

Unit 2
Capitalization
pp. 12–15

1.A	2.C	3.B	4.A	5.D
6.A	7.B	8.C	9.C	10.A
11.D	12.A	13.A	14.C	15.D
16.B	17.B	18.A	19.B	20.D
21.A	22.C	23.B	24.C	25.A

Unit 3
End Marks
pp. 16–17

1.B	2.A	3.A	4.A	5.B
6.A	7.B	8.B	9.A	10.B
11.B	12.A	13.A	14.B	15.B
16.A	17.A	18.B	19.A	20.B

The First LAP
Language Activity Pages
pp. 18–19

A: 1. sentence 2. first 3. Direction 4. pronoun 5. Names 6. title 7. inside 8. question 9. period 10. feeling; **B:** 1. professional 2. Baseball 3. Major League, camps 4. Fantasy 5. baseball 6. Major 7. Brooks 8. Florida; **C:** 1. Hockey 2. ? 3. National 4. Players 5. . 6. Camp 7. Fans 8. . 9. NHL 10. !; **D:** 1. Answers will vary. 2. Answers will vary.

Unit 4
Abbreviations
pp. 20–23

1.A	2.C	3.B	4.C	5.A
6.B	7.B	8.B	9.A	10.C
11.B	12.A	13.A	14.B	15.A
16.B	17.A	18.A	19.A	20.B
21.A	22.B	23.B	24.A	25.B
26.B	27.A	28.C	29.A	30.C
31.B	32.A	33.B	34.B	35.A
36.C	37.A	38.C		

Unit 5
Commas
pp. 24–29

1.A	2.B	3.A	4.B	5.B
6.A	7.B	8.B	9.B	10.A
11.A	12.A	13.B	14.A	15.B
16.A	17.B	18.B	19.A	20.B
21.A	22.A	23.C	24.C	25.B
26.A	27.C	28.B	29.C	30.A
31.B	32.B	33.A	34.C	35.B
36.B	37.C	38.B	39.A	40.C
41.A	42.A	43.B	44.C	45.B
46.A	47.C	48.B	49.B	50.A

Unit 6
Commas
pp. 30–35

1.C	2.B	3.D	4.D	5.A
6.C	7.C	8.B	9.A	10.B
11.C	12.B	13.A	14.A	15.C
16.A	17.B	18.C	19.B	20.B
21.A	22.C	23.B	24.D	25.B
26.C	27.D	28.A	29.C	30.B
31.A	32.D	33.A	34.B	

The Second LAP
Language Activity Pages
pp. 36–37

A: 1. one 2. Abbreviations 3. months 4. envelopes 5. periods 6. dictonary 7. Commas 8. friendly 9. closing 10. series 11. before 12. phrases; **B:** 1.A 2.C 3.A 4.B 5.A 6.C 7.C 8.B 9.A 10.B; **C:** 1. Peru, Illinois 2. Tuesday, 3. Dear Dan, 4. Seattle, 5. downtown area, 6. On Saturday, 7. however, 8. friend,; **D:** 1. Answers will vary. 2. Answers will vary.

Unit 7
Colons, Semicolons, and Hyphens
pp. 38–43

1.C	2.D	3.B	4.D	5.A
6.D	7.B	8.B	9.D	10.C
11.D	12.A	13.A	14.B	15.C
16.A	17.C	18.B	19.A	20.C
21.B	22.B	23.A	24.B	25.C
26.C	27.C	28.A		

Unit 8
Quotation Marks and Underlining
pp. 44–49

1.C	2.A	3.C	4.B	5.C
6.A	7.A	8.B	9.A	10.B
11.C	12.A	13.C	14.C	15.B
16.A	17.B	18.C	19.C	20.A
21.B	22.C	23.D	24.B	25.C
26.D	27.A	28.C	29.D	30.D
31.B	32.A			

The Third LAP
Language Activity Pages
pp. 50–51

A: 1.F 2.T 3.F 4.F 5.T 6.T 7.T 8.T 9.F 10.T 11.F 12.F; **B:** 1. fifty-nine 2. twenty-five 3. transportation-related 4. three-fourths 5. forty-five 6. two-thirds 7. sister-in-law 8. well-trained 9. great-grandmother 10. one-quarter 11. thirty-five 12. ever-present; **C:** 1. colon 2. semicolon 3. Quotation 4. hyphen 5. underline; **D:** 1. Answers will vary. 2. Answers will vary.

Unit 9
Dashes, Parentheses, Ellipses Points, and Apostrophes
pp. 52–57

1.B	2.C	3.A	4.A	5.B
6.B	7.A	8.C	9.A	10.C
11.B	12.C	13.A	14.A	15.B
16.C	17.A	18.B	19.A	20.C
21.A	22.A	23.B	24.B	25.C
26.A	27.B	28.C	29.C	30.A
31.A	32.B			

Unit 10
Capitalization and Punctuation
pp. 58–61

1.B	2.D	3.A	4.D	5.A
6.C	7.B	8.D	9.C	10.B
11.D	12.A	13.C	14.C	15.A
16.B	17.A	18.C	19.D	20.C
21.B	22.A	23.D	24.C	25.A
26.D	27.C	28.A		

The Last LAP
Language Activity Pages
pp. 62–63

A: 1.F 2.T 3.F 4.T 5.T 6.T 7.F 8.F 9.T 10.F 11.T 12.T; **B:** 1. doesn't 2. There's 3. store's 4. We'll 5. That's 6. I'd 7. You've 8. we'll 9. that's 10. I'm; **C:** 1. (1898-1988) 2. Enzo—born in Modena, Italy—knew 3. 1925-1928 4. Then—in 1929—he 5. (people devoted strongly to a cause or an interest) 6. road—no pun intended—for; **D:** 1. Answers will vary. 2. Answers will vary.

Unit 1
Capitalization
pp. 6–7

1.B	2.D	3.C	4.A	5.C
6.B	7.A	8.D	9.A	10.C
11.B	12.D	13.B	14.A	15.A
16.A	17.C	18.B	19.B	20.D

Unit 2
Capitalization
pp. 8–11

1.C	2.A	3.B	4.B	5.B
6.D	7.C	8.B	9.A	10.C
11.D	12.B	13.A	14.A	15.D
16.C	17.B	18.D	19.A	20.B
21.A	22.C	23.C	24.B	25.A
26.B	27.C	28.A	29.C	30.B

Unit 3
Capitalization
pp. 12–15

1.A	2.C	3.C	4.B	5.D
6.A	7.C	8.A	9.B	10.C
11.D	12.C	13.C	14.A	15.B
16.A	17.D	18.A	19.A	20.C
21.B	22.B	23.D	24.A	25.C
26.D				

The First LAP
Language Activity Pages
pp. 16–17

A: 1.A 2.B 3.B 4.A 5.A 6.B 7.A 8.B; **B:** 1. Don't 2. I 3. Roland 4. Ohio 5. Friday 6. Coach; **C:** 1. Hamm 2. You 3. soccer 4. Arlington 5. players 6. July 7. August 8. friends; **D:** 1. Answers will vary. 2. Answers will vary.

Unit 4
End Marks
pp. 18–19

1.B	2.B	3.A	4.B	5.B
6.A	7.A	8.B	9.B	10.B
11.B	12.A	13.A	14.A	15.B
16.B	17.B	18.A	19.B	20.A
21.B	22.A			

Unit 5
Abbreviations
pp. 20–23

1.B	2.C	3.B	4.A	5.C
6.A	7.B	8.C	9.B	10.A
11.C	12.B	13.D	14.B	15.C
16.A	17.A	18.B	19.C	20.B
21.C	22.A	23.C	24.C	25.B
26.B	27.A	28.C		

The Second LAP
Language Activity Pages
pp. 24–25

A: 1.B 2.C 3.C 4.A; **B:** 1. 33 in. 2. chap. 7 3. 2 tsp. 4. 24 hrs. 5. 96 mins. 6. 65 mph 7. jr. 8. 1 oz.; **C:** 1. it. 2. saxophone. 3. too. 4. Mr. 5. Ave. 6. CA; **D:** 1. Answers will vary. 2. Answers will vary.

Unit 6
Commas
pp. 26–29

1.B	2.B	3.A	4.A	5.A
6.A	7.B	8.A	9.B	10.B
11.A	12.B	13.A	14.A	15.A
16.B	17.A	18.B	19.A	20.C
21.A	22.B	23.C	24.D	25.C
26.A	27.B	28.D		

Unit 7
Commas
pp. 30–33

1.A.	2.B	3.A	4.C	5.C
6.B	7.C	8.A	9.B	10.B
11.C	12.C	13.A	14.C	15.C
16.C	17.A	18.B	19.C	20.B
21.A	22.B	23.C	24.C	25.C
26.A	27.C	28.B		

Unit 8
Commas
pp. 34–37

1.B	2.A	3.C	4.A	5.C
6.C	7.B	8.A	9.C	10.D
11.B	12.C	13.A	14.B	15.B
16.B	17.C	18.D	19.A	20.D

The Third LAP
Language Activity Pages
pp. 38–39

A: 1.A 2.C 3.B 4.C 5.A; **B:** 1.B 2.A 3.C 4.C; **C:** 1. After my sister and I were done eating, we went for a walk. 2. First, we put on our jackets because it was a bit windy outside. 3. Then, we set out on our way. 4. At the pond, we saw a group of ducks floating on the water. 5. Standing very still, we could hear the wind rustling the leaves of the trees around us. 6. The cattails, which had grown almost all the way around the pond, swayed in the cool breeze. **D:** 1. Answers will vary. 2. Answers will vary.

Unit 9
Colons, Semicolons, and Hyphens
pp. 40–45

1.B	2.D	3.A	4.D	5.C
6.C	7.A	8.C	9.B	10.B
11.D	12.A	13.D	14.A	15.C
16.A	17.B	18.B	19.C	20.A
21.A	22.B	23.C	24.C	25.A
26.A	27.B	28.C		

Unit 10
Quotation Marks and Underlining
pp. 46–51

1.C	2.A	3.B	4.C	5.A
6.B	7.B	8.A	9.B	10.B
11.B	12.C	13.A	14.C	15.A
16.B	17.C	18.B	19.A	20.C
21.B	22.A	23.A	24.D	25.B
26.C	27.B	28.D	29.B	30.B
31.C	32.A			

Unit 11
Other Punctuation Marks
pp. 52–57

1.B	2.C	3.A	4.A	5.B
6.C	7.A	8.A	9.A	10.B
11.B	12.C	13.A	14.A	15.B
16.C	17.A	18.A	19.C	20.B
21.B	22.C	23.C	24.C	25.A
26.A	27.C	28.C	29.C	30.A
31.C	32.B	33.B	34.C	35.A
36.B				

Unit 12
Capitalization and Punctuation
pp. 58–61

1.A	2.B	3.B	4.D	5.B
6.A	7.A	8.A	9.D	10.B
11.B	12.B	13.D	14.C	15.C
16.A	17.B	18.B	19.C	20.A
21.D	22.D	23.B	24.C	25.A
26.B	27.C	28.A		

The Last LAP
Language Activity Pages
pp. 62–63

A: 1.B 2.C 3.A 4.A 5.C 6.A; **B:** 1.A 2.B 3.B 4.A; **C:** 1. day, but 2. Mr. Minter 3. clothes— not 4. shovels, and hoes 5. lettuce. The 6. me, I 7. I've 8. farm. **D:** 1. Answers will vary. 2. Answers will vary.

Unit 1
Capitalization
pp. 6–7

1.D	2.B	3.C	4.B	5.C
6.A	7.B	8.C	9.C	10.B
11.D	12.D	13.B	14.A	15.C
16.B	17.D	18.D		

Unit 2
Capitalization
pp. 8–11

1.B	2.D	3.B	4.B	5.D
6.B	7.C	8.D	9.C	10.B
11.A	12.D	13.C	14.C	15.D
16.C	17.C	18.B	19.D	20.A
21.B	22.D	23.A	24.A	25.C
26.C	27.C	28.D		

Unit 3
Capitalization
pp. 12–15

1.D	2.C	3.D	4.C	5.A
6.D	7.C	8.B	9.C	10.D
11.C	12.B	13.D	14.D	15.C
16.C	17.B	18.D	19.A	20.D
21.C	22.D	23.D	24.D	25.B
26.A				

The First LAP
Language Activity Pages
pp. 16–17

A: 1.B 2.C 3.C 4.A 5.B; **B:** 1.A
2.B 3.A 4.B; **C:** 1. nature
2. Appalachian 3. member
4. GON 5. I 6. Rollo 7. advisor
8. Creek 9. naturalist 10. you;
D: 1. Answers will vary.
2. Answers will vary.

Unit 4
End Marks
pp. 18–19

1.A	2.B	3.A	4.A	5.B
6.A	7.B	8.B	9.A	10.B
11.B	12.B	13.B	14.B	15.A
16.A	17.B	18.A	19.A	20.A
21.B	22.A			

Unit 5
Quotation Marks
pp. 20–21

1.C	2.A	3.C	4.B	5.C
6.A	7.C	8.B	9.A	10.C

Unit 6
Abbreviations
pp. 22–27

1.B	2.A	3.A	4.B	5.C
6.B	7.B	8.A	9.C	10.B
11.A	12.C	13.A	14.C	15.B
16.B	17.C	18.A	19.B	20.B
21.C	22.B	23.A	24.C	25.A
26.B	27.A	28.A	29.C	30.B
31.B	32.C	33.A	34.A	35.C
36.A	37.B	38.C	39.B	40.A
41.B	42.B	43.C	44.A	

The Second LAP
Language Activity Pages
pp. 28–29

A: 1.C 2.B 3.B 4.A; **B:** 1. A.
Johnson; Jan. 11, 1992; Lorain,
OH; 137 cm 2. U. K. Kay; Dec.
24, 1994; Portland, OR; 139
cm 3. K. Smith; Aug. 8, 1991;
Wheeling, WV; 140 cm 4. T. J.
Kaine; July 11, 1996; Denton,
TX; 136 cm; **C:** 1. "Don't miss
this one!" 2. Mr. 3. H. 4. P.M.
5. Sat. 6. Feb. 7. Blvd. 8. SC;
D: 1. Answers will vary
2. Answers will vary.

Unit 7
Commas
pp. 30–31

1.B	2.A	3.B	4.A	5.B
6.A	7.B	8.B	9.B	10.A
11.A	12.B	13.A	14.B	15.A
16.A				

Unit 8
Commas
pp. 32–35

1.C	2.A	3.B	4.B	5.A
6.B	7.B	8.C	9.C	10.A
11.A	12.C	13.C	14.C	15.B
16.C	17.C	18.A	19.A	20.B
21.C	22.C	23.A	24.C	

Unit 9
Commas
pp. 36–41

1.B	2.D	3.D	4.C	5.A
6.B	7.C	8.C	9.A	10.B
11.A	12.C	13.A	14.B	15.B
16.C	17.B	18.A	19.A	20.C
21.B	22.B	23.D	24.A	25.B
26.C	27.A	28.C	29.D	30.D
31.B	32.D	33.B	34.C	

The Third LAP
Language Activity Pages
pp. 42–43

A: 1.B 2.A 3.B 4.A; **B:** 1.C 2.C
3.B; **C:** 1. Well, I just have to
tell you about this amazing
concert I went to last night in
Denton, Texas. 2. My brother,
my cousin, my neighbor, and I
went to town with my aunt.
3. As soon as we drove into
the parking lot, I could hear
the cheering crowd. 4. correct
5. The group was from Thies
Senegal, which is in West Africa.
6. correct 7. Wow, the rhythms
were fantastic. 8. Other
musicians played different types
of brass instruments, and there
were a few guitar players.
9. The best part of the
performance, however, was
the dancers. 10. correct
11. The enthusiastic, colorfully
dressed dancers made the
music come alive. 12. Gosh, I
want to see that group again!
D: 1. Answers will vary.
2. Answers will vary.

Unit 10
Colons and Semicolons
pp. 44–47

1.A	2.B	3.C	4.B	5.A
6.A	7.B	8.A	9.C	10.A
11.B	12.B	13.A	14.D	15.B
16.A	17.D	18.A		

Unit 11
Hyphens
pp. 48–51

1.C	2.B	3.A	4.D	5.C
6.D	7.C	8.B	9.C	10.B
11.B	12.B	13.C	14.A	15.A
16.B				

Unit 12
Underlining
pp. 52–53

1.C	2.A	3.A	4.B	5.B
6.B	7.D	8.C	9.A	10.B

Unit 13
Other Punctuation Marks
pp. 54–57

1.A	2.B	3.C	4.C	5.C
6.B	7.A	8.C	9.B	10.A
11.A	12.A	13.C	14.C	15.B
16.B	17.C	18.A		

Unit 14
Capitalization and
Punctuation
pp. 58–61

1.B	2.C	3.C	4.A	5.B
6.D	7.B	8.B	9.C	10.A
11.D	12.D	13.B	14.B	15.C
16.D	17.A	18.B	19.B	20.D
21.B	22.C	23.A	24.D	25.D
26.A	27.B	28.D		

(continued on next page)

The Last LAP
Language Activity Pages
pp. 62–63

A: 1.B 2.G 3.H 4.D 5.A 6.E
7.C 8.F; **B:** 1. dashes 2. hyphen
3. underline 4. apostrophe
5. semicolon 6. colon
7. ellipses points
8. parentheses; **C:** 1. Brook
Park, and a group 2. students
3. Saturday at 2:00
4. Landingham, Democrat,
Brook Park 5. Landingham
stated, "These kids are
committed 6. environment; I
urge 7. to help them." 8. a
brand-new song 9. "Pick It
Up" **D:** 1. Answers will vary.
2. Answers will vary.

Unit 1
Capitalization
pp. 6–7

1.D	2.B	3.B	4.C	5.D
6.B	7.A	8.D	9.A	10.D
11.B	12.D	13.A	14.A	15.C
16.B	17.D	18.D	19.B	20.D

Unit 2
Capitalization
pp. 8–11

1.D	2.C	3.C	4.C	5.C
6.A	7.D	8.D	9.B	10.C
11.C	12.B	13.B	14.B	15.A
16.D	17.C	18.A	19.C	20.C
21.C	22.C	23.B	24.D	25.C
26.D	27.A	28.A	29.C	30.D
31.D	32.A			

Unit 3
Capitalization
pp. 12–15

1.B	2.C	3.D	4.C	5.D
6.A	7.C	8.C	9.D	10.B
11.B	12.C	13.B	14.A	15.C
16.A	17.D	18.C	19.C	20.A
21.B	22.D	23.C	24.B	25.C
26.C	27.B	28.D	29.A	30.C

The First LAP
Language Activity Pages
pp. 16–17

A: 1.B 2.A 3.A 4.B 5.C;
B: 1.C 2.C 3.D 4.A; **C:** 1. July
2. I 3. For 4. Trail
5. Declaration
6. Independence 7. Fourth
8. Boston 9. English 10. Sons
11. Liberty 12. Fenway;
D: 1. Answers will vary.
2. Answers will vary.

Unit 4
End Marks
pp. 18–19

1.A	2.B	3.B	4.B	5.B
6.A	7.A	8.B	9.A	10.A
11.A	12.B	13.A	14.A	15.A
16.B	17.A	18.A	19.A	20.B

Unit 5
Abbreviations
pp. 20–23

1.B	2.B	3.A	4.A	5.C
6.C	7.A	8.C	9.A	10.B
11.A	12.C	13.A	14.A	15.B
16.B	17.C	18.B	19.A	20.C
21.B	22.B	23.A	24.A	25.C
26.B	27.A	28.C	29.B	30.A
31.C	32.B	33.A	34.A	

The Second LAP
Language Activity Pages
pp. 24–25

A: 1.C 2.A 3.A 4.B 5.A; **B:** 1.A
2.A 3.B 4.B; **C:** 1. time.
2. beach? 3. summer? 4. Mr.
5. Dr. 6. NY; **D:** 1. Answers
will vary. 2. Answers will vary.

Unit 6
Commas
pp. 26–27

1.A	2.A	3.B	4.A	5.B
6.A	7.A	8.B	9.A	10.B
11.B	12.A	13.A	14.B	15.A
16.B	17.B	18.B		

Unit 7
Commas
pp. 28–31

1.C	2.A	3.B	4.A	5.A
6.C	7.A	8.B	9.A	10.C
11.C	12.C	13.B	14.C	15.A
16.C	17.B	18.A	19.B	20.A
21.A	22.C	23.A	24.C	25.C

Unit 8
Commas
pp. 32–37

1.A	2.D	3.B	4.C	5.A
6.B	7.A	8.D	9.A	10.B
11.B	12.C	13.B	14.A	15.B
16.C	17.A	18.A	19.C	20.C
21.B	22.A	23.A	24.C	25.D
26.A	27.D	28.D	29.A	30.C
31.B	32.B	33.A	34.A	

The Third LAP
Language Activity Pages
pp. 38–39

A: 1.A 2.B 3.A 4.B 5.A; **B:** 1.A
2.B 3.C; **C:** 1. I've been
camping plenty of times with
my family, but I've always
wanted to go with my friends.
2. In fact, I know just where
we would go. 3. There's a
place called Redbird Hollow,
which is only about two hours
away. 4. It's a beautiful gorge
in Crane Hills State Park, and
I'm familiar with the area
already. 5. You can usually see
deer, turkeys, and hawks there.
6. I have lots of experience,
and I'm always careful. 7. Still,
I'm not sure what my mom
would think of the idea. 8. She
might say, "Wait until you are
older." **D:** 1. Answers will vary.
2. Answers will vary.

Unit 9
Colons, Semicolons,
and Hyphens
pp. 40–45

1.C	2.D	3.A	4.B	5.D
6.C	7.B	8.D	9.A	10.D
11.C	12.C	13.A	14.C	15.A
16.B	17.C	18.C	19.A	20.A
21.B	22.A	23.A	24.A	25.A
26.C	27.B	28.A	29.C	30.B

Unit 10
Quotation Marks
and Underlining
pp. 46–51

1.B	2.A	3.A	4.B	5.B
6.A	7.C	8.C	9.C	10.A
11.C	12.B	13.A	14.C	15.C
16.C	17.A	18.A	19.B	20.A
21.C	22.C	23.B	24.A	25.B
26.A	27.D	28.C	29.B	30.B
31.D	32.A	33.B	34.C	35.B
36.B				

Unit 11
Other Punctuation Marks
pp. 52–55

1.A	2.B	3.A	4.C	5.B
6.B	7.A	8.C	9.C	10.B
11.C	12.A	13.C	14.A	15.B
16.C	17.A	18.A	19.B	20.C
21.A	22.A			

Unit 12
Capitalization and
Punctuation
pp. 56–61

1.C	2.C	3.D	4.D	5.B
6.C	7.D	8.A	9.C	10.A
11.D	12.A	13.C	14.C	15.A
16.C	17.D	18.B	19.C	20.B
21.D	22.C	23.A	24.B	25.D
26.D	27.B	28.C	29.C	30.A
31.A	32.D	33.C	34.C	35.B
36.A	37.C	38.B	39.B	40.C
41.C	42.B	43.C	44.C	45.A
46.A	47.B	48.A	49.C	50.C

(continued on next page)

The Last LAP
Language Activity Pages
pp. 62–63
A: 1.A 2.B 3.C 4.C 5.A; **B:** 1.B
2.A 3.B 4.A 5.B; **C:** 1. On
Friday, January 28, we saw
2. In many cases, the fabric has
also become 3. silk, wool, linen,
and cotton. 4. First, he
vacuumed 5. placed the flag
between two layers of the new
fabric and carefully stitched
them 6. an acid-free panel;
D: 1. Answers will vary.
2. Answers will vary.

Unit 1
Pronunciation Strategy
pp. 6–9

1.E	2.C	3.A	4.B	5.D
6.H	7.F	8.B	9.G	10.E
11.A	12.C	13.D	14.F	15.A
16.E	17.D	18.C	19.G	20.B
21.D	22.H	23.F	24.E	25.G
26.C	27.A	28.B		

Unit 2
Pronunciation Strategy
pp. 10–13

1.C	2.A	3.B	4.B	5.A
6.E	7.F	8.C	9.G	10.D
11.B	12.A	13.C	14.B	15.A
16.A	17.C	18.B	19.B	20.A

Unit 3
Pronunciation Strategy
pp. 14–17

1.C	2.D	3.A	4.E	5.B
6.A	7.C	8.D	9.E	10.B
11.C	12.E	13.D	14.B	15.A
16.C	17.B	18.A	19.C	20.A
21.C	22.B	23.C	24.A	25.B
26.B				

The First LAP
Language Activity Pages
pp. 18–19

A: 1. consonants 2. vowel 3. words 4. sound; **B:** 1. pad, push 2. big, bell 3. man, win 4. sit, let; **C:** 1. mop, mug 2. corn, can 3. spoon, sponge 4. brush, bread 5. fan, fish 6. tea, tuna; **D:** 1. Answers will vary. 2. Answers will vary.

Unit 4
Visualization Strategy
pp. 20–25

1.A	2.B	3.B	4.A	5.B
6.B	7.A	8.A	9.B	10.B
11.A	12.A	13.A	14.A	15.B
16.B	17.A	18.B	19.B	20.A
21.A	22.B	23.B	24.A	25.B
26.B	27.B	28.A	29.A	30.B
31.A	32.B	33.B	34.A	35.B
36.A	37.B	38.A		

Unit 5
Visualization Strategy
pp. 26–27

1.B	2.A	3.C	4.A	5.B
6.C	7.A	8.B	9.B	10.A
11.C	12.A			

Unit 6
Visualization Strategy
pp. 28–31

1.A	2.A	3.B	4.A	5.B
6.B	7.A	8.B	9.B	10.A
11.B	12.A	13.B	14.A	15.B
16.B	17.A	18.A	19.A	20.B
21.A	22.B			

Unit 7
Consonant Substitution Strategy
pp. 32–35

1.A	2.C	3.B	4.B	5.C
6.B	7.C	8.A	9.B	10.C
11.E	12.C	13.D	14.B	15.A
16.E	17.B	18.D	19.F	20.G
21.C	22.A			

The Second LAP
Language Activity Pages
pp. 36–37

A: 1. vowel 2. consonants 3. words; **B:** 1. day 2. bean 3. pine 4. sight 5. load; **C:** 1. you 2. good 3. teacher 4. like 5. school 6. every 7. day 8. friend; **D:** 1. Answers will vary. 2. Answers will vary.

Unit 8
Vowel Substitution Strategy
pp. 38–41

1.D	2.A	3.F	4.G	5.I
6.B	7.C	8.E	9.H	10.C
11.J	12.B	13.F	14.G	15.E
16.H	17.D	18.A	19.I	20.A
21.B	22.B	23.A	24.A	25.B
26.A	27.B	28.B	29.A	30.B

Unit 9
Rhyming Strategy
pp. 42–47

1.A	2.C	3.B	4.C	5.A
6.C	7.B	8.C	9.A	10.B
11.B	12.C	13.C	14.A	15.B
16.A	17.B	18.C	19.C	20.B
21.A	22.A	23.B	24.C	25.A
26.B	27.B	28.C	29.B	30.C
31.A	32.B	33.C	34.A	35.C
36.B				

Unit 10
Rhyming Strategy
pp. 48–51

1.B	2.B	3.C	4.A	5.C
6.C	7.A	8.B	9.A	10.B
11.C	12.A	13.B	14.A	15.A
16.C	17.B	18.A	19.A	20.C
21.B	22.A	23.B	24.C	25.A

The Third LAP
Language Activity Pages
pp. 52–53

A: 1. vowels 2. rhyme 3. same; **B:** 1. bike 2. swim 3. tree 4. sled; **C:** 1. now 2. hot 3. rid 4. block 5. track; **D:** 1. Answers will vary. 2. Answers will vary.

Unit 11
Conventions Strategy
pp. 54–57

1.A	2.B	3.A	4.A	5.B
6.B	7.B	8.A	9.B	10.B
11.A	12.B	13.B	14.B	15.B
16.A	17.B	18.B	19.A	20.A
21.B	22.B	23.B	24.A	25.B
26.B	27.B	28.A	29.A	30.A

Unit 12
Conventions Strategy
pp. 58–61

1.A	2.B	3.A	4.B	5.A
6.B	7.A	8.A	9.B	10.B
11.A	12.B	13.A	14.A	15.B
16.A	17.B	18.A	19.B	20.B
21.A	22.A	23.B	24.B	25.A

The Last LAP
Language Activity Pages
pp. 62–63

A: 1. nouns 2. syllable 3. plural; **B:** 1. -es 2. -es 3. -s 4. -s 5. -es; **C:** 1. boxes 2. dishes 3. forks 4. spoons 5. beaches 6. parks; **D:** 1. Answers will vary. 2. Answers will vary.

Unit 1
Pronunciation Strategy
pp. 6–9

1.A	2.B	3.A	4.C	5.B
6.B	7.A	8.A	9.C	10.C
11.B	12.B	13.C	14.A	15.B
16.C	17.A	18.C	19.B	20.B
21.A	22.A	23.B	24.C	

Unit 2
Pronunciation Strategy
pp. 10–13

1.B	2.C	3.A	4.B	5.B
6.C	7.A	8.A	9.A	10.A
11.B	12.B	13.A	14.B	15.B
16.B	17.A	18.A	19.B	20.A

Unit 3
Pronunciation Strategy
pp. 14–15

1.B	2.A	3.B	4.A	5.B
6.A	7.C	8.A	9.B	10.C

Unit 4
Pronunciation Strategy
pp. 16–17

1.B	2.C	3.A	4.B	5.A
6.A	7.B	8.A	9.C	10.B

The First LAP
Language Activity Pages
pp. 18–19

A: 1.C 2.D 3.B 4.A; **B:** 1.A 2.B 3.B 4.A; **C:** 1.B 2.A 3.D 4.C; **D:** 1. Answers will vary. 2. Answers will vary.

Unit 5
Vowel Substitution Strategy
pp. 20–25

1.A	2.A	3.A	4.A	5.B
6.B	7.A	8.B	9.B	10.A
11.A	12.A	13.A	14.B	15.A
16.A	17.B	18.B	19.B	20.A
21.A	22.B	23.B	24.A	25.A
26.B	27.A	28.A	29.B	30.B
31.A	32.A	33.B	34.A	35.B
36.A				

Unit 6
Vowel Substitution Strategy
pp. 26–27

1.C	2.A	3.B	4.C	5.A
6.C	7.A	8.B	9.C	10.A
11.B	12.C			

Unit 7
Consonant Substitution Strategy
pp. 28–31

1.C	2.B	3.B	4.C	5.C
6.C	7.B	8.B	9.A	10.B
11.A	12.C	13.B	14.A	15.A
16.C	17.B	18.C	19.A	20.C
21.B	22.B	23.C	24.A	

Unit 8
Rhyming Strategy
pp. 32–35

1.B	2.A	3.C	4.A	5.A
6.B	7.A	8.C	9.A	10.B
11.C	12.A	13.B	14.A	15.C
16.B	17.A	18.B	19.C	20.B
21.A	22.B			

Unit 9
Rhyming Strategy
pp. 36–39

1.B	2.A	3.C	4.A	5.B
6.C	7.B	8.C	9.B	10.A
11.B	12.C	13.B	14.C	15.A
16.C	17.B	18.A	19.A	20.C
21.B	22.A	23.B	24.A	

The Second LAP
Language Activity Pages
pp. 40–41

A: 1.A 2.B; **B:** 1.B 2.C 3.A 4.B; **C:** 1.G 2.A 3.D 4.C 5.H 6.E 7.F 8.B; **D:** 1. We gave the dog a scrub in the tub. 2. Answers will vary.

Unit 10
Conventions Strategy
pp. 42–45

1.A	2.A	3.A	4.A	5.B
6.B	7.B	8.A	9.B	10.A
11.B	12.B	13.A	14.A	15.B
16.B	17.B	18.A	19.A	20.B

Unit 11
Conventions Strategy
pp. 46–49

1.A	2.B	3.A	4.A	5.A
6.B	7.A	8.A	9.B	10.B
11.A	12.B	13.A	14.B	15.A
16.B	17.A	18.A	19.A	20.B
21.B	22.A			

Unit 12
Conventions Strategy
pp. 50–51

1.A	2.A	3.B	4.A	5.B
6.B	7.A	8.B	9.B	10.A
11.A	12.A			

The Third LAP
Language Activity Pages
pp. 52–53

A: 1.B 2.A 3.B; **B:** 1.A 2.B 3.A; **C:** 1. landed 2. whitest 3. longer 4. strangest; **D:** 1. Answers will vary. 2. Answers will vary.

Unit 13
Compound Word Strategy
pp. 54–57

1.A	2.B	3.B	4.A	5.B
6.A	7.B	8.A	9.B	10.B
11.A	12.B	13.A	14.B	15.B
16.A	17.B	18.A	19.B	20.A
21.A	22.B	23.A	24.B	

Unit 14
Meaning Strategy
pp. 58–61

1.B	2.A	3.B	4.B	5.B
6.A	7.B	8.A	9.A	10.B
11.B	12.B	13.A	14.B	15.A
16.A	17.A	18.B	19.B	20.A
21.B	22.A			

The Last LAP
Language Activity Pages
pp. 62–63

A: 1.B 2.A; **B:** 1.A 2.B 3.A 4.B; **C:** 1. bear 2. meat 3. ate 4. horse 5. bee, **D:** 1. earth|worm, pony|tail, eye|ball, wrist|watch; Drawings will vary. 2. Answers will vary.

Unit 1
Pronunciation Strategy
pp. 6–9

1.C	2.C	3.B	4.B	5.B
6.A	7.B	8.C	9.C	10.A
11.B	12.C	13.B	14.B	15.A
16.B	17.C	18.A	19.B	20.B
21.B	22.B	23.A	24.B	

Unit 2
Pronunciation Strategy
pp. 10–13

1.C	2.A	3.B	4.C	5.A
6.C	7.B	8.C	9.C	10.A
11.B	12.B	13.A	14.A	15.B
16.C	17.C	18.B	19.C	20.A
21.B	22.C	23.B	24.C	

Unit 3
Pronunciation Strategy
pp. 14–15

1.A	2.B	3.B	4.A	5.A
6.B	7.B	8.B	9.A	10.A
11.B	12.A	13.B	14.B	15.A
16.A	17.B	18.A		

The First LAP
Language Activity Pages
pp. 16–17

A: 1.B 2.C 3.A; **B:** 1.A 2.B 3.C
4.A; **C:** 1. starfish 2. shrimp
3. squid 4. stretch 5. found;
D: 1. Answers will vary.
2. Answers will vary.

Unit 4
Rhyming Strategy
pp. 18–21

1.B	2.C	3.A	4.B	5.A
6.C	7.A	8.B	9.C	10.A
11.B	12.C	13.A	14.C	15.B
16.C	17.A	18.B	19.A	20.C
21.A	22.C	23.B	24.B	25.A
26.C	27.C	28.B	29.A	30.C
31.B	32.A	33.C	34.B	35.B

Unit 5
Rhyming Strategy
pp. 22–23

1.A	2.C	3.B	4.B	5.A
6.C	7.B	8.A	9.B	10.A
11.C	12.C	13.B	14.B	15.A
16.C	17.A	18.A		

Unit 6
Conventions Strategy
pp. 24–27

1.A	2.B	3.C	4.C	5.B
6.A	7.A	8.A	9.C	10.B
11.C	12.B	13.A	14.B	15.A
16.B	17.A	18.B	19.A	20.A
21.B	22.C	23.B	24.B	25.A
26.C	27.A	28.A	29.B	30.C

Unit 7
Conventions Strategy
pp. 28–29

1.B	2.C	3.C	4.B	5.A
6.B	7.C	8.B	9.C	10.B
11.A	12.C	13.C	14.B	15.A

The Second LAP
Language Activity Pages
pp. 30–31

A: 1.B 2.A; **B:** 1. longest
2. larger 3. formed 4. flowing
5. sandiest; **C:** 1. think 2. collar
3. day 4. part 5. name
6. black; **D:** 1. Answers will
vary. 2. Answers will vary.

Unit 8
Visualization Strategy
pp. 32–35

1.A	2.B	3.B	4.C	5.A
6.C	7.A	8.B	9.C	10.A
11.A	12.C	13.C	14.A	15.B
16.B	17.C	18.A	19.C	20.B
21.B	22.A	23.C	24.B	25.B
26.A	27.C	28.B	29.C	30.A
31.B	32.A	33.C	34.C	35.B
36.A				

Unit 9
Visualization Strategy
pp. 36–37

1.B	2.A	3.B	4.B	5.A
6.A	7.A	8.A	9.B	10.B
11.A	12.B	13.B	14.B	15.A
16.B	17.B	18.A	19.B	20.B
21.A	22.B			

Unit 10
Visualization Strategy
pp. 38–41

1.A	2.B	3.B	4.C	5.B
6.A	7.A	8.B	9.C	10.B
11.A	12.B	13.B	14.C	15.C
16.A	17.A	18.C	19.B	20.A
21.C	22.B	23.A	24.A	25.A
26.C	27.B	28.A	29.B	30.C
31.A	32.B	33.A	34.B	35.C
36.A	37.C	38.B		

Unit 11
Compound Word Strategy
pp. 42–43

1.B	2.C	3.A	4.B	5.C
6.C	7.A	8.B	9.B	10.A
11.B	12.A	13.A	14.B	

The Third LAP
Language Activity Pages
pp. 44–45

A: 1.A 2.C; **B:** 1.A 2.B 3.B
4.A; **C:** 1. climb 2. treehouse
3. caution 4. unstable
5. uncomfortable 6. sign;
D: 1. Answers will vary.
2. Answers will vary.

Unit 12
Meaning Strategy
pp. 46–49

1.B	2.B	3.A	4.B	5.B
6.B	7.B	8.B	9.A	10.B
11.A	12.B	13.A	14.B	15.A
16.B	17.B	18.B	19.A	20.B
21.B	22.A	23.B	24.B	25.A
26.B	27.B	28.B		

Unit 13
Dictionary Strategy
pp. 50–53

1.B	2.A	3.B	4.C	5.C
6.B	7.A	8.C	9.B	10.C
11.A	12.A	13.B	14.B	15.C
16.C	17.A	18.B	19.C	20.B
21.C	22.A	23.B	24.A	25.A
26.B	27.C	28.B	29.A	30.C
31.B	32.A	33.A	34.A	35.B
36.A				

Unit 14
Family Strategy
pp. 54–57

1.A	2.B	3.C	4.A	5.B
6.C	7.B	8.C	9.B	10.A
11.C	12.B	13.C	14.A	15.B
16.C	17.A	18.B	19.A	20.B
21.A	22.C	23.A	24.B	25.C
26.B	27.B	28.B	29.B	30.A
31.A	32.C	33.B	34.A	35.A
36.C	37.B	38.C		

Unit 15
Family Strategy
pp. 58–61

1.C	2.B	3.A	4.C	5.A
6.A	7.B	8.C	9.B	10.A
11.B	12.A	13.C	14.A	15.C
16.A	17.A	18.B	19.B	20.C
21.B	22.A	23.C	24.C	25.B
26.C	27.B	28.A	29.B	30.C
31.B	32.A	33.A	34.B	35.B
36.C	37.A	38.C	39.A	40.B

The Last LAP
Language Activity Pages
pp. 62–63

A: 1.A 2.C; **B:** 1.B 2.A 3.A;
C: 1. software 2. megabytes
3. break 4. pause 5. e-mail;
D: 1. Answers will vary.
2. Answers will vary.

Unit 1
Rhyming Strategy
pp. 6–11

1.B	2.C	3.A	4.B	5.A
6.D	7.B	8.C	9.A	10.D
11.C	12.A	13.C	14.B	15.D
16.A	17.D	18.B	19.A	20.C
21.D	22.A	23.B	24.C	25.B
26.D	27.A	28.B	29.D	30.C
31.C	32.D	33.B	34.A	35.B
36.B	37.A	38.C	39.B	40.A
41.D	42.C	43.B	44.D	45.A
46.C	47.B	48.D	49.A	50.C

Unit 2
Conventions Strategy
pp. 12–13

1.B	2.C	3.D	4.C	5.C
6.A	7.B	8.C	9.A	10.D
11.A	12.C	13.B	14.C	

Unit 3
Conventions Strategy
pp. 14–17

1.B	2.A	3.A	4.B	5.B
6.A	7.A	8.B	9.C	10.B
11.D	12.D	13.A	14.A	15.C
16.C	17.A	18.C	19.D	20.B
21.C	22.B	23.C	24.B	25.D
26.B	27.A	28.C		

The First LAP
Language Activity Pages
pp. 18–19

A: 1.B 2.A 3.A; **B:** Column 1: mopped, ripped, dragged; Column 2: fried, replied, copied; Column 3: tricked, laughed, destroyed; **C:** 1. running 2. birds 3. hopping 4. animals 5. tried 6. hard; **D:** 1. Answers will vary. 2. Answers will vary.

Unit 4
Visualization Strategy
pp. 20–23

1.C	2.B	3.C	4.A	5.A
6.C	7.D	8.C	9.A	10.B
11.A	12.B	13.A	14.C	15.D
16.B	17.A	18.B	19.C	20.A
21.A	22.B	23.D	24.C	25.A
26.B	27.C	28.A		

Unit 5
Visualization Strategy
pp. 24–25

1.B	2.A	3.D	4.C	5.A
6.D	7.C	8.D	9.A	10.C
11.B	12.A	13.D	14.A	15.C

Unit 6
Visualization Strategy
pp. 26–29

1.B	2.A	3.A	4.B	5.A
6.B	7.A	8.B	9.B	10.A
11.A	12.B	13.A	14.A	15.B
16.A	17.A	18.C	19.D	20.B
21.B	22.D	23.C	24.D	25.A
26.C	27.B	28.D	29.B	30.A
31.C	32.D			

The Second LAP
Language Activity Pages
pp. 30–31

A: 1.A 2.C 3.A; **B:** 1.C 2.B 3.B 4.C 5.A; **C:** 1. construction 2. final 3. direction 4. decision 5. awful 6. trouble; **D:** 1. Answers will vary. 2. Answers will vary.

Unit 7
Compound Word Strategy
pp. 32–33

1.A	2.A	3.B	4.B	5.A
6.B	7.B	8.A	9.B	10.A
11.B	12.A	13.A	14.B	15.B
16.A				

Unit 8
Meaning Strategy
pp. 34–37

1.B	2.B	3.B	4.A	5.A
6.B	7.B	8.B	9.A	10.B
11.A	12.B	13.B	14.B	15.B
16.A	17.A	18.B	19.A	20.B
21.A	22.A	23.B	24.B	25.A
26.A	27.A	28.B	29.B	30.B
31.A	32.B	33.A	34.B	35.A

Unit 9
Dictionary Strategy
pp. 38–41

1.B	2.C	3.A	4.D	5.B
6.C	7.C	8.A	9.D	10.C
11.B	12.A	13.B	14.B	15.D
16.B	17.A	18.A	19.B	20.D
21.C	22.A	23.B	24.A	25.A
26.C	27.B	28.C	29.A	30.D
31.A	32.D	33.B	34.C	35.D

The Third LAP
Language Activity Pages
pp. 42–43

A: 1.C 2.C 3.A; **B:** 1. hour 2. route 3. through 4. side 5. way; **C:** 1. grandmother's 2. hour 3. accident 4. highway 5. ambulance 6. apparent; **D:** 1. Answers will vary. 2. Answers will vary.

Unit 10
Proofreading Strategy
pp. 44–49

1.B	2.A	3.D	4.C	5.A
6.A	7.C	8.B	9.C	10.D
11.A	12.C	13.B	14.A	15.D
16.A	17.A	18.C	19.D	20.A
21.A	22.B	23.B	24.B	25.A
26.A	27.B	28.B	29.B	30.A
31.B	32.B	33.B	34.A	35.B
36.B	37.A	38.B	39.B	40.A
41.B	42.A	43.A	44.A	45.B
46.B	47.A	48.A	49.B	50.A

Unit 11
Family Strategy
pp. 50–55

1.C	2.C	3.A	4.D	5.B
6.B	7.C	8.A	9.D	10.B
11.C	12.D	13.C	14.B	15.B
16.D	17.A	18.D	19.B	20.C
21.A	22.C	23.B	24.C	25.C
26.D	27.C	28.B	29.D	30.A
31.C	32.B	33.A	34.C	35.D
36.B	37.A	38.B	39.D	40.A
41.C	42.A	43.D	44.D	45.C

Unit 12
Foreign Language Strategy
pp. 56–61

1.A	2.B	3.C	4.A	5.C
6.B	7.B	8.C	9.B	10.C
11.A	12.B	13.B	14.A	15.A
16.B	17.B	18.A	19.A	20.B
21.A	22.A	23.A	24.C	25.C
26.B	27.A	28.C	29.A	30.A
31.B	32.C	33.C	34.B	35.C
36.C	37.B	38.B	39.A	40.B
41.A	42.B	43.A	44.A	45.B

The Last LAP
Language Activity Pages
pp. 62–63

A: 1.A 2.C 3.B; **B:** 1. aque, aqueduct 2. phon, symphony 3. log, zoology 4. tele, telescope 5. equa, equator; **C:** 1. sculptors 2. human 3. Golden 4. painters 5. garden 6. visit; **D:** 1. Answers will vary. 2. Answers will vary.

Unit 1
Rhyming Strategy
pp. 6–9

1.B	2.A	3.C	4.D	5.A
6.B	7.D	8.C	9.D	10.A
11.B	12.C	13.D	14.A	15.D
16.B	17.C	18.A	19.B	20.C
21.D	22.C	23.D	24.A	25.B
26.B	27.C	28.B	29.D	30.A
31.C	32.D	33.D	34.B	35.C
36.C	37.A	38.B	39.D	40.A

Unit 2
Conventions Strategy
pp. 10–15

1.A	2.C	3.B	4.D	5.A
6.A	7.C	8.A	9.B	10.D
11.C	12.A	13.B	14.C	15.A
16.D	17.B	18.A	19.C	20.B
21.D	22.B	23.A	24.D	25.C
26.B	27.D	28.A	29.B	30.A
31.C	32.B	33.D	34.B	35.A
36.D	37.D	38.B	39.C	40.B
41.D	42.A	43.C	44.D	45.B
46.C	47.A	48.B	49.A	50.B
51.B	52.C	53.C	54.C	

The First LAP
Language Activity Pages
pp. 16–17

A: 1.F 2.F 3.T 4.T 5.T 6.T
7.T 8.T; **B:** 1. slants, glance
2. kneading, speeding 3. dare,
hair 4. round, browned
5. afford, scored; **C:** 1. light,
fight, gleaming, streaming,
wave, brave 2. air, there;
D: 1. Answers will vary.
2. Answers will vary.

Unit 3
Visualization Strategy
pp. 18–23

1.B	2.A	3.C	4.A	5.C
6.C	7.C	8.B	9.A	10.B
11.C	12.C	13.A	14.C	15.A
16.C	17.A	18.A	19.B	20.C
21.C	22.A	23.A	24.A	25.B
26.B	27.C	28.C	29.A	30.C
31.B	32.B	33.C	34.A	35.C
36.B	37.A	38.C	39.C	40.B
41.A	42.C	43.B	44.A	45.B
46.B	47.C	48.A		

Unit 4
Visualization Strategy
pp. 24–29

1.B	2.B	3.A	4.B	5.A
6.B	7.A	8.A	9.B	10.A
11.B	12.A	13.B	14.B	15.B

16.A	17.A	18.B	19.A	20.B
21.B	22.B	23.B	24.B	25.A
26.A	27.B	28.A	29.A	30.B
31.A	32.A	33.A	34.C	35.B
36.C	37.C	38.A	39.C	40.A
41.B	42.A	43.A	44.C	45.C
46.B	47.C	48.A	49.B	50.C
51.B	52.C	53.A	54.C	55.B
56.B	57.A	58.B		

The Second LAP
Language Activity Pages
pp. 30–31

A: 1. fiction 2. library
3. business 4. people
5. tremendous 6. torture
7. sufficient 8. Competition
9. commercial 10. occupation;
B: 1.A 2.B 3.B 4.A 5.A 6.A;
C: 1. title 2. level 3. trial
4. model 5. foundation 6. final
7. signal 8. cable 9. definition
10. little 11. functions
12. furniture 13. measure
14. original 15. vital;
D: 1. Answers will vary.
2. Answers will vary.

Unit 5
Compound Word Strategy
pp. 32–33

1.B	2.A	3.C	4.A	5.C
6.B	7.C	8.A	9.B	10.C
11.B	12.A	13.B	14.A	15.B
16.B	17.A	18.B	19.A	20.B
21.B	22.A			

Unit 6
Meaning Strategy
pp. 34–35

1.B	2.B	3.B	4.B	5.A
6.B	7.B	8.A	9.A	10.A
11.B	12.B	13.A	14.B	15.A
16.A	17.B	18.A	19.A	20.B

Unit 7
Dictionary Strategy
pp. 36–41

1.A	2.A	3.B	4.B	5.A
6.B	7.A	8.B	9.C	10.A
11.D	12.B	13.B	14.C	15.C
16.B	17.D	18.A	19.D	20.C
21.B	22.B	23.C	24.D	25.C
26.B	27.B	28.D	29.B	30.A
31.B	32.B	33.B	34.A	35.A
36.B	37.B	38.A	39.A	40.A
41.B	42.B	43.A	44.A	45.B
46.B	47.A	48.B	49.A	50.B
51.A	52.B	53.B	54.A	55.B
56.B	57.B	58.B		

The Third LAP
Language Activity Pages
pp. 42–43

A: 1. heel 2. navel 3. vein
4. muscles 5. blue 6. cells
7. principal 8. grays;
B: 1. indigestion 2. dislocated
3. immune 4. substance
5. nutrient 6. resistance
7. misrepresent 8. dominant;
C: 1. ball, ballpark 2. stop,
shortstop 3. shoe, shoelace
4. ache, headache 5. up,
checkup 6. wide, widespread
7. fore, forego 8. hard,
hardship; **D:** 1. misstep,
discolor, permanent, inferior,
impossible, appearance
2. Answers will vary.

Unit 8
Proofreading Strategy
pp. 44–49

1.B	2.C	3.C	4.B	5.A
6.D	7.D	8.A	9.B	10.D
11.C	12.D	13.D	14.A	15.A
16.D	17.B	18.B	19.C	20.C
21.B	22.A	23.B	24.B	25.A
26.B	27.B	28.A	29.B	30.B
31.B	32.B	33.B	34.A	35.A
36.B	37.B	38.A	39.B	40.A
41.A	42.B	43.A	44.B	45.A
46.A	47.B	48.B		

Unit 9
Family Strategy
pp. 50–55

1.C	2.D	3.A	4.B	5.A
6.C	7.C	8.A	9.B	10.D
11.A	12.C	13.D	14.B	15.A
16.C	17.B	18.A	19.D	20.C
21.B	22.D	23.C	24.A	25.C
26.D	27.B	28.A	29.B	30.B
31.A	32.B	33.D	34.D	35.C
36.D	37.A	38.B	39.C	40.D
41.A	42.A	43.C	44.B	45.D
46.C	47.B	48.A	49.A	50.C
51.B	52.C	53.A	54.C	55.C
56.B	57.B	58.A	59.A	60.A
61.A	62.C	63.B	64.A	65.B
66.A	67.C	68.C	69.B	70.C
71.A	72.A			

(continued on next page)

Unit 10
Foreign Language Strategy
pp. 56–61

1.A	2.C	3.B	4.A	5.C
6.C	7.B	8.A	9.A	10.B
11.A	12.B	13.B	14.B	15.A
16.B	17.A	18.C	19.B	20.B
21.A	22.C	23.A	24.B	25.B
26.A	27.B	28.B	29.B	30.A
31.A	32.A	33.B	34.B	35.B
36.B	37.A	38.B	39.A	40.A
41.A	42.A	43.B	44.A	45.A
46.B	47.B	48.B	49.A	50.B

The Last LAP
Language Activity Pages
pp. 62–63

A: 1. pizza 2. tortillas
3. croissant 4. pasta
5. sauerkraut 6. macaroni
7. salsa 8. mousse 9. zucchini
10. chili; **B:** 1. create
2. preserve 3. tradition
4. appetite 5. special 6. tend
7. ship 8. heart 9. incline
10. festive; **C:** 1. or, favorite
2. al, animal 3. gh, rough
4. en, different 5. ph,
geography 6. le, little 7. er,
larger 8. gh, tough 9. al,
mammal 10. on, million 11. er,
shower 12. on, discussion;
D: 1. Answers will vary.
2. Answers will vary.

Unit 1
Conventions Strategy
pp. 6–11

1.C	2.B	3.A	4.D	5.A
6.C	7.D	8.B	9.A	10.C
11.B	12.C	13.D	14.B	15.B
16.C	17.A	18.B	19.B	20.C
21.D	22.A	23.C	24.C	25.A
26.B	27.A	28.D	29.C	30.B
31.B	32.C	33.A	34.D	35.D
36.B	37.B	38.C	39.D	40.A
41.B	42.B	43.A	44.C	45.B
46.B	47.D	48.A	49.A	50.A
51.D	52.C	53.A	54.B	55.A
56.D	57.C	58.B	59.C	60.A

Unit 2
Visualization Strategy
pp. 12–17

1.C	2.A	3.B	4.C	5.A
6.D	7.D	8.B	9.A	10.C
11.D	12.B	13.D	14.A	15.C
16.C	17.A	18.A	19.C	20.B
21.B	22.D	23.A	24.C	25.A
26.D	27.A	28.B	29.C	30.D
31.D	32.B	33.C	34.A	35.C
36.D	37.A	38.C	39.C	40.B
41.D	42.B	43.C	44.C	45.B
46.A	47.B	48.C	49.C	50.C
51.C	52.C	53.C	54.B	55.C
56.C	57.B	58.C	59.C	60.A

The First LAP
Language Activity Pages
pp. 18–19

A: 1.A 2.A 3.A 4.B; **B:** 1.B
2.B 3.A 4.B 5.A; **C:** 1. people
2. justice 3. insure 4. defense
5. general 6. secure
7. blessings 8. ourselves;
D: 1. Answers will vary.
2. Answers will vary.

Unit 3
Visualization Strategy
pp. 20–25

1.B	2.A	3.A	4.B	5.A
6.A	7.B	8.B	9.A	10.A
11.B	12.A	13.A	14.B	15.B
16.B	17.B	18.B	19.A	20.A
21.B	22.B	23.A	24.A	25.B
26.B	27.A	28.B	29.B	30.A
31.A	32.A	33.B	34.A	35.B
36.B	37.C	38.A	39.C	40.C
41.B	42.B	43.A	44.C	45.B
46.B	47.C	48.B	49.A	50.C
51.A	52.B	53.C	54.B	55.A
56.A	57.C	58.B	59.A	60.D
61.B	62.A	63.B	64.D	65.D
66.A	67.C	68.B		

Unit 4
Meaning Strategy
pp. 26–29

1.B	2.A	3.A	4.B	5.B
6.A	7.B	8.B	9.B	10.A
11.B	12.A	13.B	14.B	15.A
16.A	17.B	18.B	19.A	20.A
21.B	22.B	23.A	24.B	25.B
26.B	27.A	28.A	29.B	30.A
31.B	32.A	33.B	34.A	35.A
36.A	37.B	38.B	39.B	40.A
41.B	42.A			

The Second LAP
Language Activity Pages
pp. 30–31

A: 1.B 2.B 3.A 4.C; **B:** 1.B 2.A
3.B 4.B 5.B; **C:** 1. separate
2. resistance 3. tyranny
4. sacrifice 5. secede;
D: 1. Answers will vary.
2. Answers will vary.

Unit 5
Dictionary Strategy
pp. 32–37

1.B	2.B	3.C	4.B	5.C
6.A	7.C	8.B	9.C	10.A
11.B	12.B	13.A	14.A	15.B
16.A	17.A	18.A	19.B	20.B
21.B	22.B	23.A	24.A	25.B
26.A	27.B	28.B	29.B	30.B
31.A	32.A	33.B	34.B	35.B
36.A	37.B	38.A	39.A	40.B
41.B	42.B	43.B	44.C	45.D
46.B	47.C	48.B	49.D	50.B
51.C	52.B	53.A	54.D	

Unit 6
Proofreading Strategy
pp. 38–45

1.A	2.B	3.B	4.A	5.B
6.C	7.C	8.B	9.C	10.C
11.C	12.A	13.B	14.C	15.B
16.A	17.C	18.C		

The Third LAP
Language Activity Pages
pp. 46–47

A: 1.B 2.D 3.B 4.A 5.B;
B: 1. authors 2. inauguration
3. commander 4. responsible
5. foreign 6. impeached;
C: 1. Wren 2. excessively
3. nautical 4. climbed
5. surprise; **D:** 1. Answers will
vary. 2. Answers will vary.

Unit 7
Family Strategy
pp. 48–53

1.C	2.D	3.B	4.A	5.D
6.C	7.D	8.B	9.A	10.D
11.C	12.B	13.C	14.C	15.D
16.A	17.C	18.D	19.C	20.A
21.A	22.C	23.B	24.D	25.A
26.B	27.A	28.B	29.A	30.B
31.B	32.A	33.C	34.B	35.A
36.B	37.A	38.B	39.C	40.D
41.C	42.C	43.D	44.C	45.B
46.C	47.A	48.A	49.A	50.B
51.A	52.B	53.A	54.B	55.C
56.B	57.A	58.B	59.A	60.C
61.B	62.A	63.B	64.A	65.C

Unit 8
Foreign Language Strategy
pp. 54–61

1.B	2.B	3.C	4.C	5.A
6.C	7.B	8.C	9.C	10.B
11.B	12.B	13.C	14.B	15.A
16.A	17.C	18.A	19.B	20.B
21.B	22.C	23.C	24.C	25.C
26.C	27.A	28.C	29.A	30.C
31.B	32.B	33.A	34.A	35.B
36.B	37.A	38.A	39.B	40.A
41.B	42.A	43.A	44.B	45.A
46.A	47.A	48.B	49.A	50.A
51.B	52.A	53.B	54.A	55.B
56.A	57.A	58.B	59.B	60.A
61.B	62.B	63.B	64.A	65.A
66.A	67.B	68.B	69.B	70.A
71.B	72.B	73.B	74.B	75.B
76.A	77.A	78.B	79.B	80.A
81.B	82.B			

The Last LAP
Language Activity Pages
pp. 62–63

A: 1.C 2.B 3.A 4.B; **B:** 1.B
2.C 3.B 4.C; **C:** 1. reflection
2. autograph 3. script
4. pedestrian 5. pepperoni
6. uniform 7. cycles 8. evolves;
D: 1. Answers will vary.
2. Answers will vary.

Unit 1
Conventions Strategy
pp. 6–11

1.C	2.A	3.B	4.B	5.C
6.A	7.C	8.A	9.C	10.B
11.A	12.C	13.B	14.C	15.A
16.C	17.A	18.B	19.B	20.A
21.A	22.B	23.B	24.A	25.A
26.B	27.A	28.B	29.A	30.A
31.B	32.A	33.B	34.C	35.C
36.B	37.A	38.C	39.C	40.C
41.B	42.B	43.C	44.C	45.A
46.A	47.A	48.A	49.B	50.B
51.B	52.B	53.B	54.A	55.B

Unit 2
Visualization Strategy
pp. 12–19

1.C	2.C	3.A	4.B	5.A
6.C	7.C	8.C	9.C	10.A
11.A	12.B	13.A	14.C	15.C
16.B	17.B	18.B	19.C	20.C
21.B	22.B	23.A	24.C	25.A
26.C	27.B	28.A	29.B	30.A
31.B	32.A	33.C	34.C	35.A
36.C	37.B	38.C	39.A	40.B
41.A	42.B	43.B	44.B	45.A
46.B	47.B	48.C	49.B	50.B
51.B	52.C	53.C	54.C	55.C
56.B	57.C	58.C	59.B	60.C
61.A	62.C	63.B	64.B	65.A
66.A	67.B	68.A	69.B	70.A
71.A	72.A	73.A	74.B	75.B
76.A	77.B	78.A	79.A	80.B
81.A	82.A	83.B	84.A	

The First LAP
Language Activity Pages
pp. 20–21

A: 1.A 2.B 3.A 4.A 5.B;
B: 1. correct 2. general
3. enculturation 4. appreciation
5. correct 6. civilization;
C: 1. Once 2. creature
3. couple 4. magnificent
5. possession 6. universe
7. lettuce 8. delicious
9. fiercely 10. miserable;
D: 1. Answers will vary.
2. Answers will vary.

Unit 3
Visualization Strategy
pp. 22–25

1.B	2.B	3.A	4.B	5.A
6.B	7.A	8.B	9.A	10.B
11.A	12.A	13.B	14.B	15.A
16.B	17.A	18.B	19.A	20.B
21.A	22.A	23.C	24.B	25.C
26.C	27.A	28.C	29.B	30.A
31.C	32.C	33.B	34.C	35.A
36.B	37.A	38.C	39.B	40.A
41.C	42.B			

Unit 4
Meaning Strategy
pp. 26–29

1.B	2.B	3.A	4.B	5.B
6.A	7.B	8.B	9.A	10.B
11.A	12.B	13.B	14.A	15.B
16.B	17.B	18.A	19.A	20.A
21.B	22.B	23.A	24.A	25.B
26.A	27.B	28.B	29.B	30.A
31.B	32.B	33.B	34.B	35.A
36.A	37.B	38.B	39.A	40.A
41.B	42.B			

The Second LAP
Language Activity Pages
pp. 30–31

A: 1.A 2.C 3.B 4.A 5.A 6.C;
B: 1. foreward 2. perfect
3. peace 4. Continental
5. reasons; **C:** 1. rode 2. which
3. scepter 4. pair 5. scanty
6. tail 7. gate 8. daylight
9. way 10. all; **D:** 1. Answers
will vary. 2. Answers will vary.

Unit 5
Dictionary Strategy
pp. 32–37

1.C	2.C	3.B	4.C	5.B
6.A	7.C	8.B	9.B	10.B
11.C	12.B	13.C	14.B	15.A
16.A	17.A	18.A	19.A	20.A
21.B	22.B	23.B	24.B	25.B
26.A	27.A	28.A	29.A	30.A
31.A	32.B	33.A	34.A	35.B
36.B	37.A	38.A	39.B	40.B
41.B	42.A	43.A	44.B	45.B
46.A	47.A	48.C	49.B	50.B
51.C	52.A	53.C	54.C	55.A
56.C	57.B	58.C		

Unit 6
Proofreading Strategy
pp. 38–45

1.B	2.A	3.A	4.B	5.C
6.B	7.C	8.C	9.A	10.C
11.C	12.A	13.A	14.C	

The Third LAP
Language Activity Pages
pp. 46–47

A: 1.D 2.A 3.C 4.B 5.D 6.C;
B: 1. acquire 2. knowledge
3. Teachers 4. character
5. psychomotor
6. administrators; **C:** 1. rough
2. creature 3. herd 4. predator
5. haunches 6. animal

7. succumbs 8. awful 9. terror
10. caught; **D:** 1. Answers will
vary. 2. Answers will vary.

Unit 7
Family Strategy
pp. 48–53

1.C	2.B	3.D	4.D	5.A
6.C	7.B	8.D	9.A	10.C
11.C	12.A	13.A	14.D	15.C
16.B	17.C	18.B	19.C	20.A
21.B	22.D	23.D	24.C	25.A
26.B	27.C	28.D	29.C	30.A
31.C	32.B	33.B	34.D	35.D
36.A	37.B	38.C	39.D	40.A
41.C	42.B	43.B	44.A	45.D
46.C	47.A	48.B	49.C	50.A
51.A	52.B	53.C	54.A	55.B
56.B	57.C	58.A	59.B	60.B
61.B	62.A	63.C	64.B	65.C
66.C				

Unit 8
Foreign Language Strategy
pp. 54–61

1.A	2.B	3.C	4.C	5.A
6.B	7.B	8.A	9.C	10.B
11.A	12.A	13.B	14.A	15.C
16.A	17.B	18.C	19.C	20.A
21.C	22.A	23.A	24.B	25.B
26.A	27.C	28.A	29.B	30.B
31.A	32.B	33.A	34.B	35.A
36.B	37.B	38.B	39.A	40.B
41.B	42.A	43.A	44.A	45.A
46.B	47.A	48.B	49.A	50.A
51.B	52.A	53.B	54.B	55.A
56.B	57.A	58.B	59.A	60.B
61.A	62.B	63.B	64.A	65.A
66.B	67.A	68.B	69.A	70.A
71.A	72.B	73.B	74.B	75.A
76.A	77.B	78.A	79.A	80.B

The Last LAP
Language Activity Pages
pp. 62–63

A: 1.A 2.B 3.A 4.B 5.B 6.B;
B: 1. Adobe bricks are often
used in southwestern land-
scapes. 2. The Italians create
beautiful civic plazas. 3. The
main ingredient in quiche is
egg. 4. A patio can be a very
private getaway with proper
landscaping. **C:** 1. uninterrupted
2. tourists 3. psychologist
4. autograph 5. laborious
6. massages 7. hydrating
8. symphony 9. macaroni
10. strudel; **D:** 1. Answers will
vary. 2. Answers will vary.

Unit 1
Conventions Strategy
pp. 6–11

1.C	2.B	3.C	4.A	5.D
6.B	7.B	8.C	9.D	10.D
11.B	12.C	13.B	14.A	15.B
16.A	17.B	18.A	19.A	20.B
21.B	22.B	23.A	24.A	25.B
26.A	27.B	28.B	29.A	30.B
31.B	32.B	33.A	34.A	35.A
36.B	37.A	38.A	39.A	40.B
41.A	42.A	43.B	44.B	45.B
46.A	47.B	48.B	49.B	50.B

Unit 2
Visualization Strategy
pp. 12–19

1.A	2.C	3.C	4.B	5.A
6.C	7.B	8.A	9.C	10.A
11.B	12.C	13.C	14.A	15.C
16.A	17.C	18.B	19.A	20.C
21.B	22.A	23.C	24.C	25.A
26.C	27.B	28.A	29.A	30.A
31.C	32.B	33.A	34.C	35.C
36.A	37.B	38.A	39.C	40.B
41.C	42.C	43.A	44.A	45.A
46.A	47.C	48.A	49.C	50.A
51.C	52.C	53.C	54.C	55.B
56.B	57.B	58.A	59.B	60.A
61.A	62.A	63.A	64.A	65.A
66.B	67.A	68.A	69.A	70.B
71.B	72.A	73.B	74.A	75.B
76.A	77.B	78.A		

The First LAP
Language Activity Pages
pp. 20–21

A: 1.A 2.A 3.B 4.B 5.B;
B: 1. agricultural 2. natural
3. textile 4. correct
5. inventions; **C:** 1. clouds
2. victorious 3. bruised
4. measures 5. wrinkled
6. adversaries 7. nimbly
8. pleasing; **D:** 1. Answers will
vary. 2. Answers will vary.

Unit 3
Visualization Strategy
pp. 22–25

1.B	2.A	3.B	4.A	5.B
6.A	7.A	8.B	9.B	10.A
11.B	12.B	13.A	14.A	15.A
16.B	17.B	18.B	19.A	20.B
21.D	22.C	23.B	24.D	25.A
26.C	27.D	28.A	29.B	30.A
31.D	32.A	33.B	34.C	35.D
36.B	37.A	38.D	39.C	40.B
41.B	42.C			

Unit 4
Meaning Strategy
pp. 26–29

1.A	2.B	3.B	4.B	5.A
6.B	7.B	8.B	9.B	10.B
11.A	12.A	13.B	14.B	15.B
16.A	17.A	18.A	19.A	20.B
21.A	22.B	23.B	24.A	25.B
26.B	27.A	28.B	29.A	30.A
31.B	32.B	33.B	34.B	35.B
36.A	37.B	38.A	39.B	40.B
41.B	42.B			

The Second LAP
Language Activity Pages
pp. 30–31

A: 1.A 2.B 3.A 4.B 5.A 6.B;
B: 1. conceived 2. proposition
3. great 4. forfeit 5. principle;
C: 1. half 2. no 3. knew
4. sent 5. emissaries 6. traveled
7. whole 8. not 9. night
10. son 11. poor 12. heard;
D: 1. Answers will vary.
2. Answers will vary.

Unit 5
Dictionary Strategy
pp. 32–37

1.A	2.C	3.B	4.A	5.A
6.A	7.B	8.B	9.A	10.B
11.B	12.A	13.B	14.A	15.B
16.B	17.A	18.A	19.A	20.A
21.B	22.B	23.A	24.B	25.A
26.C	27.B	28.C	29.B	30.B
31.A	32.B	33.C	34.B	35.A
36.A	37.B	38.B	39.A	40.B
41.A	42.A	43.A	44.A	45.B
46.B	47.A	48.B	49.B	50.B

Unit 6
Proofreading Strategy
pp. 38–45

1.A	2.A	3.B	4.B	5.C
6.B	7.C	8.B	9.B	10.D
11.D	12.C	13.A	14.C	15.C

The Third LAP
Language Activity Pages
pp. 46–47

A: 1.A 2.A 3.D 4.B 5.C 6.D;
B: 1. abundant 2. oxygen
3. vital 4. organs 5. muscular
6. esophagus 7. stomach
8. human; **C:** 1. interrupts
2. ensues 3. brightness
4. consoling 5. embrace
6. irreplaceable 7. obedience
8. improbable 9. irresistible
10. impossible; **D:** 1. Answers
will vary. 2. Answers will vary.

Unit 7
Family Strategy
pp. 48–53

1.C	2.B	3.D	4.C	5.B
6.A	7.B	8.D	9.D	10.A
11.C	12.B	13.B	14.A	15.D
16.C	17.C	18.A	19.C	20.D
21.A	22.D	23.C	24.C	25.C
26.B	27.C	28.D	29.A	30.A
31.B	32.B	33.A	34.B	35.C
36.A	37.B	38.C	39.B	40.C
41.A	42.B	43.C	44.B	45.A
46.C	47.A	48.B	49.A	50.C
51.A	52.C	53.B	54.A	55.B
56.C	57.A	58.B	59.B	60.A
61.B	62.A	63.C	64.B	65.A
66.C	67.B	68.A	69.C	70.C

Unit 8
Foreign Language Strategy
pp. 54–61

1.C	2.A	3.C	4.B	5.C
6.A	7.B	8.B	9.A	10.C
11.A	12.C	13.A	14.B	15.B
16.C	17.A	18.B	19.A	20.A
21.C	22.C	23.B	24.B	25.A
26.A	27.C	28.C	29.B	30.C
31.A	32.B	33.A	34.A	35.A
36.B	37.A	38.B	39.A	40.B
41.B	42.A	43.A	44.A	45.B
46.B	47.A	48.A	49.B	50.B
51.B	52.A	53.A	54.B	55.B
56.A	57.B	58.A	59.B	60.A
61.A	62.B	63.B	64.A	65.B
66.A	67.B	68.A	69.A	70.B
71.A	72.A	73.B	74.A	75.B

(continued on next page)

■■■■ **The Last LAP** ■■■■
Language Activity Pages
pp. 62–63

A: 1.B 2.C 3.B 4.C 5.B 6.C
7.A 8.A; **B:** 1. Wood blocks,
tambourines, and maracas are
often used in rhythm bands.
2. An alphorn is used to call
cattle in the mountain regions
of Switzerland. 3. Timpani,
sometimes called kettledrums,
are the only drums capable of
producing true musical notes.
4. A crescendo in music
indicates that the musician
should gradually play louder.
C: 1. laborious 2. motion
3. audible 4. sympathy
5. entourage 6. fatigue
7. morsels 8. sustenance
9. interrupted 10. manually
11. morale 12. termination;
D: 1. captivate, concert,
castanet, symphony, cantata;
Paragraphs will vary.
2. Answers will vary.

Unit 1
Categories
pp. 6–11

1.C	2.B	3.A	4.A	5.C
6.B	7.C	8.A	9.C	10.B
11.C	12.A	13.B	14.C	15.A
16.B	17.C	18.C	19.A	20.D
21.B	22.A	23.C	24.B	25.E
26.D				

Unit 2
Categories
pp. 12–15

1.B	2.A	3.D	4.C	5.C
6.E	7.D	8.B	9.A	10.C
11.D	12.A	13.B	14.E	15.A
16.D	17.B	18.C		

The First LAP
Language Activity Pages
pp. 16–17

A: 1. category 2. words
3. alike; **B:** 1. cat 2. bear
3. rabbit 4. dog 5. lion;
C: 1. blue 2. green 3. yellow
4. purple; **D:** 1. Answers will
vary. 2. Answers will vary.

Unit 3
Synonyms
pp. 18–23

1.A	2.B	3.B	4.A	5.A
6.B	7.A	8.B	9.A	10.A
11.A	12.B	13.C	14.E	15.A
16.B	17.F	18.D	19.D	20.G
21.A	22.C	23.F	24.E	25.B
26.A	27.B	28.A	29.A	30.B
31.B	32.A	33.A	34.A	35.B

Unit 4
Antonyms
pp. 24–29

1.A	2.B	3.B	4.A	5.B
6.A	7.B	8.A	9.A	10.B
11.A	12.B	13.F	14.B	15.E
16.A	17.C	18.D	19.B	20.D
21.A	22.F	23.G	24.C	25.E
26.B	27.B	28.A	29.A	30.B
31.A	32.B	33.A	34.B	35.A

The Second LAP
Language Activity Pages
pp. 30–31

A: 1. Synonyms 2. Antonyms
3. *giant* 4. *loud*; **B:** 1. sad
2. clean 3. far 4. cool 5. hard
6. run; **C:** 1. cloudy 2. foggy
3. bright 4. hot; **D:** 1. Answers
will vary. 2. Answers will vary.

Unit 5
Homographs
pp. 32–35

1.D	2.B	3.A	4.C	5.C
6.E	7.A	8.B	9.D	10.A
11.E	12.B	13.C	14.D	15.B
16.D	17.C	18.A	19.F	20.E

Unit 6
Homophones
pp. 36–39

1.B	2.C	3.A	4.D	5.A
6.E	7.B	8.C	9.A	10.B
11.D	12.C	13.F	14.E	15.G
16.H	17.B	18.A	19.C	20.D
21.E	22.F	23.H	24.G	25.J
26.I				

Unit 7
Compound Words
pp. 40–43

1.C	2.D	3.A	4.B	5.F
6.C	7.E	8.B	9.A	10.D
11.D	12.C	13.A	14.B	15.E
16.C	17.F	18.A	19.D	20.B

Unit 8
Prefixes
pp. 44–47

1.C	2.A	3.B	4.C	5.C
6.B	7.A	8.C	9.B	10.A
11.D	12.C	13.A	14.B	15.F
16.E	17.A	18.C	19.D	20.B

Unit 9
Suffixes
pp. 48–51

1.B	2.A	3.D	4.C	5.F
6.A	7.B	8.E	9.D	10.C
11.D	12.A	13.B	14.C	15.E
16.B	17.F	18.A	19.C	20.D

The Third LAP
Language Activity Pages
pp. 52–53

A: 1. compound
2. Homophones
3. Homographs 4. prefix
5. suffix; **B:** 1. sunshine
2. chalkboard 3. anyone
4. board 5. sun 6. one; **C:** 1. left
2. left 3. kind 4. kind 5. like
6. like **D:** 1. Answers will vary.
2. Answers will vary.

Unit 10
Guide Words
pp. 54–57

1.B	2.C	3.A	4.C	5.B
6.A	7.B	8.A	9.C	10.C
11.B	12.C	13.A	14.C	15.A
16.C	17.A	18.B	19.C	20.A

Unit 11
Definitions
pp. 58–61

1.B	2.D	3.A	4.C	5.E
6.C	7.A	8.F	9.B	10.D
11.B	12.E	13.G	14.C	15.F
16.D	17.A	18.G	19.A	20.E
21.D	22.B	23.C	24.F	

The Last LAP
Language Activity Pages
pp. 62–63

A: 1. dictionary 2. Definitions
3. Guide 4. words;
B: 1. beginning 2. middle
3. end 4. beginning 5. boy
6. brain; **C:** 1. Dear 2. day
3. deck 4. December 5. deep;
D: 1. Answers will vary.
2. Answers will vary.

Unit 1
Categories
pp. 6–9

1.D	2.C	3.A	4.B	5.E
6.F	7.D	8.A	9.F	10.H
11.E	12.C	13.I	14.B	15.G
16.H	17.D	18.I	19.A	20.E
21.F	22.C	23.G	24.B	25.A
26.C	27.B	28.A	29.C	30.C
31.B	32.A			

Unit 2
Synonyms
pp. 10–13

1.B	2.A	3.A	4.B	5.A
6.B	7.A	8.A	9.B	10.B
11.A	12.B	13.B	14.A	15.B
16.B	17.B	18.B.	19.A	20.B
21.B	22.B	23.B	24.A	25.A
26.B	27.A	28.B		

Unit 3
Antonyms
pp. 14–17

1.B	2.A	3.A	4.B	5.A
6.A	7.B	8.B	9.B	10.A
11.A	12.B	13.A	14.A	15.B
16.B	17.B	18.A	19.A	20.A
21.A	22.A	23.A	24.B	25.B
26.B	27.B	28.A	29.B	30.A
31.A	32.A			

The First LAP
Language Activity Pages
pp. 18–19

A: 1. synonyms 2. categories
3. antonyms 4. antonyms;
B: 1. bicycle 2. delight
3. scissors 4. desk
5. tablecloth; **C:** 1. unknown
2. shy 3. country 4. big
5. boring 6. polite;
D: 1. Answers will vary.
2. Answers will vary.

Unit 4
Homographs
pp. 20–21

1.A	2.B	3.B	4.A	5.A
6.B	7.A	8.B	9.B	10.A

Unit 5
Homophones
pp. 22–23

1.B	2.A	3.A	4.B	5.B
6.A	7.A	8.B	9.B	10.A
11.A	12.B	13.B	14.A	

Unit 6
Word Maps
pp. 24–29

1.B	2.A	3.B	4.A	5.B
6.C	7.A	8.D	9.D	10.A
11.B	12.C	13.A	14.D	15.B
16.C	17.C	18.B	19.A	20.D
21.C	22.A	23.D	24.B	25.C
26.B	27.D	28.A	29.B	30.A
31.C	32.D	33.A	34.C	35.B
36.D	37.B	38.A	39.C	40.D

Unit 7
Linear Graphs
pp. 30–31

1.A	2.B	3.B	4.B	5.A
6.B	7.B	8.A	9.B	10.B

The Second LAP
Language Activity Pages
pp. 32–33

A: 1. Homophones 2. Linear
graphs 3. Word maps
4. Homographs; **B:** 1. Meet
2. blue 3. hear 4. ate; **C:** 1.C
2.B 3.D 4.A; **D:** 1. Answers
will vary. 2. Answers will vary.

Unit 8
Compound Words
pp. 34–35

1.B	2.A	3.A	4.B	5.A
6.B	7.A	8.B		

Unit 9
Prefixes
pp. 36–37

1.A	2.B	3.A	4.A	5.B
6.B	7.B	8.A	9.B	10.B

Unit 10
Suffixes
pp. 38–39

1.A	2.A	3.B	4.B	5.B
6.B	7.A	8.A	9.B	10.B
11.B	12.A			

Unit 11
Base Words
pp. 40–43

1.B	2.A	3.C	4.B	5.B
6.A	7.C	8.C	9.A	10.B
11.B	12.A	13.B	14.C	15.B
16.C	17.B	18.C	19.C	20.A
21.A	22.B	23.A	24.B	25.B
26.A	27.A	28.B	29.A	30.B

The Third LAP
Language Activity Pages
pp. 44–45

A: 1. base 2. suffix
3. compound 4. prefix;

B: 1. un-law-ful
2. dis-connect-ed
3. pre-view-ed 4. good-ness
5. over-flow-ing; **C:** 1. digger
2. powerful 3. mouthful
4. unearthed 5. darkness;
D: 1. rewrite, driver, forceful,
speechless 2. Answers will
vary.

Unit 12
Context Clues
pp. 46–49

1.A	2.B	3.B	4.A	5.B
6.A	7.B	8.A	9.B	10.A
11.B	12.A	13.B	14.A	15.B
16.B				

Unit 13
Context Clues
pp. 50–53

1.A	2.A	3.B	4.B	5.A
6.B	7.A	8.B	9.A	10.B
11.A	12.A	13.B	14.A	15.B
16.B				

Unit 14
Guide Words
pp. 54–55

1.C	2.A	3.A	4.B	5.B
6.A	7.B	8.C	9.B	10.A
11.C	12.C	13.C	14.B	

Unit 15
Syllables
pp. 56–57

1.B	2.A	3.B	4.C	5.B
6.C	7.B	8.A	9.A	10.B
11.B	12.A			

Unit 16
Parts of a Dictionary Entry
pp. 58–59

1.C	2.A	3.D	4.B	5.D
6.C	7.A	8.B.	9.D	10.C

Unit 17
Multiple-Meaning Words
pp. 60–61

1.B	2.B	3.A	4.B	5.A
6.A	7.B	8.A		

The Last LAP
Language Activity Pages
pp. 62–63

A: 1. Comparison 2. Guide
3. Contrast 4. Multiple-
meaning; **B:** 1.A 2.D 3.B 4.C;
C: 1.A 2.A 3.B; **D:** 1. Answers
will vary. 2. Answers will vary.

Unit 1
Categories
pp. 6–7

1.A	2.F	3.D	4.B	5.E.
6.C	7.I	8.E	9.A	10.D
11.L	12.J	13.B	14.F	15.H
16.K	17.C	18.G		

Unit 2
Synonyms
pp. 8–9

1.C	2.A	3.B	4.A	5.C
6.B	7.A	8.A	9.B	10.C
11.B	12.C	13.A	14.B	15.A
16.B				

Unit 3
Antonyms
pp. 10–11

1.A	2.C	3.B	4.A	5.B
6.C	7.B	8.A	9.C	10.B
11.A	12.C	13.A	14.B	15.C
16.A				

Unit 4
Idioms
pp. 12–15

1.B	2.A	3.A	4.B	5.B
6.A	7.A	8.A	9.B	10.A
11.B	12.A	13.A	14.B	15.B
16.A	17.A	18.A	19.B	20.A
21.B	22.A	23.A	24.B	

Unit 5
Similes and Metaphors
pp. 16–19

1.A	2.B	3.A	4.B	5.B
6.A	7.A	8.A	9.B	10.B
11.A	12.B	13.B	14.A	15.A
16.B	17.B	18.A	19.B	20.A
21.A	22.B	23.B	24.A	25.B
26.B	27.A	28.A		

The First LAP
Language Activity Pages
pp. 20–21

A: 1.B 2.A 3.C; **B:** 1.A 2.B
3.C 4.A 5.C 6.B; **C:** 1.B 2.A
3.F 4.D 5.E 6.C; **D:** 1. Answers
will vary. 2. Answers will vary.

Unit 6
Homographs
pp. 22–23

1.B	2.A	3.B	4.A	5.B
6.A	7.A	8.B	9.B	10.A
11.B	12.A			

Unit 7
Homophones
pp. 24–25

1.B	2.A	3.A	4.B	5.A
6.B	7.A	8.B	9.B	10.A
11.A	12.B			

Unit 8
Word Maps
pp. 26–29

1.B	2.A	3.B	4.C	5.D
6.A	7.B	8.C	9.D	10.A
11.C	12.A	13.B	14.D	15.D
16.A	17.B	18.C	19.A	20.B
21.D	22.C	23.D	24.A	25.B
26.C				

Unit 9
Linear Graphs
pp. 30–31

1.B	2.A	3.B	4.A	5.B
6.B	7.B	8.A	9.A	10.B
11.A	12.B	13.A	14.A	15.B
16.A				

The Second LAP
Language Activity Pages
pp. 32–33

A: 1.B 2.A; **B:** 1.A 2.B 3.B
4.A; **C:** 1. one 2. sun 3. blue
4. two 5. hole 6. do 7. knows
8. way; **D:** 1. Answers will
vary. 2. living things → animal
→ insect → butterfly

Unit 10
Compound Words
pp. 34–35

1.A	2.B	3.B	4.A	5.B
6.A	7.B	8.A	9.A	10.B

Unit 11
Prefixes
pp. 36–37

1.C	2.B	3.A	4.C	5.B
6.A	7.A	8.B	9.C	10.B
11.C	12.A	13.B	14.C	15.A

Unit 12
Suffixes
pp. 38–39

1.B	2.C	3.A	4.B	5.A
6.A	7.C	8.B	9.A	10.B
11.C	12.A			

Unit 13
Base Words
pp. 40–43

1.B	2.A	3.C	4.A	5.A
6.B	7.C	8.B	9.A	10.A
11.B	12.A	13.B	14.C	15.C
16.B	17.B	18.C	19.A	20.C
21.B	22.B	23.A	24.C	25.A
26.B	27.A	28.A	29.C	30.A
31.C	32.A	33.C	34.A	35.C

The Third LAP
Language Activity Pages
pp. 44–45

A: 1.B 2.C 3.A 4.A;
B: 1. actor 2. retake
3. careless 4. untie
5. impatient 6. regularly;
C: 1. birthday 2. afternoon
3. baseball 4. highlight
5. downtown; **D:** 1. Answers
will vary. 2. Answers will vary.

Unit 14
Context Clues
pp. 46–47

1.B	2.A	3.A	4.B	5.A
6.B	7.B	8.A	9.B	10.B
11.A	12.B	13.B	14.A	

Unit 15
Context Clues
pp. 48–49

1.A	2.B	3.A	4.A	5.B
6.A	7.B	8.B	9.A	10.A
11.B	12.B	13.A	14.B	

Unit 16
Context Clues
pp. 50–53

1.A	2.B	3.B	4.A	5.B
6.B	7.A	8.B	9.B	10.A
11.B	12.A	13.B	14.A	15.A
16.B	17.A	18.B	19.A	20.A
21.A	22.B			

Unit 17
Guide Words
pp. 54–55

1.A	2.A	3.B	4.C	5.A
6.C	7.B	8.C	9.A	10.C
11.B	12.A	13.B	14.B	15.A
16.C				

Unit 18
Syllables
pp. 56–57

1.B	2.C	3.C	4.B	5.C
6.A	7.B	8.A	9.B	10.A
11.A	12.B	13.B	14.A	

Unit 19
Parts of a Dictionary Entry
pp. 58–59

1.C	2.A	3.D	4.B	5.C
6.B	7.A	8.D	9.C	10.B

(continued on next page)

▰▰▰ Unit 20 ▰▰▰
Multiple-Meaning Words
pp. 60–61

1.B   2.A   3.B   4.B   5.A
6.B   7.B   8.B   9.B   10.A
11.A 12.A

▰▰▰ The Last LAP ▰▰▰
Language Activity Pages
pp. 62–63

A: 1.A 2.C 3.C 4.A; **B:** 1.D
2.A 3.C 4.B; **C:** 1. Kelp is a
kind of seaweed. 2. A sea otter
is a mammal. 3. Webbed feet
are feet in which the toes are
joined by skin. **D:** 1. Answers
will vary. 2. sim-ple,
kind-ness, fa-vor-ite

Unit 1
Categorization
pp. 6–7

1.E	2.A	3.C	4.G	5.B
6.H	7.F	8.D	9.C	10.G
11.E	12.H	13.D	14.A	15.B
16.F	17.A	18.H	19.E	20.D
21.B	22.F	23.C	24.G	

Unit 2
Synonyms and Antonyms
pp. 8–9

1.C	2.B	3.A	4.B	5.C
6.B	7.A	8.A	9.B	10.A
11.B	12.A	13.B	14.C	15.A
16.B	17.A	18.B		

Unit 3
Idioms
pp. 10–11

1.B	2.B	3.A	4.A	5.B
6.A	7.A	8.B	9.A	10.A
11.B	12.B	13.A	14.A	15.A

Unit 4
Similes and Metaphors
pp. 12–13

1.A	2.A	3.B	4.B	5.B
6.A	7.B	8.A	9.B	10.B
11.A	12.A	13.B	14.B	15.A

Unit 5
Homonyms
pp. 14–17

1.B	2.A	3.B	4.A	5.A
6.A	7.B	8.B	9.A	10.B
11.A	12.A	13.B	14.A	15.B
16.A	17.A	18.B	19.B	20.B
21.A	22.A	23.A	24.B	25.A
26.A	27.B	28.A	29.A	30.B
31.B	32.A	33.B	34.A	35.B

The First LAP
Language Activity Pages
pp. 18–19

A: 1.B 2.B 3.C 4.C 5.B;
B: 1. Areas of a Country
2. Desert Words 3. Skilled
Workers 4. Natural Building
Materials; **C:** 1. close 2. lead
3. eight 4. lead 5. close 6. ate
7. dessert 8. desert 9. sighed
10. side; **D:** 1. Answers will
vary. 2. Answers will vary.

Unit 6
Word Maps
pp. 20–21

1.C	2.D	3.A	4.B	5.A
6.C	7.B	8.D	9.D	10.A
11.B	12.C	13.B	14.C	15.D
16.A	17.A	18.D	19.C	20.B

Unit 7
Analogies
pp. 22–25

1.B	2.A	3.A	4.B	5.A
6.B	7.B	8.A	9.B	10.A
11.A	12.B	13.A	14.A	15.B
16.A	17.A	18.B	19.A	20.A
21.A	22.B	23.A	24.A	25.A
26.A	27.B	28.B	29.B	30.A
31.A	32.B	33.A	34.A	35.A
36.B	37.A	38.B	39.A	40.B

Unit 8
Compound Words
pp. 26–27

1.B	2.A	3.A	4.B	5.A
6.A	7.B	8.B	9.A	10.B
11.A	12.B	13.A	14.B	15.A

Unit 9
Prefixes
pp. 28–29

1.B	2.C	3.B	4.A	5.B
6.A	7.B	8.A	9.B	10.C
11.A	12.C	13.B	14.A	15.C
16.A				

Unit 10
Suffixes
pp. 30–31

1.B	2.C	3.A	4.C	5.C
6.B	7.B	8.A	9.B	10.C
11.A	12.A	13.C	14.C	15.B
16.C				

Unit 11
Base Words
pp. 32–33

1.D	2.C	3.B	4.D	5.A
6.D	7.C	8.A	9.B	10.C
11.C	12.D	13.B	14.A	15.B
16.A	17.B	18.B		

The Second LAP
Language Activity Pages
pp. 34–35

A: 1.C 2.C 3.B 4.A 5.B; **B:**
1. rarely 2. frequently 3. how
often it snows in the springtime
4. how often the average person
brushes his or her teeth;
C: 1.D 2.F 3.B 4.C 5.E 6.A;
D: 1. Answers will vary.
2. Answers will vary.

Unit 12
Greek and Latin Roots
pp. 36–39

1.B	2.A	3.B	4.A	5.A
6.B	7.B	8.A	9.B	10.A
11.A	12.A	13.A	14.B	15.A
16.A	17.A	18.B	19.B	20.A
21.A	22.B	23.A	24.A	25.B
26.B				

Unit 13
Context Clues
pp. 40–41

1.A	2.B	3.A	4.B	5.A
6.A	7.B	8.B		

Unit 14
Context Clues
pp. 42–43

1.B	2.B	3.A	4.A	5.A
6.A	7.B	8.A		

Unit 15
Context Clues
pp. 44–45

1.B	2.A	3.A	4.B	5.A
6.A	7.A	8.A		

Unit 16
Context Clues
pp. 46–47

1.B	2.A	3.B	4.A	5.A
6.B	7.A	8.A		

The Third LAP
Language Activity Pages
pp. 48–49

A: 1. root 2. cause-and-effect
3. example 4. contrast;
B: 1. century 2. pedestrian
3. dehydrate 4. epigraph
5. Phonetic; **C:** 1. something
that helps or betters a person
or thing 2. done in a quick or
careless way 3. great suffering
of body or mind; **D:** 1. Answers
will vary. 2. Answers will vary.

Unit 17
Guide Words
pp. 50–51

1.C	2.A	3.A	4.B	5.C
6.C	7.B	8.B	9.A	10.B
11.A	12.C	13.B	14.B	15.B
16.A	17.A	18.B		

(continued on next page)

Unit 18
Syllables
pp. 52–53

1.B	2.B	3.A	4.B	5.A
6.A	7.B	8.A	9.A	10.B
11.B	12.A	13.A	14.A	15.B

Unit 19
Parts of a Dictionary Entry
pp. 54–55

1.C	2.E	3.D	4.A	5.A
6.B	7.D	8.C		

Unit 20
Multiple-Meaning Words
pp. 56–59

1.A	2.B	3.A	4.A	5.B
6.B	7.B	8.A	9.A	10.A
11.A	12.A	13.B	14.A	15.C
16.A	17.C	18.B	19.C	20.B
21.A	22.B	23.B	24.C	25.A

Unit 21
Word Origins
pp. 60–61

1.C	2.D	3.A	4.B	5.E
6.A	7.F	8.C	9.B	10.D

The Last LAP
Language Activity Pages
pp. 62–63

A: 1.B 2.A 3.B 4.B 5.C;
B: 1.D 2.E 3.B 4.A 5.C 6.B
7.A 8.C 9.A 10.C; **C:** 1. e-ven
2. fro-zen 3. wa-ter 4. camp-ing
5. weath-er; **D:** 1. Column 1:
intense, intent, interconnect.
Column 2: interested,
interesting, intermediate.
2. Answers will vary.

Unit 1
Categorization
pp. 6–7

1.D	2.E	3.F	4.A	5.B
6.G	7.C	8.H	9.I	10.J
11.K	12.E	13.A	14.D	15.C
16.B	17.F	18.E	19.C	20.D
21.G	22.B	23.A	24.F	

Unit 2
Synonyms and Antonyms
pp. 8–9

1.B	2.D	3.A	4.D	5.B
6.B	7.B	8.B	9.D	10.B
11.A	12.C	13.D	14.A	

Unit 3
Idioms
pp. 10–11

1.A	2.B	3.B	4.A	5.A
6.A	7.A	8.B	9.B	10.A
11.A	12.B	13.A	14.B	

Unit 4
Similes and Metaphors
pp. 12–13

1.A	2.A	3.B	4.B	5.B
6.A	7.A	8.C	9.A	10.B
11.C	12.A	13.B	14.B	15.A
16.B	17.C	18.B		

Unit 5
Homonyms
pp. 14–17

1.A	2.B	3.B	4.A	5.A
6.A	7.B	8.A	9.A	10.B
11.A	12.A	13.B	14.B	15.A
16.A	17.A	18.B	19.A	20.A
21.A	22.A	23.B	24.B	25.A
26.B	27.B	28.A		

The First LAP
Language Activity Pages
pp. 18–19

A: 1.A 2.B 3.B 4.C 5.A;
B: 1.D 2.B 3.C 4.A; **C:** 1.H
2.E 3.L 4.B 5.C 6.K;
D: 1. Answers will vary.
2. Answers will vary.

Unit 6
Word Maps
pp. 20–21

1.B	2.A	3.C	4.D	5.C
6.A	7.B	8.D	9.B	10.C
11.D	12.A	13.A	14.D	15.C
16.B	17.D	18.B	19.C	20.A

Unit 7
Analogies
pp. 22–25

1.A	2.A	3.B	4.A	5.A
6.B	7.B	8.A	9.A	10.B
11.B	12.A	13.B	14.B	15.B
16.B	17.A	18.A	19.B	20.A
21.A	22.A	23.B	24.A	25.B
26.B	27.B	28.A	29.B	30.A
31.B	32.B	33.B	34.B	35.A
36.A				

Unit 8
Prefixes
pp. 26–27

1.B	2.B	3.A	4.A	5.A
6.C	7.B	8.C	9.C	10.A
11.B	12.C	13.B	14.A	15.B
16.C				

Unit 9
Suffixes
pp. 28–29

1.A	2.A	3.C	4.C	5.A
6.C	7.C	8.B	9.A	10.A
11.A	12.C	13.B	14.A	

Unit 10
Base Words
pp. 30–31

1.C	2.D	3.A	4.A	5.D
6.C	7.D	8.D	9.B	10.C
11.A	12.B	13.C	14.C	15.B
16.A				

The Second LAP
Language Activity Pages
pp. 32–33

A: 1.A 2.C 3.C 4.A 5.B;
B: 1. secondary 2. superior
3. an employee of a business
4. the owner of a business;
C: 1.H 2.C 3.A 4.G 5.B 6.E;
D: 1. Answers will vary.
2. co-owner, coexist,
coworker, fourth word with
the prefix *co-* will vary; basic,
geometric, angelic, fourth word
with the suffix *-ic* will vary

Unit 11
Greek and Latin Roots
pp. 34–39

1.A	2.B	3.A	4.B	5.B
6.B	7.B	8.A	9.A	10.B
11.A	12.B	13.A	14.A	15.B
16.B	17.A	18.B	19.B	20.A
21.A	22.B	23.A	24.A	25.B
26.A	27.A	28.A	29.B	30.A
31.A	32.B	33.B	34.A	35.B
36.A	37.A	38.B	39.A	40.B

Unit 12
Context Clues
pp. 40–41

1.B	2.B	3.A	4.A	5.B
6.A	7.B	8.A	9.A	10.B

Unit 13
Context Clues
pp. 42–43

1.A	2.B	3.A	4.B	5.A
6.A	7.B	8.B		

Unit 14
Context Clues
pp. 44–45

1.A	2.B	3.A	4.B	5.A
6.A	7.B	8.A		

Unit 15
Context Clues
pp. 46–47

1.B	2.B	3.A	4.B	5.B
6.A	7.A	8.B	9.A	10.B

The Third LAP
Language Activity Pages
pp. 48–49

A: 1.E 2.D 3.F 4.B;
B: 1. conjunction 2. facsimile
3. aerophobia 4. auditory;
C: 1.C 2.E 3.A 4.B 5.D;
D: 1. Answers will vary.
2. Answers will vary.

Unit 16
Guide Words
pp. 50–51

1.C	2.A	3.B	4.C	5.C
6.A	7.B	8.A	9.C	10.B
11.A	12.C	13.A	14.B	15.A
16.A	17.C	18.A	19.B	20.C

Unit 17
Syllables
pp. 52–53

1.B	2.A	3.B	4.B	5.A
6.A	7.B	8.B	9.B	10.B
11.B	12.A	13.A	14.A	15.B

Unit 18
Parts of a Dictionary Entry
pp. 54–55

1.B	2.C	3.D	4.D	5.E
6.A	7.E	8.C		

Unit 19
Multiple-Meaning Words
pp. 56–57

1.A	2.B	3.A	4.B	5.B
6.A	7.A	8.B	9.A	10.B
11.B	12.A			

(continued on next page)

Unit 20
Word Origins
pp. 58–59

1.E 2.A 3.C 4.B 5.D
6.B 7.F 8.D 9.G 10.A
11.E 12.H 13.I 14.C

Unit 21
Content-Area Words
pp. 60–61

1.F 2.E 3.H 4.B 5.C
6.A 7.G 8.D 9.D 10.F
11.J 12.B 13.A 14.C 15.H
16.I

The Last LAP
Language Activity Pages
pp. 62–63

A: 1.B 2.C 3.B 4.A 5.A;
B: 1.B 2.C 3.A 4.D 5.E 6.D
7.E 8.A 9.D 10.E;
C: 1. vi-olent, vio-lent 2. pressure 3. sud-den 4. frighten-
ing, fright-ening;
D: 1. Answers will vary.
2. Answers will vary.

Unit 1
Categorization
pp. 6–7

1.D 2.A 3.G 4.J 5.B
6.H 7.K 8.L 9.C 10.E
11.F 12.I 13.H 14.D 15.B
16.G 17.F 18.A 19.E 20.C
21.C 22.G 23.A 24.D 25.B
26.H 27.E 28.F

Unit 2
Synonyms and Antonyms
pp. 8–9

1.A 2.C 3.B 4.B 5.A
6.D 7.C 8.A 9.B 10.A
11.D 12.B 13.B 14.C 15.D
16.A 17.A 18.B

Unit 3
Figurative Language
pp. 10–11

1.B 2.A 3.B 4.B 5.B
6.B 7.B 8.A 9.B 10.A
11.B 12.B 13.A 14.B

Unit 4
Homonyms
pp. 12–13

1.A 2.A 3.B 4.B 5.A
6.B 7.A 8.A 9.A 10.B
11.B 12.B 13.A 14.B 15.A
16.A

Unit 5
Word Maps
pp. 14–15

1.A 2.C 3.B 4.D 5.A
6.D 7.C 8.B 9.C 10.A
11.B 12.D

The First LAP
Language Activity Pages
pp. 16–17

A: 1.C 2.B 3.B 4.A 5.B;
B: 1. Endurance Sports
2. Reptiles 3. Travel Terms
4. Layers of the Rain Forest
5. Computer Parts 6. In the
Laboratory 7. Time 8. Garden;
C: 1. great 2. do 3. heir
4. through 5. isle 6. where;
D: 1. Answers will vary.
2. Answers will vary.

Unit 6
Analogies
pp. 18–23

1.A 2.B 3.A 4.A 5.B
6.A 7.A 8.B 9.A 10.B
11.A 12.A 13.B 14.A 15.B
16.B 17.A 18.B 19.A 20.B
21.A 22.A 23.B 24.B 25.A
26.B 27.A 28.A 29.A 30.B
31.A 32.B 33.A 34.A 35.A
36.B 37.A 38.B 39.B 40.A
41.B 42.A 43.A 44.A 45.B
46.B 47.A 48.B 49.B 50.A
51.B 52.B 53.A 54.A 55.A
56.B 57.B 58.A 59.B 60.B

Unit 7
Prefixes
pp. 24–25

1.B 2.B 3.A 4.B 5.B
6.A 7.B 8.A 9.C 10.C
11.C 12.A 13.C 14.C 15.A

Unit 8
Suffixes
pp. 26–27

1.C 2.B 3.A 4.A 5.C
6.C 7.B 8.A 9.A 10.A
11.A 12.B 13.A 14.B 15.C
16.A

Unit 9
Base Words
pp. 28–29

1.B 2.B 3.D 4.D 5.C
6.A 7.B 8.B 9.A 10.B
11.B 12.A 13.A 14.B 15.C
16.A 17.C 18.D 19.A 20.B
21.A 22.C

The Second LAP
Language Activity Pages
pp. 30–31

A: 1.A 2.B 3.B 4.C 5.B 6.C;
B: 1.B 2.A 3.B 4.B 5.A 6.B;
C: 1. identify 2. recovered
3. distaste 4. irrational
5. removed 6. involuntarily
7. widened 8. multifaceted
9. unlikely; **D:** 1. Answers will
vary. 2. Answers will vary.

Unit 10
Greek and Latin Roots
pp. 32–37

1.C 2.A 3.A 4.B 5.C
6.C 7.C 8.C 9.A 10.C
11.A 12.B 13.A 14.A 15.A
16.A 17.A 18.B 19.A 20.A
21.C 22.A 23.B 24.C 25.C
26.B 27.A 28.B 29.A 30.C
31.B 32.A 33.A 34.C 35.B
36.A 37.A 38.B 39.C 40.B
41.B 42.A 43.C 44.A 45.A
46.C 47.A 48.B

Unit 11
Context Clues
pp. 38–39

1.A 2.A 3.B 4.B 5.B
6.A 7.B 8.A 9.A 10.B

Unit 12
Context Clues
pp. 40–41

1.B 2.A 3.A 4.B 5.A
6.B 7.B 8.A 9.A 10.A

Unit 13
Context Clues
pp. 42–43

1.B 2.A 3.A 4.B 5.A
6.B 7.A 8.A 9.A 10.B
11.A 12.A

Unit 14
Context Clues
pp. 44–45

1.B 2.A 3.A 4.B 5.B
6.B 7.A 8.A 9.B 10.A
11.B 12.B

The Third LAP
Language Activity Pages
pp. 46–47

A: 1. cause-and-effect
2. comparison 3. definition
4. general 5. example;
B: 1. panacea 2. pathogen
3. geode 4. Proceed
5. malady 6. inscription
7. Circumference 8. optical;
C: 1.B 2.A 3.B 4.C 5.A;
D: 1. Answers will vary.
2. Answers will vary.

Unit 15
**Connotation and Shades
of Meaning**
pp. 48–49

1.B 2.A 3.B 4.B 5.A
6.A 7.A 8.B 9.A 10.A
11.A 12.B 13.A 14.B 15.C

Unit 16
Syllables
pp. 50–51

1.C 2.A 3.B 4.A 5.C
6.B 7.A 8.C 9.A 10.B
11.A 12.A 13.A 14.A 15.B

Unit 17
Parts of a Dictionary Entry
pp. 52–53

1.A 2.A 3.B 4.B 5.A
6.B 7.D 8.B 9.A 10.C
11.D 12.B

(continued on next page)

Unit 18
Multiple-Meaning Words
pp. 54–55

1.A	2.A	3.A	4.B	5.B
6.A	7.A	8.B	9.B	10.B
11.B	12.A	13.B	14.A	

Unit 19
Word Origins
pp. 56–57

1.F	2.A	3.D	4.C	5.B
6.E	7.C	8.G	9.F	10.B
11.E	12.D	13.H	14.A	

Unit 20
Foreign Words and Phrases
pp. 58–59

1.F	2.A	3.C	4.J	5.H
6.D	7.G	8.B	9.E	10.I
11.C	12.G	13.J	14.A	15.E
16.F	17.B	18.D	19.I	20.H

Unit 21
Content-Area Words
pp. 60–61

1.C	2.D	3.A	4.G	5.F
6.H	7.E	8.B	9.A	10.J
11.K	12.B	13.H	14.G	15.C
16.E	17.D	18.F		

The Last LAP
Language Activity Pages
pp. 62–63

A: 1.B 2.B 3.C 4.A 5.C;
B: 1.B 2.A 3.C 4.E 5.D 6.E
7.D 8.E 9.D 10.C 11.E 12.D;
C: 1. negative 2. negative
3. positive 4. negative
5. negative 6. negative
7. neutral 8. neutral 9. neutral
10. neutral 11. negative
12. positive; **D:** 1. Answers will
vary. 2. Answers will vary.

Unit 1
Categorization
pp. 6–7

1.G	2.B	3.A	4.I	5.M
6.C	7.D	8.K	9.E	10.L
11.F	12.H	13.J	14.D	15.F
16.G	17.A	18.B	19.C	20.E
21.E	22.C	23.A	24.F	25.B
26.D				

Unit 2
Synonyms and Antonyms
pp. 8–9

1.C	2.B	3.C	4.B	5.C
6.A	7.C	8.A	9.C	10.A
11.A	12.B	13.A	14.C	15.B
16.C	17.A	18.B		

Unit 3
Figurative Language
pp. 10–11

1.B	2.A	3.A	4.B	5.B
6.A	7.A	8.B	9.A	10.B
11.A	12.B			

Unit 4
Homonyms
pp. 12–13

1.A	2.B	3.B	4.A	5.B
6.A	7.A	8.A	9.A	10.B
11.B	12.A	13.A	14.B	15.A
16.B				

Unit 5
Word Maps
pp. 14–15

1.A	2.D	3.B	4.C	5.D
6.B	7.A	8.C	9.A	10.C
11.D	12.B			

Unit 6
Analogies
pp. 16–21

1.B	2.A	3.A	4.A	5.B
6.A	7.B	8.B	9.B	10.A
11.B	12.A	13.A	14.A	15.B
16.B	17.A	18.B	19.B	20.A
21.A	22.B	23.A	24.A	25.B
26.A	27.B	28.B	29.A	30.A
31.A	32.B	33.A	34.A	35.B
36.A	37.B	38.A	39.B	40.A
41.B	42.A	43.A	44.A	45.A
46.B	47.B	48.A	49.A	50.B
51.A	52.B	53.A	54.B	55.B
56.A	57.A	58.A	59.B	60.A

The First LAP
Language Activity Pages
pp. 22–23

A: 1.C 2.A 3.B 4.C 5.C 6.B 7.A 8.A; **B:** 1.C 2.E 3.A 4.B 5.D; **C:** 1. homograph 2. metaphor 3. idiom 4. homophone 5. homophone 6. simile; **D:** 1. Answers will vary. 2. Answers will vary.

Unit 7
Base Words and Affixes
pp. 24–29

1.C	2.E	3.C	4.A	5.E
6.D	7.A	8.B	9.B	10.E
11.D	12.A	13.B	14.E	15.C
16.A	17.B	18.A	19.A	20.C
21.C	22.B	23.A	24.C	25.B
26.C	27.A	28.D	29.B	30.C
31.A	32.B	33.D	34.C	35.A
36.C	37.B	38.A	39.B	40.C
41.A	42.B	43.A	44.C	45.A
46.B	47.B	48.A	49.C	50.A

Unit 8
Greek and Latin Roots and Affixes
pp. 30–35

1.A	2.A	3.A	4.B	5.B
6.A	7.B	8.A	9.B	10.A
11.A	12.B	13.B	14.A	15.B
16.B	17.A	18.B	19.A	20.B
21.A	22.A	23.A	24.A	25.B
26.B	27.A	28.B	29.A	30.A
31.A	32.B	33.B	34.A	35.A
36.B	37.B	38.A	39.B	40.A
41.B	42.B	43.B	44.A	45.A
46.B				

Unit 9
Anglo-Saxon Roots
pp. 36–37

1.B	2.A	3.A	4.A	5.B
6.B	7.B	8.B	9.B	10.A
11.A	12.B			

The Second LAP
Language Activity Pages
pp. 38–39

A: 1.B 2.A 3.B 4.A 5.C; **B:** 1. postdate 2. counteroffensive 3. knowhow 4. strictures 5. paramedics 6. ornithology; **C:** minimalist/E; intersecting/D; structure/C; inscribed/B; memorial/A; **D:** 1. Answers will vary. 2. Answers will vary.

Unit 10
Context Clues
pp. 40–41

1.B	2.A	3.B	4.B	5.B
6.A	7.A	8.A	9.A	10.B

Unit 11
Context Clues
pp. 42–43

1.B	2.A	3.A	4.B	5.A
6.B	7.A	8.A	9.A	10.B

Unit 12
Context Clues
pp. 44–45

1.A	2.B	3.B	4.A	5.B
6.A	7.B	8.A	9.A	10.B

Unit 13
Connotation and Shades of Meaning
pp. 46–47

1.A	2.A	3.B	4.B	5.B
6.A	7.B	8.A	9.B	10.A
11.A	12.A	13.B	14.A	15.B

The Third LAP
Language Activity Pages
pp. 48–49

A: 1.B 2.C 3.B 4.C 5.B; **B:** 1. witty/sarcastic 2. barter/haggle 3. confident/smug 4. helper/subordinate 5. visit/harass; **C:** 1.F 2.C 3.B 4.D 5.E 6.A; **D:** 1. Answers will vary. 2. Answers will vary.

Unit 14
Syllables
pp. 50–51

1.C	2.C	3.A	4.A	5.B
6.C	7.A	8.B	9.B	10.B
11.A	12.A	13.B	14.A	15.B

Unit 15
Parts of a Dictionary Entry
pp. 52–53

1.B	2.A	3.B	4.B	5.B
6.B	7.D	8.C	9.D	10.A

Unit 16
Multiple-Meaning Words
pp. 54–55

1.A	2.A	3.B	4.B	5.B
6.B	7.A	8.A	9.B	10.B
11.A	12.A			

(continued on next page)

Unit 17
Word Origins
pp. 56–57

1.B	2.F	3.A	4.D	5.C
6.E	7.H	8.G	9.A	10.I
11.D	12.F	13.B	14.C	15.E
16.J				

Unit 18
Foreign Words and Phrases
pp. 58–59

1.G	2.E	3.A	4.H	5.B
6.F	7.C	8.D	9.D	10.I
11.A	12.B	13.J	14.G	15.H
16.E	17.C	18.F		

Unit 19
Content-Area Words
pp. 60–61

1.A	2.D	3.F	4.G	5.E
6.B	7.C	8.H	9.H	10.A
11.E	12.D	13.B	14.C	15.G
16.F				

The Last LAP
Language Activity Pages
pp. 62–63

A: 1.F 2.T 3.T 4.F 5.T 6.T 7.T 8.T; **B:** 1. revolution 2. four 3. adjective 4. yes; **C:** 1. carpe diem 2. pedigree 3. chagrin 4. confetti 5. loco 6. strudel; **D:** 1. Answers will vary. 2. Answers will vary.

Unit 1
Categorization
pp. 6–7

1.J	2.E	3.H	4.F	5.L
6.A	7.M	8.C	9.D	10.I
11.G	12.B	13.K	14.F	15.B
16.E	17.A	18.G	19.D	20.C
21.E	22.D	23.F	24.B	25.C
26.A				

Unit 2
Synonyms and Antonyms
pp. 8–9

1.D	2.A	3.C	4.B	5.A
6.C	7.A	8.A	9.D	10.B
11.D	12.A	13.B	14.A	15.B
16.D	17.D	18.C		

Unit 3
Figurative Language
pp. 10–13

1.A	2.B	3.A	4.B	5.B
6.A	7.A	8.A	9.B	10.A
11.A	12.B	13.A	14.B	15.A
16.B	17.C	18.A	19.B	20.C
21.B	22.A	23.B	24.B	25.A
26.C	27.C	28.B	29.A	30.B
31.C	32.B			

Unit 4
Homonyms
pp. 14–15

1.B	2.A	3.B	4.B	5.A
6.A	7.B	8.B	9.A	10.B
11.A	12.B	13.B	14.A	15.A
16.B	17.B	18.A		

Unit 5
Word Maps
pp. 16–17

1.B	2.D	3.A	4.C	5.D
6.A	7.B	8.C	9.B	10.C
11.A	12.D	13.D	14.C	15.B
16.A				

Unit 6
Analogies
pp. 18–21

1.A	2.B	3.B	4.B	5.B
6.A	7.A	8.B	9.B	10.B
11.B	12.A	13.B	14.A	15.B
16.A	17.B	18.B	19.B	20.A
21.A	22.A	23.B	24.B	25.A
26.B	27.A	28.B	29.A	30.B
31.B	32.A	33.A	34.B	35.A
36.B				

The First LAP
Language Activity Pages
pp. 22–23

A: 1.C 2.A 3.B 4.A 5.D 6.D;
B: 1.B 2.C 3.A 4.D 5.F 6.E;
C: 1. homophone 2. homograph
3. idiom 4. homograph
5. homograph 6. homophone
7. simile 8. homophone;
D: 1. Answers will vary.
2. Answers will vary.

Unit 7
Base Words and Affixes
pp. 24–29

1.D	2.D	3.A	4.D	5.B
6.C	7.A	8.A	9.E	10.B
11.E	12.D	13.E	14.C	15.C
16.B	17.A	18.B	19.D	20.D
21.A	22.B	23.E	24.B	25.D
26.E	27.E	28.B	29.D	30.A
31.C	32.B	33.A	34.C	35.B
36.A	37.D	38.B	39.C	40.A
41.C	42.A	43.B	44.B	45.B
46.B	47.B	48.A	49.C	50.C
51.A	52.A			

Unit 8
Greek and Latin Roots and Affixes
pp. 30–35

1.B	2.A	3.A	4.B	5.B
6.A	7.B	8.A	9.A	10.A
11.B	12.B	13.A	14.A	15.B
16.A	17.B	18.A	19.B	20.B
21.B	22.A	23.B	24.B	25.A
26.B	27.A	28.B	29.B	30.A
31.A	32.A	33.B	34.A	35.A
36.B	37.B	38.A	39.B	40.A
41.A	42.B	43.A	44.A	45.B
46.B	47.A	48.B	49.B	50.A
51.B	52.A			

Unit 9
Anglo-Saxon Roots
pp. 36–37

1.A	2.B	3.A	4.A	5.B
6.A	7.B	8.A	9.A	10.A
11.A	12.B	13.A	14.B	

The Second LAP
Language Activity Pages
pp. 38–39

A: 1.B 2.A 3.C 4.A;
B: 1. connect 2. join
3. consider 4. construct;
C: 1. acknowledged
2. international 3. unusual
4. open 5. transportation
6. distinguished 7. named
8. absolute; **D:** 1. Answers will
vary. 2. Answers will vary.

Unit 10
Context Clues
pp. 40–41

1.B	2.A	3.A	4.A	5.B
6.B	7.A	8.B	9.A	10.B

Unit 11
Context Clues
pp. 42–43

1.A	2.B	3.A	4.B	5.A
6.B	7.B	8.B	9.B	10.A

Unit 12
Context Clues
pp. 44–45

1.A	2.B	3.A	4.B	5.A
6.B	7.A	8.B	9.B	10.A

Unit 13
Connotation and Shades of Meaning
pp. 46–47

1.B	2.A	3.A	4.A	5.A
6.B	7.B	8.B	9.B	10.B
11.B	12.B	13.B	14.B	15.A
16.A				

The Third LAP
Language Activity Pages
pp. 48–49

A: 1.B 2.B 3.C 4.A 5.B;
B: 1. nuisance 2. nefarious
3. screeching 4. clatter
5. invasion 6. oppose;
C: 1.C 2.D 3.E 4.A 5.B;
D: 1. Answers will vary.
2. Answers will vary.

Unit 14
Syllables
pp. 50–51

1.C	2.B	3.A	4.B	5.C
6.B	7.A	8.C	9.B	10.A
11.C	12.A	13.B	14.C	15.A
16.B	17.C	18.B	19.B	20.C
21.B	22.B			

(continued on next page)

Unit 15
Parts of a Dictionary Entry
pp. 52–53

1.A 2.B 3.C 4.A 5.A
6.A 7.C 8.A 9.B 10.A

Unit 16
Multiple-Meaning Words
pp. 54–55

1.B 2.A 3.B 4.B 5.B
6.A 7.B 8.B 9.A 10.A
11.B 12.A 13.B 14.B 15.A
16.B

Unit 17
Word Origins
pp. 56–57

1.B 2.E 3.F 4.A 5.D
6.C 7.B 8.D 9.G 10.A
11.H 12.E 13.F 14.C

Unit 18
Foreign Words and Phrases
pp. 58–59

1.E 2.G 3.B 4.H 5.A
6.F 7.D 8.C 9.D 10.I
11.G 12.J 13.C 14.A 15.B
16.F 17.H 18.E

Unit 19
Content-Area Words
pp. 60–61

1.B 2.A 3.F 4.C 5.D
6.E 7.D 8.G 9.H 10.A
11.F 12.B 13.E 14.C

The Last LAP
Language Activity Pages
pp. 62–63

A: 1.F 2.F 3.F 4.T 5.F 6.F
7.T 8.F; **B:** 1. four 2. three
3. adjective, noun
4. immediately following the
entry word; **C:** 1. Pardonnez
moi 2. Au contraire 3. objet
d'art 4. status quo 5. ad hoc
6. faux pas; **D:** 1. Answers will
vary. 2. Answers will vary.

Unit 1

Building Sentences with Nouns
pp. 6–9

1.C 2.B 3.C 4.B 5.B
6.A 7.A 8.B 9.C 10.C
11.B 12.A 13.A 14.A 15.A
16.A 17.B 18.C 19.B 20.A

Unit 2

Building Sentences with Verbs
pp. 10–13

1.C 2.A 3.B 4.C 5.A
6.C 7.B 8.B 9.A 10.C
11.B 12.A 13.C 14.B 15.A
16.A 17.A 18.C 19.B 20.C

Unit 3

Building Sentences with Nouns and Verbs
pp. 14–17

1.E 2.C 3.A 4.F 5.D
6.B 7.A 8.D 9.H 10.F
11.G 12.B 13.C 14.E 15.C
16.H 17.A 18.D 19.G 20.F
21.E 22.B 23.D 24.A 25.G
26.C 27.B 28.E 29.F 30.H

The First LAP

Language Activity Pages
pp. 18–19

A: 1. sentence 2. names 3. tells
4. noun 5. verbs; **B:** 1.N 2.T
3.T 4.T 5.N; **C:** 1. brother
2. feels 3. sweater 4. knows
5. keep; **D:** 1. Answers will
vary. 2. Answers will vary.

Unit 4

Building Sentences with Adjectives
pp. 20–23

1.A 2.B 3.C 4.B 5.A
6.B 7.C 8.A 9.B 10.C
11.B 12.B 13.A 14.A 15.B
16.A 17.B 18.B 19.A 20.A
21.B 22.B 23.A 24.A

Unit 5

Building Sentences with Prepositions
pp. 24–27

1.C 2.A 3.A 4.B 5.A
6.C 7.B 8.B 9.A 10.C
11.C 12.A 13.C 14.B 15.C
16.A 17.B 18.B 19.C 20.A

The Second LAP

Language Activity Pages
pp. 28–29

A: 1. Adjectives 2. Prepositions
3. smart 4. under; **B:** 1. Old, in
2. eight, on 3. Pretty, across
4. hot, near; **C:** 1.A 2.A 3.P
4.A 5.P 6.P; **D:** 1. Answers
will vary. 2. Answers will vary.

Unit 6

Combining Sentences
pp. 30–35

1.B 2.A 3.B 4.A 5.B
6.A 7.A 8.B 9.B 10.A
11.A 12.A 13.B 14.B 15.A
16.B 17.B 18.A 19.A 20.A
21.B 22.A 23.A 24.B

Unit 7

Combining Sentences
pp. 36–39

1.B 2.A 3.A 4.B 5.A
6.A 7.B 8.A 9.A 10.B
11.A 12.A 13.B 14.B 15.A

Unit 8

Putting Words in the Correct Order
pp. 40–45

1.A 2.B 3.B 4.B 5.A
6.A 7.A 8.B 9.B 10.A
11.C 12.B 13.A 14.C 15.B
16.B 17.A 18.C 19.B 20.A
21.C 22.B 23.C 24.B 25.A
26.C

The Third LAP

Language Activity Pages
pp. 46–47

A: 1. Sentences 2. Adjectives
3. after 4. before; **B:** 1. Yes
2. The white cat eats some
food. 3. The black cat naps.
4. The striped cat is fast. 5. Yes;
C: 1. Yes 2. No 3. Yes 4. Yes
5. No; **D:** 1. Answers will vary.
2. Answers will vary.

Unit 9

Agreement with Verbs and Adjectives
pp. 48–53

1.A 2.A 3.B 4.A 5.B
6.B 7.A 8.B 9.A 10.A
11.B 12.A 13.A 14.B 15.C
16.A 17.A 18.B 19.A 20.C
21.B 22.A 23.B 24.B 25.A
26.B 27.B 28.B 29.A 30.A

Unit 10

Sentence Problems
pp. 54–57

1.A 2.B 3.A 4.B 5.A
6.A 7.B 8.A 9.A 10.B
11.B 12.A 13.A 14.B 15.A
16.A 17.B 18.A

Unit 11

Adding Prepositional Phrases
pp. 58–61

1.C 2.B 3.A 4.C 5.A
6.A 7.B 8.A 9.B 10.B
11.B 12.C 13.B 14.A 15.C

The Last LAP

Language Activity Pages
pp. 62–63

A: 1. noun 2. verbs 3. phrase
4. preposition; **B:** 1. hop
2. longer 3. smallest 4. dusted;
C: 1. otters 2. swim 3. like
4. has 5. fur; **D:** 1. Answers
will vary. 2. Answers will vary.

Unit 1
Building Sentences with Nouns and Verbs
pp. 6–9

1.C	2.B	3.D	4.A	5.C
6.B	7.A	8.C	9.D	10.B
11.B	12.A	13.D	14.A	15.D
16.C	17.A	18.D	19.C	20.B
21.D	22.A	23.C	24.A	25.B
26.C	27.B	28.A	29.A	30.D
31.C	32.B			

Unit 2
Building Sentences with Nouns and Verbs
pp. 10–13

1.D	2.E	3.A	4.B	5.C
6.G	7.C	8.A	9.E	10.B
11.F	12.D	13.E	14.F	15.D
16.C	17.A	18.G	19.B	20.B
21.E	22.C	23.F	24.G	25.D
26.A				

The First LAP
Language Activity Pages
pp. 14–15

A: 1.C 2.A; **B:** 1. circle *teams*, underline *played* 2. circle *marbles*, underline *clinked* 3. circle *puzzle*, underline *looks* 4. circle *Dominos*, underline *covered* 5. circle *goal*, underline *win* 6. circle *I*, underline *like*; **C:** 1. game 2. drove 3. finished 4. left 5. Peter; **D:** 1. Answers will vary. 2. Answers will vary.

Unit 3
Building Sentences with Adjectives
pp. 16–19

1.C	2.A	3.C	4.B	5.A
6.B	7.C	8.B	9.A	10.B
11.C	12.C	13.B	14.A	15.A
16.B	17.B	18.A	19.B	20.A
21.A	22.B	23.A	24.B	25.B
26.A	27.B	28.A	29.A	30.B
31.A	32.B			

Unit 4
Building Sentences with Adverbs
pp. 20–23

1.B	2.C	3.C	4.B	5.A
6.B	7.B	8.A	9.C	10.B
11.A	12.A	13.B	14.A	15.A
16.B	17.B	18.A	19.B	20.A
21.B	22.B			

The Second LAP
Language Activity Pages
pp. 24–25

A: 1.B 2.A; **B:** 1. The cheerful baby smiled sweetly at the camera. 2. My lazy dog never gets enough sleep. 3. A green balloon floated above the crowd. **C:** 1. wet 2. loudly 3. neatly 4. angrily 5. great; **D:** 1. Answers will vary. 2. Answers will vary.

Unit 5
Combining Sentences
pp. 26–31

1.A	2.A	3.B	4.B	5.A
6.B	7.B	8.A	9.B	10.A
11.B	12.A	13.A	14.A	15.B
16.A	17.A	18.B	19.A	20.A

Unit 6
Combining Sentences
pp. 32–35

1.A	2.B	3.A	4.A	5.B
6.A	7.B	8.B	9.A	10.B
11.B	12.B	13.A	14.A	15.A
16.B				

Unit 7
Correct Word Order in a Sentence
pp. 36–41

1.A	2.B	3.B	4.A	5.B
6.B	7.A	8.A	9.B	10.B
11.A	12.C	13.B	14.A	15.A
16.B	17.C	18.B	19.B	20.C
21.A	22.C	23.A	24.B	25.A
26.C				

The Third LAP
Language Activity Pages
pp. 42–43

A: 1.C 2.B; **B:** 1. Frogs and spiders eat flies. 2. Can you stay, or do you have to go? 3. The cat has short ears, but its tail is long. **C:** 1. The universe is huge and contains many galaxies. 2. Matter and energy fill the universe. 3. The universe is rapidly expanding. *or* The universe is expanding rapidly. **D:** 1. Answers will vary. 2. Answers will vary.

Unit 8
Parallelism
pp. 44–49

1.A	2.C	3.D	4.C	5.A
6.D	7.C	8.B	9.A	10.B
11.B	12.A	13.C	14.C	15.A
16.C	17.B	18.C	19.A	20.A
21.B	22.A	23.B	24.B	25.A
26.A	27.B	28.B	29.A	30.A
31.B	32.B			

Unit 9
Sentence Problems
pp. 50–53

1.A	2.B	3.B	4.A	5.B
6.B	7.A	8.A	9.B	10.B
11.A	12.A	13.B	14.B	15.A
16.B	17.B	18.A	19.A	20.B
21.A	22.A			

Unit 10
Sentence Problems
pp. 54–57

1.A	2.B	3.B	4.A	5.A
6.B	7.A	8.A	9.B	10.A
11.A	12.B	13.B	14.A	15.B
16.B	17.A	18.B	19.A	20.B

Unit 11
Adding Prepositional Phrases
pp. 58–61

1.B	2.A	3.B	4.C	5.B
6.C	7.C	8.A	9.B	10.A
11.A	12.C	13.C	14.B	15.B
16.B				

The Last LAP
Language Activity Pages
pp. 62–63

A: 1.B 2.C; **B:** 1.B 2.A; **C:** 1. My cat Max snuck out this morning, and I couldn't find him anywhere. 2. By lunchtime I was confused and worried. 3. Where could he be? 4. The babysitter helped me look for him, but we still couldn't find him. 5. We called his name and offered him treats. 6. By the time Mom got home, we were scared. 7. Finally, just as I was about to go to sleep, my mom and I heard a meow. 8. Max was home! **D:** 1. Answers will vary. 2. Answers will vary.

Unit 1
Building Sentences
pp. 6–9

1.C	2.A	3.A	4.D	5.B
6.D	7.B	8.C	9.A	10.D
11.C	12.D	13.D	14.B	15.A
16.C	17.B	18.C	19.D	20.A
21.B	22.A	23.C	24.A	25.A
26.D	27.B	28.C	29.D	30.A
31.B	32.A	33.C	34.D	35.A
36.C	37.D	38.C	39.B	40.D
41.B	42.A	43.C	44.D	45.D
46.B				

Unit 2
Building Sentences
pp. 10–15

1.B	2.G	3.H	4.A	5.D
6.C	7.I	8.J	9.F	10.E
11.G	12.L	13.A	14.B	15.F
16.K	17.C	18.M	19.E	20.P
21.O	22.I	23.N	24.D	25.J
26.H	27.A	28.C	29.D	30.A
31.B	32.D	33.B	34.B	35.C
36.A	37.C	38.A	39.B	40.D
41.B	42.B	43.D	44.A	45.D
46.A				

Unit 3
Building Sentences
pp. 16–17

1.C	2.A	3.A	4.B	5.C
6.B	7.C	8.B	9.B	10.A
11.A	12.B	13.C	14.C	15.A

The First LAP
Language Activity Pages
pp. 18–19

A: 1.B 2.A 3.A; **B:** 1.B 2.B 3.A 4.B; **C:** 1. Tim 2. stood 3. remembered 4. bus 5. run; **D:** 1. Answers will vary. 2. Answers will vary.

Unit 4
Building Sentences
pp. 20–21

1.B	2.A	3.A	4.B	5.B
6.A	7.B	8.A	9.B	10.A
11.B	12.A	13.B	14.A	15.B
16.A	17.A	18.B	19.A	20.B
21.A	22.B			

Unit 5
Building Sentences
pp. 22–23

1.B	2.A	3.A	4.C	5.C
6.C	7.C	8.A	9.A	10.C
11.B	12.C	13.A	14.B	15.C
16.B	17.C	18.A		

Unit 6
Building Sentences
pp. 24–27

1.B	2.A	3.D	4.D	5.B
6.A	7.D	8.B	9.B	10.C
11.B	12.D	13.A	14.C	15.D
16.A	17.A	18.D	19.D	20.A
21.C	22.C	23.D	24.A	25.D
26.B	27.B	28.D	29.B	30.D
31.A	32.B	33.C	34.A	35.B
36.D	37.A	38.C	39.D	40.B
41.C	42.A	43.B	44.C	45.B
46.D	47.A	48.D	49.C	50.B

The Second LAP
Language Activity Pages
pp. 28–29

A: 1.B 2.C 3.A 4.C; **B:** 1.A 2.B 3.B 4.C; **C:** 1. always/ adverb 2. helped/verb 3. winding/adjective 4. They/pronoun 5. deer/noun; **D:** 1. Answers will vary. 2. Answers will vary.

Unit 7
Combining Sentences
pp. 30–31

1.C	2.C	3.A	4.C	5.B
6.A	7.B	8.A		

Unit 8
Combining Sentences
pp. 32–33

1.B	2.A	3.A	4.A	5.C
6.C	7.B	8.C		

Unit 9
Combining Sentences
pp. 34–35

1.C	2.C	3.A	4.C	5.C
6.B	7.A	8.B		

Unit 10
Combining Sentences
pp. 36–37

1.A	2.A	3.C	4.C	5.A
6.A	7.C	8.A		

Unit 11
Combining Sentences
pp. 38–41

1.B	2.B	3.A	4.A	5.A
6.B	7.C	8.A	9.B	10.A
11.C	12.B	13.C	14.B	15.B
16.B				

Unit 12
Correct Word Order
pp. 42–45

1.B	2.A	3.B	4.B	5.A
6.A	7.B	8.A	9.B	10.B
11.B	12.B	13.C	14.B	15.B
16.A	17.B	18.C	19.A	20.C
21.B	22.B	23.C	24.B	

The Third LAP
Language Activity Pages
pp. 46–47

A: 1.B 2.C 3.A; **B:** 1. I eat salad with Italian dressing and croutons. 2. I don't like cold soup or warm milk. 3. Open a can of diced tomatoes. 4. Lots of people put ketchup and mustard on hot dogs. 5. Dried apricots are a good source of iron and fiber. **C:** 1. Boil two cups of water in a pan. 2. noodles 3. Drain 4. stir 5. well; **D:** 1. Answers will vary. 2. Answers will vary.

Unit 13
Parallelism
pp. 48–51

1.A	2.B	3.B	4.B	5.B
6.B	7.A	8.A	9.B	10.B
11.B	12.A	13.B	14.B	15.B
16.B	17.B	18.A	19.A	20.B
21.A	22.B	23.B	24.B	25.B
26.A	27.B	28.B		

Unit 14
Sentence Fluency
pp. 52–55

1.B	2.A	3.A	4.A	5.B
6.B	7.B	8.A	9.B	10.B
11.A	12.A	13.B	14.B	15.A
16.B	17.A	18.B		

Unit 15
Sentence Problems
pp. 56–59

1.B	2.A	3.B	4.A	5.A
6.B	7.A	8.B	9.A	10.A
11.A	12.B	13.A	14.B	15.A
16.B	17.B	18.A	19.A	20.B
21.A	22.B	23.A	24.B	25.A
26.A	27.A	28.B	29.A	30.A
31.B	32.B	33.A	34.A	

Unit 16
Sentence Problems
pp. 60–61

1.A	2.B	3.A	4.A	5.B
6.A	7.A	8.A	9.A	10.B
11.B	12.A	13.B	14.B	

The Last LAP
Language Activity Pages
pp. 62–63

A: 1.C 2.A 3.B; **B:** 1. verb 2. subject 3. subject 4. verb 5. verb; **C:** 1. fun 2. gives 3. learn 4. helps; **D:** 1. Answers will vary. 2. Answers will vary.

Unit 1
Building Sentences
pp. 6–7

1.B	2.B	3.A	4.C	5.A
6.C	7.C	8.B	9.A	10.C

Unit 2
Building Sentences
pp. 8–9

1.E	2.G	3.A	4.F	5.H
6.B	7.I	8.C	9.D	10.B
11.D	12.F	13.C	14.A	15.K
16.J	17.H	18.I	19.E	20.G

Unit 3
Building Sentences
pp. 10–11

1.A	2.C	3.A	4.B	5.B
6.C	7.B	8.A	9.A	10.C
11.B	12.C	13.A	14.B	

Unit 4
Building Sentences
pp. 12–13

1.A	2.C	3.B	4.C	5.D
6.A	7.B	8.A	9.C	10.D
11.D	12.C	13.B	14.D	15.A
16.C	17.B	18.A	19.D	20.B
21.A	22.C			

Unit 5
Building Sentences
pp. 14–15

1.A	2.B	3.A	4.C	5.C
6.B	7.A	8.B	9.C	10.A
11.A	12.C			

Unit 6
Building Sentences
pp. 16–17

1.B	2.A	3.B	4.C	5.A
6.B	7.C	8.B	9.A	10.B

The First LAP
Language Activity Pages
pp. 18–19

A: 1.B 2.A 3.C 4.B; **B:** 1.D
2.C 3.B 4.C 5.C 6.B;
C: 1. presidents/had
2. Thomas Jefferson/received
3. Abraham Lincoln/lived
4. pony/rode 5. cow/provided;
D: 1. Answers will vary.
2. Answers will vary.

Unit 7
Combining Sentences
pp. 20–25

1.B	2.B	3.B	4.A	5.C
6.B	7.A	8.B	9.A	10.A
11.C	12.C	13.A	14.B	15.B
16.A	17.C	18.B	19.A	20.A
21.C	22.B	23.C	24.A	

Unit 8
Combining Sentences
pp. 26–31

1.B	2.A	3.A	4.C	5.B
6.A	7.C	8.B	9.C	10.C
11.A	12.B	13.C	14.C	15.B
16.C	17.B	18.C	19.A	20.B
21.A	22.A	23.C	24.C	25.A
26.B	27.A	28.C	29.A	30.C

Unit 9
Combining Sentences
pp. 32–33

1.A	2.C	3.A	4.C	5.C
6.B	7.B	8.C		

The Second LAP
Language Activity Pages
pp. 34–35

A: 1.B 2.C 3.C; **B:** 1.B 2.A
3.B; **C:** 1. Ringing loudly/P
2. my neighbor/A 3. escaped
from the zoo/A 4. Quite
confused/P 5. the trickster/A
6. Handing me the
newspaper/P;
D: 1. Answers will vary.
2. Answers will vary.

Unit 10
Correct Word Order
pp. 36–37

1.A	2.B	3.A	4.B	5.B
6.A	7.A	8.B	9.A	10.A
11.B	12.A	13.B	14.B	

Unit 11
The Sound of Language
pp. 38–43

1.A	2.C	3.C	4.B	5.C
6.B	7.A	8.A	9.B	10.C
11.C	12.A	13.C	14.B	15.B
16.A	17.A	18.C	19.A	20.C
21.C	22.B	23.A	24.B	25.B
26.A	27.A	28.B	29.A	30.B
31.B	32.B	33.A	34.A	35.B
36.B	37.A	38.B	39.A	40.A
41.B	42.A			

The Third LAP
Language Activity Pages
pp. 44–45

A: 1.A 2.B 3.B 4.B; **B:** 1.C 2.B
3.D 4.E 5.A; **C:** 1. alliteration
2. assonance 3. onomatopoeia
4. rhyme 5. repetition;
D: 1. Answers will vary.
2. Answers will vary.

Unit 12
Sentence Fluency
pp. 46–49

1.B	2.B	3.A	4.B	5.A
6.B	7.A	8.A	9.B	10.A
11.A	12.B	13.A	14.A	

Unit 13
Parallelism
pp. 50–55

1.A	2.B	3.A	4.B	5.B
6.A	7.B	8.B	9.A	10.B
11.B	12.B	13.A	14.A	15.B
16.A	17.B	18.B	19.A	20.A
21.B	22.B	23.A	24.B	25.A
26.A	27.B	28.B	29.A	30.A
31.B	32.B	33.A	34.B	35.B

Unit 14
Sentence Problems
pp. 56–57

1.B	2.A	3.A	4.B	5.B
6.A	7.B	8.A	9.A	10.A
11.B	12.A	13.B	14.B	15.B
16.A				

Unit 15
Sentence Problems
pp. 58–59

1.A	2.A	3.B	4.B	5.A
6.B	7.B	8.A	9.A	10.B
11.A	12.B	13.B	14.A	

Unit 16
Sentence Problems
pp. 60–61

1.B	2.B	3.A	4.B	5.A
6.A	7.A	8.B	9.B	10.A
11.B	12.A	13.B	14.A	15.B

The Last LAP
Language Activity Pages
pp. 62–63

A: 1.B 2.C 3.B 4.C;
B: 1. fragment 2. fragment
3. correct 4. run-on
5. fragment 6. correct 7. run-
on 8. fragment; **C:** 1. waited
2. colder 3. jumped 4. most
boring 5. most thrilling 6. paid;
D: 1. Answers will vary.
2. Answers will vary.

Unit 1
Building Sentences
pp. 6–7

1.C 2.B 3.C 4.A 5.C
6.A 7.A 8.B 9.A 10.C
11.C 12.C 13.B 14.B 15.A
16.C

Unit 2
Building Sentences
pp. 8–11

1.F 2.J 3.C 4.L 5.G
6.H 7.A 8.B 9.D 10.E
11.K 12.I 13.D 14.N 15.H
16.F 17.P 18.B 19.A 20.C
21.O 22.I 23.J 24.M 25.K
26.G 27.E 28.L 29.C 30.A
31.B 32.B 33.A 34.A 35.C
36.B 37.C 38.C 39.A 40.B

Unit 3
Building Sentences
pp. 12–15

1.B 2.A 3.C 4.C 5.A
6.A 7.B 8.C 9.A 10.B
11.A 12.A 13.C 14.A 15.A
16.B 17.B 18.A 19.C 20.B
21.A 22.B 23.C 24.C

Unit 4
Building Sentences
pp. 16–21

1.A 2.C 3.B 4.B 5.A
6.B 7.C 8.C 9.A 10.A
11.B 12.B 13.C 14.A 15.A
16.B 17.C 18.B 19.A 20.C
21.C 22.B 23.C 24.A 25.A
26.B 27.C 28.C 29.A 30.C
31.B 32.C 33.B 34.A

The First LAP
Language Activity Pages
pp. 22–23

A: 1. Complete 2. Compound
3. Subordinate 4. conjunction
5. semicolon; **B:** 1. CDP 2. CES
3. CDS 4. CEP 5. CES 6. CDP
7. CDS 8. CES 9. CEP 10. CDP;
C: 1.A 2.B 3.F 4.G 5.J;
D: 1. Answers will vary.
2. Answers will vary.

Unit 5
Combining Sentences
pp. 24–27

1.B 2.A 3.C 4.C 5.A
6.B 7.B 8.A 9.C 10.A
11.C 12.A 13.B 14.B 15.C
16.B 17.A 18.C

Unit 6
Combining Sentences
pp. 28–33

1.A 2.C 3.A 4.B 5.B
6.C 7.C 8.A 9.A 10.A
11.C 12.B 13.C 14.A 15.B
16.C 17.B 18.A 19.B 20.C
21.A 22.C 23.C 24.B 25.A

Unit 7
Combining Sentences
pp. 34–35

1.C 2.B 3.C 4.A 5.C
6.A 7.B 8.C

The Second LAP
Language Activity Pages
pp. 36–37

A: 1. or 2. and 3. repetition
4. Participles 5. Compound
6. Complex 7. Appositives
8. appositive; **B:** 1.X 2.D 3.D
4.X 5.X; **C:** 1. Karen Hesse,
the author of 1997s Out of the
Dust, wanted to be a writer
from an early age.
2. Encouraged by her fifth-
grade teacher, Hesse gained
confidence to pursue her
writing. 3. Hesse's first book,
Wish on a Unicorn, was
published in 1991.
4. Dedicated to quality writing
for children and young adults,
Hesse offers something for
many age groups. 5. Hesse,
the recipient of the impressive
Newbery Award for Out of the
Dust, has received many
awards for her writing.
6. A unique novel that includes
poems and dated entries, Out
of the Dust was inspired by
people's desperate need for
rain. **D:** 1. Answers will vary.
2. Answers will vary.

Unit 8
The Sound of Language
pp. 38–43

1.A 2.C 3.C 4.A 5.B
6.B 7.B 8.A 9.C 10.B
11.A 12.B 13.C 14.B 15.A
16.B 17.A 18.C 19.C 20.A
21.A 22.C 23.B 24.C 25.A
26.B 27.A 28.B 29.B 30.A
31.B 32.A 33.A 34.B 35.B
36.B 37.B 38.A 39.A 40.B
41.A 42.B

Unit 9
Sentence Fluency
pp. 44–47

1.A 2.B 3.C 4.A 5.B
6.A 7.B 8.B 9.A 10.B

The Third LAP
Language Activity Pages
pp. 48–49

A: 1.T 2.F 3.T 4.F 5.F 6.T
7.T 8.F 9.T 10.T; **B:** 1.D 2.A
3.F 4.B 5.E 6.C; **C:** 1.B 2.C
and E 3.A 4.F 5.D 6.G;
D: 1. Answers will vary.
2. Answers will vary.

Unit 10
Parallelism
pp. 50–53

1.B 2.B 3.A 4.B 5.A
6.B 7.A 8.B 9.A 10.B
11.A 12.B 13.A 14.B 15.A
16.A 17.B 18.B 19.A 20.A
21.A 22.A 23.A 24.B 25.B
26.A 27.B 28.B 29.B 30.A
31.B 32.B 33.A 34.A

Unit 11
Sentence Problems
pp. 54–59

1.B 2.A 3.A 4.B 5.B
6.A 7.B 8.A 9.A 10.B
11.A 12.B 13.A 14.B 15.B
16.A 17.A 18.B 19.B 20.A
21.A 22.A 23.B 24.A 25.B
26.B 27.B 28.A 29.B 30.A
31.B 32.B 33.B 34.B 35.B
36.B 37.A 38.B 39.A 40.B
41.B 42.A

Unit 12
Expanding Sentences
pp. 60–61

1.B 2.C 3.B 4.A 5.B
6.C 7.A 8.A 9.B 10.A

The Last LAP
Language Activity Pages
pp. 62–63

A: 1.T 2.F 3.T 4.T 5.T 6.T
7.T 8.F; **B:** 1. dreads
2. explained 3. quiet 4. easily
5. editing 6. fire 7. happy
8. thoroughly; **C:** 1.G 2.G 3.R
4.U 5.R 6.G 7.U 8.R;
D: 1. Answers will vary.
2. Answers will vary.

Unit 1

Building Sentences
pp. 6–7

1.B	2.C	3.A	4.B	5.A
6.C	7.B	8.A	9.C	10.C
11.B	12.A	13.B	14.A	

Unit 2

Building Sentences
pp. 8–9

1.C	2.A	3.B	4.C	5.B
6.A	7.A	8.C	9.B	10.C
11.A	12.B			

Unit 3

Building Sentences
pp. 10–13

1.A	2.C	3.B	4.A	5.C
6.C	7.B	8.A	9.C	10.A
11.B	12.C	13.A	14.A	15.C
16.C	17.B	18.A	19.C	20.B
21.A	22.C	23.C	24.B	25.B
26.C				

Unit 4

Building Sentences
pp. 14–19

1.B	2.B	3.A	4.A	5.C
6.B	7.A	8.C	9.A	10.B
11.B	12.A	13.C	14.B	15.A
16.B	17.A	18.B	19.C	20.C
21.A	22.C	23.B	24.A	25.B
26.C	27.A	28.B	29.C	30.A
31.A	32.A	33.B	34.C	35.B
36.A	37.B	38.A		

The First LAP

Language Activity Pages
pp. 20–21

A: 1.B 2.A 3.A 4.C 5.B;
B: 1.D 2.C 3.B 4.E 5.G 6.F
7.A 8.H; **C:** 1.E 2.B 3.D 4.A
5.C; **D:** 1. Answers will vary.
2. Answers will vary.

Unit 5

Combining Sentences
pp. 22–27

1.C	2.A	3.C	4.A	5.C
6.B	7.B	8.A	9.B	10.C
11.C	12.A	13.C	14.A	15.C
16.B	17.A	18.A	19.B	20.B
21.C	22.C	23.A	24.B	25.A
26.C	27.B	28.C	29.A	30.B

Unit 6

Combining Sentences
pp. 28–33

1.B	2.C	3.B	4.C	5.C
6.A	7.C	8.A	9.A	10.A
11.B	12.A	13.C	14.B	15.A
16.C	17.A	18.C	19.A	20.B
21.C	22.C	23.B	24.A	25.C
26.B				

The Second LAP

Language Activity Pages
pp. 34–35

A: 1.B 2.A 3.A; **B:** 1.A 2.A;
C: 1.C 2.E 3.A 4.D 5.B;
D: 1. Answers will vary.
2. Answers will vary.

Unit 7

The Sound of Language
pp. 36–41

1.C	2.C	3.A	4.B	5.B
6.C	7.B	8.A	9.A	10.C
11.B	12.A	13.B	14.C	15.B
16.A	17.B	18.A	19.C	20.A
21.A	22.C	23.B	24.B	25.A
26.A	27.A	28.A	29.B	30.A
31.B	32.A	33.A	34.B	35.A
36.B	37.B	38.A	39.A	40.A
41.B	42.A	43.B	44.B	

Unit 8

Sentence Fluency
pp. 42–45

1.C	2.B	3.C	4.A	5.C
6.A	7.C	8.A	9.B	10.C

Unit 9

Parallelism
pp. 46–51

1.B	2.A	3.B	4.B	5.A
6.A	7.B	8.B	9.A	10.B
11.B	12.B	13.B	14.A	15.B
16.A	17.B	18.A	19.A	20.B
21.B	22.B	23.B	24.B	25.A
26.B	27.B	28.A	29.A	30.A
31.B	32.A	33.A	34.B	35.B
36.B	37.B	38.B	39.A	40.B
41.A	42.B			

The Third LAP

Language Activity Pages
pp. 52–53

A: 1.A 2.C 3.B 4.C; **B:** 1.B
2.A 3.B 4.B; **C:** 1. do 2. slowly
3. way 4. moos 5. chews
6. shoes 7. instead 8. head
9. grow 10. clatter 11. matter
12. see; **D:** 1. Answers will
vary. 2. Answers will vary.

Unit 10

Sentence Problems
pp. 54–59

1.B	2.B	3.A	4.C	5.A
6.A	7.B	8.A	9.C	10.A
11.A	12.B	13.B	14.B	15.A
16.B	17.B	18.A	19.B	20.B
21.A	22.B	23.B	24.B	25.A
26.B	27.A	28.A	29.B	30.B
31.A	32.B	33.B	34.B	35.A
36.B	37.B	38.A	39.B	40.B
41.B	42.B	43.A	44.B	45.B
46.B	47.B	48.B		

Unit 11

Expanding Sentences
pp. 60–61

1.B	2.C	3.B	4.A	5.A
6.C	7.C	8.A	9.C	10.C

The Last LAP

Language Activity Pages
pp. 62–63

A: 1.B 2.C 3.C 4.B; **B:** 1.B
2.B 3.C 4.A 5.A 6.C; **C:** 1.A
2.B 3.C 4.F 5.D 6.E;
D: 1. Answers will vary.
2. Answers will vary.

Unit 1
Building Sentences
pp. 6–9

1.A 2.B 3.B 4.C 5.A
6.C 7.C 8.A 9.C 10.C
11.B 12.A 13.A 14.B 15.C
16.B 17.B 18.B 19.A 20.C
21.C 22.A

Unit 2
Combining Sentences
pp. 10–15

1.B 2.A 3.C 4.C 5.A
6.A 7.A 8.B 9.A 10.A
11.B 12.C 13.C 14.A 15.C
16.B 17.B 18.A 19.B 20.B
21.C 22.C 23.A 24.C 25.B
26.C 27.A 28.B

Unit 3
Combining Sentences
pp. 16–19

1.B 2.C 3.B 4.A 5.A
6.B 7.A 8.A 9.C 10.A
11.B 12.A 13.B 14.C

The First LAP
Language Activity Pages
pp. 20–21

A: 1.A 2.C 3.B; **B:** 1.B 2.A;
C: 1. signs that warned…
2. Upon the arrival of…
3. Although the Spanish
conquerors were
outnumbered… 4. culture as
they took over… 5. some
artifacts remain that give…;
D: 1. Answers will vary.
2. Answers will vary.

Unit 4
The Sound of Language
pp. 22–25

1.B 2.B 3.B 4.A 5.A
6.A 7.B 8.A 9.A 10.B
11.B 12.B 13.A 14.A 15.B
16.A 17.B 18.A 19.A 20.B
21.B 22.A 23.B 24.B 25.A
26.A 27.B 28.B 29.A 30.B
31.A 32.B 33.A 34.B

Unit 5
Sentence Fluency
pp. 26–29

1.A 2.B 3.B 4.C 5.A
6.A 7.B 8.C

Unit 6
Parallelism
pp. 30–31

1.B 2.A 3.B 4.A 5.A
6.B 7.B 8.A 9.A 10.B
11.A 12.B 13.A 14.B 15.A
16.B 17.A 18.B 19.A 20.A

Unit 7
Parallelism
pp. 32–35

1.B 2.A 3.B 4.B 5.A
6.B 7.A 8.A 9.B 10.A
11.B 12.A 13.B 14.A 15.B
16.B 17.B 18.A 19.B 20.A
21.B 22.A

The Second LAP
Language Activity Pages
pp. 36–37

A: 1.B 2.B 3.B 4.A; **B:** 1.B 2.A
3.B 4.A; **C:** 1. onomatopoeia
2. repetition 3. assonance
4. alliteration 5. end rhyme;
D: 1. Answers will vary.
2. Answers will vary.

Unit 8
Sentence Problems
pp. 38–41

1.B 2.A 3.A 4.B 5.B
6.A 7.B 8.A 9.B 10.B
11.A 12.C 13.B 14.C 15.A
16.B 17.A 18.A 19.A 20.A
21.B 22.C 23.A 24.C 25.A

Unit 9
Sentence Problems
pp. 42–47

1.B 2.B 3.A 4.B 5.A
6.B 7.B 8.B 9.A 10.A
11.B 12.A 13.B 14.B 15.A
16.B 17.B 18.B 19.A 20.B
21.A 22.B 23.B 24.B 25.A
26.A 27.B 28.B 29.B 30.B
31.A 32.A 33.B 34.B 35.B
36.A 37.A 38.B 39.C 40.B
41.B 42.A 43.B 44.B 45.A

The Third LAP
Language Activity Pages
pp. 48–49

A: 1.A 2.A 3.C 4.B; **B:** 1.A
2.C 3.A; **C:** 1. fragment
2. misplaced modifier
3. redundant 4. run-on
sentence 5. unclear antecedent
6. redundant 7. fragment
8. dangling modifier;
D: 1. Answers will vary.
2. Answers will vary.

Unit 10
Expanding Sentences
pp. 50–55

1.B 2.C 3.B 4.A 5.A
6.B 7.C 8.B 9.A 10.A
11.A 12.A 13.B 14.C 15.B
16.C 17.A 18.B 19.C 20.C
21.B 22.A 23.A 24.C 25.C
26.B 27.A 28.C

Unit 11
Diagramming Sentences
pp. 56–61

1.B 2.B 3.A 4.A 5.B
6.A 7.A 8.B 9.A 10.B
11.B 12.A 13.B 14.B 15.B
16.B 17.A 18.A 19.B 20.A
21.A 22.B 23.A 24.B 25.B
26.B 27.A 28.B 29.B 30.A

The Last LAP
Language Activity Pages
pp. 62–63

A: 1.A 2.B 3.A 4.A 5.B;
B: 1.

2. he | took | lessons

3. parents | taught | things

4. music | was played

5. band | played

6. you | Have heard | "Take the 'A' Train"

C: 1. appositive phrase
2. dependent clause
3. participial phrase
4. adjective clause 5. participial
phrase; **D:** 1. Answers will
vary. 2. Answers will vary.

Unit 1
Building Sentences
pp. 6–9

1.B 2.A 3.A 4.C 5.A
6.B 7.A 8.C 9.B 10.C
11.A 12.C 13.A 14.C 15.B
16.A 17.B 18.A 19.B 20.B
21.A 22.C 23.C 24.A

Unit 2
Combining Sentences
pp. 10–13

1.A 2.B 3.A 4.C 5.C
6.A 7.A 8.B 9.A 10.A
11.A 12.B 13.B 14.A 15.A
16.B 17.A 18.B 19.B 20.A

Unit 3
Combining Sentences
pp. 14–17

1.B 2.C 3.C 4.A 5.B
6.C 7.B 8.A 9.B 10.B
11.A 12.A 13.A 14.A 15.C
16.A 17.C 18.B

The First LAP
Language Activity Pages
pp. 18–19

A: 1.A 2.C 3.C; **B:** 1.A 2.C
3.B 4.A; **C:** 1.D 2.A 3.F 4.E
5.B 6.C 7.G; **D:** 1. Answers
will vary. 2. Answers will vary.

Unit 4
The Sound of Language
pp. 20–23

1.B 2.A 3.B 4.B 5.A
6.A 7.A 8.B 9.A 10.A
11.A 12.B 13.B 14.A 15.B
16.A 17.A 18.A 19.B 20.A
21.B 22.B 23.A 24.B 25.A
26.A 27.B 28.A 29.A 30.B
31.A 32.B 33.B 34.A 35.A
36.A 37.B 38.A 39.B 40.B
41.B 42.A

Unit 5
Sentence Fluency
pp. 24–27

1.A 2.B 3.A 4.C 5.A
6.A 7.B 8.C

Unit 6
Parallelism
pp. 28–31

1.A 2.B 3.A 4.A 5.A
6.B 7.A 8.B 9.B 10.A
11.A 12.A 13.A 14.B 15.A
16.B 17.A 18.B 19.A 20.B
21.A 22.B

Unit 7
Parallelism
pp. 32–35

1.B 2.B 3.A 4.B 5.A
6.B 7.A 8.B 9.B 10.B
11.B 12.A 13.A 14.B 15.A
16.A 17.A 18.B 19.A 20.A
21.B 22.B

The Second LAP
Language Activity Pages
pp. 36–37

A: 1.C 2.B 3.C 4.C; **B:** 1.B
2.A; **C:** 1. alliteration,
assonance, rhyme;
2. alliteration; 3. alliteration,
onomatopoeia, assonance;
4. repetition, rhyme, assonance;
5. assonance; **D:** 1. Answers
will vary. 2. Answers will vary.

Unit 8
Sentence Problems
pp. 38–43

1.B 2.A 3.A 4.B 5.B
6.A 7.A 8.B 9.A 10.B
11.A 12.B 13.A 14.B 15.B
16.A 17.B 18.A 19.A 20.B
21.A 22.A 23.C 24.B 25.B
26.C 27.A 28.C 29.A 30.B
31.B 32.B 33.A 34.B 35.B
36.A 37.A 38.B 39.B 40.B
41.B 42.A 43.A 44.B 45.A
46.B

Unit 9
Sentence Problems
pp. 44–49

1.A 2.A 3.B 4.A 5.B
6.B 7.B 8.A 9.B 10.B
11.A 12.B 13.B 14.A 15.A
16.A 17.B 18.A 19.A 20.B
21.B 22.B 23.A 24.B 25.B
26.A 27.A 28.A 29.A 30.B
31.B 32.B 33.B 34.B 35.B
36.B 37.B 38.A 39.B 40.B
41.A 42.B 43.C 44.A 45.B
46.A

The Third LAP
Language Activity Pages
pp. 50–51

A: 1.B 2.A 3.C 4.B 5.A;
B: 1.A 2.A 3.B; **C:** 1. awkward
2. run-on sentence 3. incorrect
pronoun-antecedent agreement
4. fragment 5. redundant
6. fragment 7. dangling modifier
8. incorrect pronoun-antecedent
agreement 9. dangling modifier
10. run-on sentence;

D: 1. Answers will vary.
2. Answers will vary.

Unit 10
Expanding Sentences
pp. 52–55

1.B 2.C 3.B 4.A 5.A
6.A 7.B 8.B 9.C 10.A
11.B 12.C 13.A 14.B 15.A
16.B

Unit 11
Diagramming Sentences
pp. 56–61

1.A 2.A 3.B 4.B 5.B
6.A 7.A 8.A 9.A 10.B
11.B 12.A 13.B 14.B 15.A
16.B 17.B 18.B 19.A 20.A

The Last LAP
Language Activity Pages
pp. 62–63

A: 1.D 2.A 3.A;
B: 1.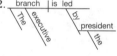

2.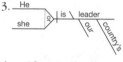

3. He / she is leader our country's

4. you | Can name | branch another of government our

5. (you) | Think about it carefully

6.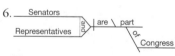

7. They | form | branch the legislative

8. Congress | makes | laws and Supreme Court | explains | laws the

C: 1.B 2.D 3.A 4.C 5.E 6.G
7.F; **D:** 1. Answers will vary.
2. Answers will vary.

Unit 1
Types of Paragraphs
pp. 6–9

1.B   2.A   3.B   4.B   5.A
6.B   7.B   8.A   9.A   10.B
11.A   12.A

Unit 2
Types of Paragraphs
pp. 10–13

1.A   2.B   3.A   4.B   5.B
6.A   7.A   8.A   9.B   10.A
11.B   12.B

Unit 3
Using a Web
pp. 14–19

1.A   2.C   3.A   4.B   5.D
6.C   7.A   8.C   9.B   10.D

The First LAP
Language Activity Pages
pp. 20–21

A: 1. paragraph 2. true 3. Webs
4. topic; **B:** skates, sleds;
C: 1. I play with toys. 2. I eat
fruit. 3. I lost a watch.
D: 1. Answers will vary.
2. Answers will vary.

Unit 4
Topic Sentences
pp. 22–25

1.A   2.B   3.B   4.C   5.A
6.A   7.C   8.A   9.C   10.B

Unit 5
Topic Sentences
pp. 26–29

1.B   2.C   3.A   4.C   5.A
6.B   7.A   8.C   9.B   10.A
11.C   12.A

Unit 6
Details
pp. 30–35

1.B   2.C   3.A   4.C   5.B
6.A   7.C   8.A   9.A   10.C
11.B   12.C   13.B   14.B   15.A
16.C   17.A   18.B   19.C   20.B
21.B   22.C   23.A   24.A

The Second LAP
Language Activity Pages
pp. 36–37

A: 1. sentence 2. topic
3. details; **B:** B; **C:** 1.A 2.C 3.E
4.F 5.H; **D:** 1. Answers will
vary. 2. Answers will vary.

Unit 7
Closing Sentences
pp. 38–43

1.C   2.B   3.A   4.C   5.B
6.B   7.C   8.A   9.B   10.B
11.A   12.C   13.A   14.B   15.C
16.C   17.B   18.A

Unit 8
Complete Paragraphs
pp. 44–49

1.A   2.C   3.B   4.B   5.A
6.C   7.C   8.B   9.A   10.C
11.A   12.B   13.B   14.C   15.A
16.A   17.C   18.B

The Third LAP
Language Activity Pages
pp. 50–51

A: 1. Complete 2. topic
3. Details 4. closing; **B:** C;
C: 1.J 2.D 3.G 4.H;
D: 1. Answers will vary.
2. Answers will vary.

Unit 9
Staying on Topic
pp. 52–57

1.C   2.B   3.D   4.C   5.A
6.C   7.B   8.D   9.C   10.A
11.B   12.D   13.C   14.A   15.B
16.D   17.B   18.C   19.A   20.D
21.B   22.C

Unit 10
Time and Order Words
pp. 58–61

1.A   2.B   3.A   4.B   5.A
6.A   7.B   8.A   9.A   10.B
11.B   12.B   13.A   14.A   15.A
16.B

The Last LAP
Language Activity Pages
pp. 62–63

A: 1. topic 2. when 3. detail;
B: 1. yes 2. yes 3. yes 4. yes
5. no 6. yes; **C:** 1.C 2.E 3.F
4.H 5.J; **D:** 1. Answers will
vary. 2. Answers will vary.

Unit 1
Types of Paragraphs
pp. 6–11

1.A	2.A	3.B	4.C	5.A
6.A	7.C	8.A	9.A	10.C
11.A	12.B			

Unit 2
Using a Web
pp. 12–17

1.A	2.A	3.A	4.B	5.C
6.B	7.C	8.B	9.B	10.A

The First LAP
Language Activity Pages
pp. 18–19

A: 1.B 2.B; **B:** *Middle circle:* The children's museum is a great place to visit. *Connecting circles:* It has a neat underwater tunnel. You can learn about children from different countries. There is a science center. **C:** describe how something looks; **D:** 1. Answers will vary. 2. Answers will vary.

Unit 3
Topic Sentences
pp. 20–25

1.B	2.A	3.C	4.C	5.A
6.B	7.B	8.C	9.C	10.C
11.C	12.C	13.A	14.B	

Unit 4
Details
pp. 26–29

1.C	2.A	3.C	4.B	5.A
6.C	7.A	8.A	9.B	10.B
11.C	12.A	13.B	14.B	15.A
16.B				

Unit 5
Closing Sentences
pp. 30–33

1.A	2.B	3.A	4.B	5.A
6.B	7.A	8.A		

The Second LAP
Language Activity Pages
pp. 34–35

A: 1.B 2.B 3.A; **B:** 1.B; **C:** 1. Deserts can be colorful places. 2. Answers will vary but should include the second, third, or fourth sentence. 3. It is surprising how colorful deserts can be. **D:** 1. Answers will vary. 2. Answers will vary.

Unit 6
Complete Sentences
pp. 36–41

1.B	2.A	3.C	4.A	5.C
6.B	7.C	8.A	9.B	10.C
11.B	12.C	13.A	14.B	

Unit 7
Staying on Topic
pp. 42–47

1.D	2.D	3.B	4.D	5.C
6.C	7.C	8.A	9.D	10.C
11.C	12.D	13.B	14.D	15.C
16.B	17.C	18.D		

The Third LAP
Language Activity Pages
pp. 48–49

A: 1.D 2.A; **B:** 1.D 2.T 3.D 4.C; **C:** D, H; **D:** 1. Answers will vary. 2. Answers will vary.

Unit 8
Time and Order Words
pp. 50–53

1.A	2.B	3.A	4.A	5.B
6.A	7.B	8.B	9.A	10.A
11.B	12.B	13.A	14.B	

Unit 9
Using Dialogue
pp. 54–57

1.B	2.A	3.C	4.B	5.A
6.C	7.A	8.C		

Unit 10
Making Comparisons
pp. 58–61

1.A	2.A	3.B	4.B	5.A
6.B	7.A	8.A	9.A	10.B
11.B	12.A	13.B	14.B	15.B
16.B	17.A	18.B	19.A	20.A

The Last LAP
Language Activity Pages
pp. 62–63

A: 1. simile 2. Time 3. dialogue 4. metaphor 5. Order; **B:** 1. glass 2. mountain 3. bear 4. treasure; **C:** 1. this morning 2. this afternoon 3. First 4. Then; **D:** 1. Answers will vary. 2. Answers will vary.

Unit 1
Types of Paragraphs
pp. 6–11

1.A	2.B	3.C	4.A	5.B
6.B	7.B	8.A	9.C	10.C
11.A	12.A	13.C	14.A	15.C
16.B				

Unit 2
Using a Web
pp. 12–17

1.C	2.A	3.B	4.C	5.B
6.A	7.A	8.C	9.B	10.B

The First LAP
Language Activity Pages
pp. 18–19

A: 1.B 2.C 3.A; **B:** 1. persuasive
2. expository 3. narrative
4. descriptive; **C:** C;
D: 1. Answers will vary.
2. Answers will vary.

Unit 3
Topic Sentences
pp. 20–25

1.A	2.C	3.B	4.C	5.C
6.A	7.C	8.C	9.C	10.B
11.A	12.A	13.C	14.A	15.C
16.A				

Unit 4
Details
pp. 26–29

1.C	2.C	3.B	4.A	5.A
6.C	7.A	8.B	9.A	10.A
11.B	12.C	13.B	14.C	15.B
16.A	17.B	18.B		

Unit 5
Closing Sentences
pp. 30–33

1.A	2.A	3.B	4.A	5.C
6.B	7.C	8.A	9.B	10.C

The Second LAP
Language Activity Pages
pp. 34–35

A: 1.A 2.C 3.A; **B:** B; **C:** 1.D
2.E 3.B 4.A; **D:** 1. Answers
will vary. 2. Answers will vary.

Unit 6
Complete Paragraphs
pp. 36–41

1.C	2.A	3.C	4.C	5.A
6.B	7.C	8.A	9.C	10.A
11.A	12.A	13.B	14.A	15.A
16.A				

Unit 7
Staying on Topic
pp. 42–47

1.D	2.C	3.B	4.D	5.D
6.B	7.C	8.B	9.D	10.C
11.D	12.A	13.C	14.C	15.C
16.B	17.B	18.B	19.D	20.A

The Third LAP
Language Activity Pages
pp. 48–49

A: 1.A 2.B; **B:** B; **C:** 3, 5, 7;
D: 1. Answers will vary.
2. Answers will vary.

Unit 8
Time and Order Words
pp. 50–53

1.B	2.A	3.A	4.B	5.B
6.A	7.B	8.B	9.B	10.A
11.B	12.A	13.B	14.B	15.A
16.A	17.A	18.A	19.A	20.B
21.A	22.B	23.B	24.B	25.A
26.A	27.B	28.A	29.B	30.B
31.A	32.A	33.B	34.A	35.A
36.B	37.A	38.B	39.A	40.B

Unit 9
Dialogue
pp. 54–57

1.B	2.C	3.C	4.B	5.C
6.C	7.B	8.A	9.B	10.C
11.A	12.A	13.B	14.C	

Unit 10
Making Comparisons
pp. 58–61

1.A	2.B	3.A	4.A	5.B
6.B	7.A	8.B	9.A	10.B
11.A	12.B	13.A	14.B	15.A
16.A	17.B	18.A	19.B	20.B
21.A	22.B	23.A	24.A	25.B
26.B	27.A	28.A	29.B	30.B
31.A	32.A	33.B	34.B	35.A
36.B				

The Last LAP
Language Activity Pages
pp. 62–63

A: 1.C 2.B 3.B; **B:** 1.A 2.B
3.B 4.A; **C:** Would you like to
learn how to make a strawberry
smoothie? First, you will need
to gather six large strawberries,
a small carton of yogurt, and
four ounces of lemonade. Then,
put all the ingredients into a
blender. Next, turn on the
blender just long enough to
mix the ingredients and chop
the strawberries. Finally, pour
your strawberry smoothie into
a glass and enjoy!
D: 1. Answers will vary.
2. Answers will vary.

Unit 1
Types of Paragraphs
pp. 6–9

1.A	2.A	3.A	4.B	5.A
6.C	7.B	8.B	9.C	10.A

Unit 2
Using a Web
pp. 10–15

1.C	2.A	3.B	4.A	5.C
6.A	7.C	8.A	9.A	10.B
11.C	12.A			

The First LAP
Language Activity Pages
pp. 16–17

A: 1.C 2.A 3.A;
B: 1. expository 2. persuasive
3. narrative 4. expository
5. descriptive; **C:** 1. outer
circle 2. middle circle 3. not
in web 4. outer circle 5. not
in web 6. outer circle;
D: 1. Answers will vary.
2. Answers will vary.

Unit 3
Topic Sentences
pp. 18–23

1.B	2.A	3.C	4.B	5.B
6.A	7.A	8.C	9.C	10.B
11.A	12.A	13.C	14.C	

Unit 4
Details
pp. 24–27

1.B	2.C	3.A	4.B	5.C
6.B	7.C	8.A	9.B	10.A
11.C	12.A	13.B	14.A	15.B
16.A	17.C	18.B	19.A	20.C

Unit 5
Closing Sentences
pp. 28–31

1.B	2.A	3.C	4.B	5.A
6.C	7.A	8.C		

The Second LAP
Language Activity Pages
pp. 32–33

A: 1.C 2.A 3.A; **B:** 1. narrative
2. persuasive 3. expository
4. descriptive; **C:** 1. detail
2. topic sentence 3. detail
4. closing sentence 5. detail
6. detail; **D:** 1. Answers will
vary. 2. Answers will vary.

Unit 6
Complete Paragraphs
pp. 34–39

1.B	2.C	3.C	4.B	5.C
6.A	7.B	8.A	9.A	10.C
11.A	12.C	13.B	14.B	15.C
16.A				

Unit 7
Staying on Topic
pp. 40–45

1.B	2.C	3.D	4.B	5.C
6.C	7.C	8.C	9.A	10.C
11.C	12.A	13.B	14.B	15.B
16.C	17.D	18.A	19.C	20.C

The Third LAP
Language Activity Pages
pp. 46–47

A: 1.C 2.B; **B:** 1.A 2.C; **C:** 1.C
2.A 3.B; **D:** 1. Answers will
vary. 2. Answers will vary.

Unit 8
Transition Words
pp. 48–51

1.A	2.B	3.B	4.B	5.B
6.A	7.A	8.B	9.A	10.A
11.B	12.B	13.A	14.A	15.B
16.A	17.B	18.A	19.A	20.B
21.A	22.B	23.A	24.A	25.A
26.B	27.B	28.B	29.B	30.A
31.B	32.A	33.B	34.B	35.A
36.A	37.A	38.B	39.B	40.A
41.B	42.A	43.A	44.A	

Unit 9
Sentence Variety
pp. 52–53

1.B	2.B	3.A	4.A	5.A
6.A	7.B	8.B		

Unit 10
Using Dialogue
pp. 54–57

1.B	2.A	3.B	4.C	5.C
6.B	7.C	8.B		

Unit 11
Figurative Language
pp. 58–61

1.B	2.A	3.B	4.C	5.B
6.A	7.C	8.A	9.B	10.B
11.C	12.B	13.A	14.B	15.C
16.A	17.A	18.A	19.A	20.B
21.A	22.A	23.B	24.A	25.A
26.A	27.A	28.B	29.A	30.A

The Last LAP
Language Activity Pages
pp. 62–63

A: 1.B 2.C; **B:** 1. last 2. blew
its scorching breath
3. mercilessly hit 4. precious
5. as the inside of a volcano
6. walk in the park; **C:** 4, 7, 6,
8, 2, 1, 3, 5; **D:** 1. Answers will
vary. 2. Answers will vary.

Unit 1
Narrative Paragraphs
pp. 6–7
1.C 2.A 3.B 4.B 5.C

Unit 2
Narrative Paragraphs
pp. 8–13
1.B 2.D 3.B 4.A 5.C
6.C 7.D 8.A 9.B 10.D
11.C 12.A 13.B 14.B 15.A
16.A

Unit 3
Narrative Paragraphs
pp. 14–17
1.B 2.B 3.C 4.A 5.B
6.A 7.C 8.C 9.B 10.A

Unit 4
Narrative Paragraphs
pp. 18–19
1.A 2.B 3.A 4.A 5.C

The First LAP
Language Activity Pages
pp. 20–21
A: 1.F 2.T 3.T 4.T 5.T 6.F
7.F 8.F 9.T 10.T; **B:** 1.D 2.E
3.F 4.H 5.I; **C:** 1.B 2.A 3.B
4.B 5.A; **D:** 1. Answers will
vary. 2. Answers will vary.

Unit 5
Persuasive Paragraphs
pp. 22–23
1.C 2.A 3.A 4.C 5.B

Unit 6
Persuasive Paragraphs
pp. 24–29
1.A 2.C 3.B 4.B 5.C
6.A 7.C 8.A 9.C 10.A
11.A 12.B 13.B 14.C

Unit 7
Persuasive Paragraphs
pp. 30–31
1.B 2.A 3.C 4.B 5.C

The Second LAP
Language Activity Pages
pp. 32–33
A: 1.F 2.F 3.T 4.T 5.T 6.F
7.T 8.T 9.F 10.F; **B:** 1. opinion
2. fact 3. fact 4. opinion
5. opinion 6. fact 7. fact
8. fact; **C:** 1.C 2.E 3.G 4.H;
D: 1. Answers will vary.
2. Answers will vary.

Unit 8
Expository Paragraphs
pp. 34–35
1.A 2.B 3.C 4.A 5.B

Unit 9
Expository Paragraphs
pp. 36–39
1.D 2.A 3.F 4.B 5.C
6.E 7.A 8.B 9.B 10.A
11.A 12.B

Unit 10
Expository Paragraphs
pp. 40–41
1.C 2.A 3.C 4.C 5.B

Unit 11
Writing Paragraphs
pp. 42–45
1.B 2.A 3.B 4.B 5.A
6.A 7.B 8.A 9.A 10.B

The Third LAP
Language Activity Pages
pp. 46–47
A: 1.T 2.F 3.T 4.T 5.T 6.F
7.F 8.T 9.F 10.F; **B:** 1.P 2.E
3.N 4.P 5.E; **C:** 1.B 2.A 3.A
4.A; **D:** 1. Answers will vary.
2. Answers will vary.

Unit 12
Writing Paragraphs
pp. 48–51
1.A 2.A 3.B 4.B 5.A
6.B 7.A 8.B 9.C 10.A
11.B 12.C 13.A 14.C 15.C
16.A 17.B 18.C 19.B 20.C
21.A 22.B 23.C 24.B 25.A
26.C 27.C 28.B 29.A 30.A
31.C 32.C 33.B 34.A 35.C

Unit 13
Writing Paragraphs
pp. 52–55
1.E 2.C 3.G 4.D 5.A
6.F 7.B 8.B 9.A 10.A
11.A 12.A 13.B 14.B 15.A
16.B 17.A 18.B 19.A 20.B
21.B 22.A 23.B 24.A 25.B

Unit 14
Writing Paragraphs
pp. 56–57
1.B 2.C 3.C 4.A 5.C
6.B 7.A 8.B 9.C 10.B
11.B 12.C 13.B 14.A 15.C
16.C 17.B 18.A 19.A 20.C

Unit 15
Writing Paragraphs
pp. 58–61
1.A 2.A 3.B 4.C 5.C
6.B 7.A 8.C 9.A 10.A
11.B 12.C

The Last LAP
Language Activity Pages
pp. 62–63
A: 1. metaphor 2. simile
3. Transitions 4. descriptive
5. Personification
6. Exaggeration 7. expository
8. audience 9. dialogue
10. Organization; **B:** 1. angry
2. a chance in a million
3. like the wind 4. buckets
5. moaned; **C:** 1.B 2.B 3.C
4.A 5.A; **D:** 1. Answers will
vary. 2. Answers will vary.

Unit 1
Narrative Paragraphs
pp. 6–9

1.A 2.D 3.D 4.A 5.D
6.C 7.A 8.B 9.B 10.C

Unit 2
Narrative Paragraphs
pp. 10–11

1.D 2.A 3.B 4.B 5.D
6.A

Unit 3
Narrative Paragraphs
pp. 12–15

1.B 2.A 3.C 4.B 5.A
6.A 7.C 8.A 9.C 10.C

Unit 4
Narrative Paragraphs
pp. 16–17

1.C 2.A 3.B 4.A 5.C

The First LAP
Language Activity Pages
pp. 18–19

A: 1.B 2.A 3.B 4.C 5.A; **B:** C;
C: 1.B 2.H 3.K 4.L;
D: 1. Answers will vary.
2. Answers will vary.

Unit 5
Persuasive Paragraphs
pp. 20–21

1.C 2.A 3.B 4.A 5.C

Unit 6
Persuasive Paragraphs
pp. 22–27

1.A 2.B 3.C 4.B 5.A
6.A 7.C 8.B 9.C 10.B
11.C 12.A 13.A 14.B 15.A
16.C

Unit 7
Persuasive Paragraphs
pp. 28–29

1.A 2.C 3.B 4.C 5.A

The Second LAP
Language Activity Pages
pp. 30–31

A: 1.A 2.B 3.A 4.C; **B:** C;
C: B, E; **D:** 1. Answers will
vary. 2. Answers will vary.

Unit 8
Expository Paragraphs
pp. 32–33

1.C 2.B 3.A 4.A 5.C

Unit 9
Expository Paragraphs
pp. 34–37

1.C 2.B 3.A 4.D 5.C
6.B 7.A 8.C 9.B 10.B
11.C 12.D

Unit 10
Expository Paragraphs
pp. 38–39

1.B 2.A 3.C 4.B 5.A

Unit 11
Writing Paragraphs
pp. 40–43

1.B 2.A 3.A 4.A 5.B
6.A 7.B 8.B 9.A

The Third LAP
Language Activity Pages
pp. 44–45

A: 1.C 2.A 3.B 4.C; **B:** 1.B
2.A; **C:** 1.C 2.E 3.F 4.G 5.H;
D: 1. Answers will vary.
2. Answers will vary.

Unit 12
Writing Paragraphs
pp. 46–49

1.C 2.D 3.B 4.B 5.B
6.D 7.A 8.B 9.D 10.A
11.B 12.D 13.C 14.A 15.D

Unit 13
Writing Paragraphs
pp. 50–53

1.A 2.A 3.B 4.B 5.B
6.B 7.A 8.B 9.C 10.A
11.A 12.C 13.B 14.C 15.B

Unit 14
Writing Paragraphs
pp. 54–57

1.C 2.C 3.B 4.B 5.A
6.C 7.C 8.B 9.C 10.A
11.B 12.B 13.C 14.B 15.B
16.A 17.C 18.A 19.B 20.B
21.C 22.B 23.C 24.A 25.B
26.C 27.A 28.A 29.C 30.A
31.B 32.B 33.A 34.C 35.C
36.B 37.B 38.C 39.A 40.A
41.C 42.A 43.C 44.C

Unit 15
Writing Paragraphs
pp. 58–61

1.C 2.B 3.C 4.C 5.A
6.B 7.B 8.C 9.A 10.B
11.A 12.C

The Last LAP
Language Activity Pages
pp. 62–63

A: 1.C 2.C 3.A 4.C; **B:** 1.B
2.A 3.C 4.A; **C:** 1. trek
2. proudly raised its shoulders
3. grueling 4. as toothpicks
5. lead weight 6. taunted us
7. sharp, craggy 8. collapsed
9. revived 10. absorbed
11. magnificent 12. felt like I
was far above Earth;
D: 1. Answers will vary.
2. Answers will vary.

Unit 1
Narrative Paragraphs
pp. 6–9

1.A 2.A 3.B 4.B 5.A
6.C 7.B 8.B 9.A 10.B

Unit 2
Narrative Paragraphs
pp. 10–11

1.B 2.E 3.B 4.D 5.E
6.B 7.B 8.E

Unit 3
Narrative Paragraphs
pp. 12–15

1.A 2.B 3.C 4.C 5.B
6.B 7.A 8.C 9.A 10.B

Unit 4
Narrative Paragraphs
pp. 16–17

1.B 2.C 3.C 4.B 5.B

The First LAP
Language Activity Pages
pp. 18–19

A: 1.A 2.B 3.A 4.B 5.A;
B: 1, 5, 2, 6, 3, 4; **C:** 1. Walt
Whitman was also a famous
poet at the time. 2. The
United States had declared its
independence from the English
in 1776. 3. Many people also
consider firefighters to be
heroes. 4. I always stand up
for what I believe.
D: 1. Answers will vary.
2. Answers will vary.

Unit 5
Persuasive Paragraphs
pp. 20–21

1.B 2.A 3.B 4.A 5.C

Unit 6
Persuasive Paragraphs
pp. 22–25

1.C 2.A 3.B 4.C 5.A
6.A 7.D 8.C 9.A 10.D

Unit 7
Persuasive Paragraphs
pp. 26–29

1.A 2.A 3.B 4.B 5.A
6.B 7.A 8.A 9.B 10.A
11.A 12.B

Unit 8
Persuasive Paragraphs
pp. 30–31

1.A 2.A 3.C 4.A 5.C

The Second LAP
Language Activity Pages
pp. 32–33

A: 1.F 2.T 3.T 4.F 5.F;
B: 1. The first paragraph
appeals to the reader's
emotions. 2. The second
paragraph includes the topic
sentence. 3. The writer's
claim is to save landmarks from
destruction. 4. The third
paragraph appeals to the
reader's logic. **C:** 1.C 2.B 3.A
4.3 5.6; **D:** 1. Answers will
vary. 2. Answers will vary.

Unit 9
Expository Paragraphs
pp. 34–35

1.C 2.C 3.C 4.B 5.A

Unit 10
Expository Paragraphs
pp. 36–39

1.D 2.D 3.B 4.C 5.E
6.C 7.E 8.D 9.C 10.B
11.C 12.E 13.A 14.E

Unit 11
Expository Paragraphs
pp. 40–41

1.A 2.A 3.C 4.C 5.A

Unit 12
Writing Paragraphs
pp. 42–45

1.A 2.C 3.A 4.A 5.C
6.C 7.B 8.A 9.B 10.B
11.C 12.A 13.B 14.B 15.C
16.A 17.B 18.C

The Third LAP
Language Activity Pages
pp. 46–47

A: 1.C 2.B 3.C 4.A; **B:** The
appropriate way to display the
American flag is for the pole to
appear on the left-hand side.
Touching the pole should be
the field of blue with white
stars. The field of blue should
also appear at the top of the
left corner. Below the field of
blue will be the red and white
stripes. These stripes should
continue horizontally across
the flag to the right-hand side.
C: 6, 7; **D:** 1. Answers will
vary. 2. Answers will vary.

Unit 13
Writing Paragraphs
pp. 48–49

1.B 2.A 3.B 4.B 5.A
6.A 7.B 8.B

Unit 14
Writing Paragraphs
pp. 50–53

1.C 2.B 3.A 4.A 5.C
6.B 7.A 8.B 9.C 10.B
11.B 12.A 13.B 14.A 15.C
16.B

Unit 15
Writing Paragraphs
pp. 54–57

1.C 2.C 3.A 4.A 5.B
6.C 7.C 8.B 9.A 10.B
11.A 12.B 13.C 14.A 15.A
16.B 17.C 18.A 19.A 20.C

Unit 16
Writing Paragraphs
pp. 58–61

1.B 2.A 3.B 4.A 5.A
6.A 7.B 8.A 9.B 10.A
11.B 12.A

The Last LAP
Language Activity Pages
pp. 62–63

A: 1.C 2.A 3.A 4.C;
B: 1. their worst nightmares
2. violent 3. swirl 4. the
funnel cloud of a tornado
5. machine 6. strikes
7. unleashes its fury
8. demolishing; **C:** 1. The
opening paragraph states the
main idea from the beginning.
2. However 3. In trying to get
the wolves to help her 4. The
closing paragraph restates the
main idea. **D:** 1. Answers will
vary. 2. Answers will vary.

Unit 1
Narrative Paragraphs
pp. 6–9
1.D 2.A 3.A 4.A 5.C
6.B 7.A 8.C 9.B 10.A

Unit 2
Narrative Paragraphs
pp. 10–11
1.D 2.A 3.D 4.D 5.B
6.B 7.D 8.A

Unit 3
Narrative Paragraphs
pp. 12–15
1.B 2.C 3.A 4.B 5.A
6.C 7.B 8.A 9.A 10.B
11.C 12.C

Unit 4
Narrative Paragraphs
pp. 16–17
1.B 2.B 3.B 4.A 5.B
6.B

The First LAP
Language Activity Pages
pp. 18–19
A: 1. topic sentence
2. narrative paragraph
3. Dialogue
4. Staying on topic 5. closing
sentence; B: B; C: 1.C 2.F
3.H 4.J; D: 1. Answers will
vary. 2. Answers will vary.

Unit 5
Persuasive Paragraphs
pp. 20–21
1.C 2.A 3.C 4.A 5.A

Unit 6
Persuasive Paragraphs
pp. 22–25
1.A 2.C 3.B 4.C 5.A
6.A 7.C 8.D 9.B 10.D
11.D 12.C

Unit 7
Persuasive Paragraphs
pp. 26–29
1.A 2.A 3.B 4.B 5.A
6.B 7.A 8.B 9.A 10.A
11.A 12.A

Unit 8
Persuasive Paragraphs
pp. 30–31
1.C 2.A 3.B 4.A 5.B

The Second LAP
Language Activity Pages
pp. 32–33
A: 1.T 2.T 3.T 4.F 5.T 6.F
7.T 8.T; B: 1.C 2.A 3.B; C: B,
E; D: 1. Answers will vary.
2. Answers will vary.

Unit 9
Expository Paragraphs
pp. 34–35
1.C 2.A 3.C 4.B 5.A

Unit 10
Expository Paragraphs
pp. 36–39
1.D 2.B 3.A 4.D 5.A
6.B 7.A 8.D 9.C 10.C
11.B 12.C 13.B 14.A 15.D

Unit 11
Expository Paragraphs
pp. 40–41
1.B 2.C 3.A 4.C 5.A

Unit 12
Writing Paragraphs
pp. 42–45
1.B 2.C 3.C 4.B 5.C
6.A 7.A 8.A 9.B 10.B
11.D 12.A 13.D 14.C 15.D
16.A

The Third LAP
Language Activity Pages
pp. 46–47
A: 1.A 2.A 3.B 4.A; B: 1. a
focal point 2. left to right;
C: B, F; D: 1. Answers will
vary. 2. Answers will vary.

Unit 13
Writing Paragraphs
pp. 48–49
1.A 2.B 3.B 4.A 5.B
6.B 7.A 8.A 9.B 10.B

Unit 14
Writing Paragraphs
pp. 50–53
1.C 2.C 3.A 4.B 5.C
6.C 7.A 8.A 9.B 10.C
11.A 12.C 13.A 14.C 15.B
16.A

Unit 15
Writing Paragraphs
pp. 54–57
1.A 2.B 3.C 4.C 5.A
6.C 7.B 8.A 9.B 10.A
11.A 12.C 13.B 14.B 15.B
16.B 17.C 18.A 19.A 20.C

Unit 16
Writing Paragraphs
pp. 58–61
1.B 2.A 3.B 4.A 5.A
6.B 7.A 8.A 9.A 10.A
11.B 12.A 13.A 14.A 15.B
16.B

The Last LAP
Language Activity Pages
pp. 62–63
A: 1.B 2.A 3.C 4.A;
B: 1. Personification
2. Exaggeration 3. Simile
4. Transition Word
5. Metaphor; C: 1. first night
2. Because 3. before 4. Until
5. today 6. then 7. As soon as
8. so; D: 1. Answers will vary.
2. Answers will vary.

Unit 1
Getting Ideas
pp. 6–9

1.A   2.C   3.B   4.C   5.B
6.C   7.A   8.C   9.B   10.A
11.C 12.B 13.C 14.A

Unit 2
Planning
pp. 10–13

1.B   2.A   3.B   4.A   5.B
6.A   7.A   8.A   9.B   10.B
11.A 12.A 13.B 14.A

Unit 3
Planning
pp. 14–17

1.B   2.B   3.B   4.A   5.B
6.B   7.A   8.B   9.A   10.B
11.B 12.B 13.A 14.A 15.B

The First LAP
Language Activity Pages
pp. 18–19

A: 1. ideas 2. topic
3. planning 4. sense; **B:** 1.C
2.E 3.A 4.B 5.D; **C:** 1.B 2.D
3.E 4.G 5.H; **D:** 1. Answers
will vary. 2. Answers will vary.

Unit 4
Writing
pp. 20–25

1.A   2.B   3.B   4.A   5.B
6.B   7.A   8.A   9.B   10.B

The Second LAP
Language Activity Pages
pp. 26–27

A: 1. sentences 2. topic
3. details 4. closing; **B:** 1.A
2.B 3.E 4.F 5.H; **C:** 1.A 2.C
3.D 4.F; **D:** 1. Answers will
vary. 2. Answers will vary.

Unit 5
Revising
pp. 28–33

1.A   2.A   3.B   4.A   5.B
6.A   7.B   8.A   9.A   10.B
11.A 12.A 13.A 14.B 15.A
16.A 17.A 18.B

Unit 6
Revising
pp. 34–39

1.B   2.A   3.A   4.B   5.A
6.A   7.B   8.B   9.A   10.B
11.B 12.B 13.B 14.A 15.B
16.A 17.A 18.B 19.A 20.A
21.B 22.A

Unit 7
Revising
pp. 40–45

1.A   2.B   3.B   4.A   5.B
6.A   7.A   8.A   9.B   10.A
11.B 12.A 13.B 14.A 15.A
16.B 17.B 18.B

The Third LAP
Language Activity Pages
pp. 46–47

A: 1. revise 2. add 3. topic
4. proper 5. clear 6. order;
B: 1. Today 2. Grandpa
3. house 4. early; **C:** Thank
you for the ride on your boat.
I hope to go on it again. Please
write back soon. **D:** 1. Answers
will vary. 2. Answers will vary.

Unit 8
Checking
pp. 48–51

1.B   2.A   3.A   4.A   5.B
6.A   7.B   8.A   9.B   10.B
11.A 12.B 13.A 14.B 15.A
16.B 17.A 18.A 19.A 20.A
21.B 22.A

Unit 9
Checking
pp. 52–57

1.A   2.B   3.A   4.A   5.B
6.A   7.B   8.B   9.A   10.A
11.B 12.A 13.B 14.A 15.B
16.B 17.B 18.A 19.A 20.B
21.A 22.A 23.B 24.B 25.A

Unit 10
Sharing
pp. 58–61

1.B   2.A   3.B   4.A   5.B
6.E   7.D   8.C   9.B   10.A
11.B 12.A 13.C 14.E 15.D

The Last LAP
Language Activity Pages
pp. 62–63

A: 1. check 2. Capital
3. spelled 4. proofreading
5. Sharing; **B:** 1. On Sunday it
was not windy enough to fly
kites. 2. Rick and I hoped to
fly our kites. 3. We played
catch instead. 4. I cannot wait
to try again! 5. After Rick left I
went inside to eat. **C:** 1. friend
2. I 3. kites 4. Saturday
5. lots 6. color. 7. green
8. The 9. them. 10. orange;
D: 1. Answers will vary.
2. Answers will vary.

Unit 1
Getting Ideas
pp. 6–9

1.A 2.B 3.A 4.A 5.A
6.C 7.C 8.A 9.A 10.A
11.A 12.A 13.C 14.B

Unit 2
Planning
pp. 10–13

1.B 2.A 3.A 4.B 5.A
6.B 7.B 8.B

Unit 3
Planning
pp. 14–17

1.A 2.B 3.A 4.B 5.B
6.B 7.B 8.A 9.B 10.A

The First LAP
Language Activity Pages
pp. 18–19

A: 1.D 2.C; **B:** 1.A; **C:** 1. yes
2. no 3. yes 4. yes;
D: 1. Answers will vary.
2. Answers will vary.

Unit 4
Writing
pp. 20–25

1.A 2.B 3.B 4.A 5.B
6.A 7.A 8.A 9.A 10.A

The Second LAP
Language Activity Pages
pp. 26–27

A: 1.D; **B:** 1.B; **C:** 1.B;
D: 1. Answers will vary.
2. Answers will vary.

Unit 5
Revising
pp. 28–33

1.A 2.B 3.A 4.B 5.A
6.B 7.A 8.B 9.A 10.A
11.B 12.B 13.B 14.B 15.A
16.A

Unit 6
Revising
pp. 34–35

1.A 2.B 3.A 4.A 5.A
6.B 7.B 8.A 9.A 10.B

Unit 7
Revising
pp. 36–39

1.A 2.B 3.A 4.B 5.B
6.B 7.A 8.A 9.B 10.B
11.B 12.A

Unit 8
Revising
pp. 40–45

1.B 2.A 3.A 4.B 5.A
6.A 7.B 8.B 9.A 10.A
11.B 12.A 13.A 14.B 15.A
16.A 17.B 18.B

The Third LAP
Language Activity Pages
pp. 46–47

A: 1.C 2.A 3.A; **B:** 1. daisies
and mums 2. Miami Beach
3. ants; **C:** Sentences 3 and 6
do not belong. **D:** 1. Fill a pan
with water. When the water is
boiling, add the pasta. Cook
the pasta for 12 minutes. Drain
the water, and empty the
cooked pasta into a bowl.
2. Answers will vary.

Unit 9
Checking
pp. 48–51

1.B 2.B 3.A 4.A 5.B
6.A 7.B 8.A 9.A 10.B
11.B 12.A 13.A 14.B 15.A
16.B 17.B 18.A 19.A 20.B
21.A 22.B

Unit 10
Checking
pp. 52–57

1.B 2.A 3.B 4.B 5.A
6.A 7.B 8.B 9.A 10.B
11.A 12.A 13.B 14.A 15.B
16.B 17.A 18.B 19.A 20.B
21.A 22.B 23.A 24.A 25.A

Unit 11
Sharing
pp. 58–61

1.B 2.A 3.B 4.A 5.B
6.B 7.A 8.A 9.B 10.A
11.B 12.A 13.A 14.B 15.A
16.B

The Last LAP
Language Activity Pages
pp. 62–63

A: 1.A 2.B 3.A 4.B; **B:** 1.A
2.B 3.B; **C:** Polar bears are the
largest of all bears. They have
huge bodies covered with
thick white fur. Polar bears live
in freezing climates where the
land is covered with ice and
snow year round. These
animals swim in the icy
water to hunt for food.
D: 1. Answers will vary.
2. Answers will vary.

Unit 1
Getting Ideas
pp. 6–9

1.B 2.B 3.C 4.A 5.A
6.A 7.B 8.C 9.B 10.A
11.C 12.B 13.A 14.B 15.C
16.A 17.A 18.B

Unit 2
Planning
pp. 10–11

1.B 2.C 3.A 4.C 5.B
6.B

Unit 3
Planning
pp. 12–17

1.A 2.C 3.C 4.B 5.A
6.C 7.A 8.B 9.C 10.B
11.C 12.B 13.A 14.C 15.C
16.C

The First LAP
Language Activity Pages
pp. 18–19

A: 1.B 2.A; **B:** 1.B 2.A 3.B;
C: The following answers to
1–4 can be in any order: A, D,
E, H; **D:** 1. Answers will vary.
2. Answers will vary.

Unit 4
Drafting
pp. 20–23

1.A 2.B 3.C 4.A 5.A
6.A 7.C 8.A

Unit 5
Drafting
pp. 24–27

1.A 2.B 3.A 4.B 5.B
6.C

The Second LAP
Language Activity Pages
pp. 28–29

A: 1.A 2.C; **B:** 1.A 2.B; **C:** B;
D: 1. Answers will vary.
2. Answers will vary.

Unit 6
Revising
pp. 30–33

1.B 2.A 3.B 4.A 5.B
6.B 7.B 8.B 9.A 10.A
11.A 12.A 13.B 14.B

Unit 7
Revising
pp. 34–37

1.B 2.C 3.B 4.B 5.B
6.C 7.B 8.B 9.A 10.B
11.A 12.A 13.C 14.A 15.B
16.A 17.A 18.C 19.B 20.B

Unit 8
Revising
pp. 38–43

1.A 2.B 3.B 4.B 5.A
6.B 7.A 8.A 9.B 10.B
11.C 12.C 13.C 14.A 15.B
16.B 17.B 18.B 19.C 20.A

Unit 9
Revising
pp. 44–47

1.B 2.A 3.B 4.B 5.A
6.A 7.A 8.B 9.B 10.A

The Third LAP
Language Activity Pages
pp. 48–49

A: 1.A 2.C 3.B; **B:** 1.D 2.B;
C: If you want a good
sandwich, try a tomato and
mayonnaise sandwich. Here is
how you make one. First slice
a tomato into thin pieces.
Then get two slices of bread.
Cover one of the slices with
mayonnaise. If you want to,
you can even put the bread in
the toaster—before you spread
the mayonnaise, of course! Last
put the tomatoes on the other
slice of bread, and then put the
two together. Enjoy!
D: 1. Answers will vary.
2. Answers will vary.

Unit 10
Editing and Proofreading
pp. 50–53

1.B 2.C 3.A 4.B 5.A
6.C 7.A 8.B 9.A 10.C
11.B 12.A 13.C 14.B 15.B
16.C 17.A 18.C 19.B 20.A

Unit 11
Proofreading Marks
pp. 54–57

1.C 2.B 3.B 4.A 5.A
6.B 7.C 8.A 9.C 10.C
11.B 12.A 13.B 14.B 15.A

Unit 12
Publishing
pp. 58–61

1.A 2.B 3.B 4.B 5.D
6.E 7.F 8.A 9.C 10.B
11.D 12.E 13.A 14.B 15.C
16.F

The Last LAP
Language Activity Pages
pp. 62–63

A: 1.A 2.B 3.A; **B:** 1.A 2.B
3.B 4.A; **C:** Check student
work for correct proofreading
marks. New words to be
inserted are, in order: *huge,*
gases, hard, far away from,
millions, hot, day, heat;
D: 1. Answers will vary.
2. Answers will vary.

Unit 1
Getting Ideas
pp. 6–9

1.B	2.C	3.D	4.D	5.D
6.C	7.D	8.B	9.A	10.A
11.B	12.C	13.C	14.D	15.D
16.C	17.D	18.B	19.B	20.A

Unit 2
Planning
pp. 10–15

1.B	2.C	3.C	4.B	5.A
6.C	7.B	8.C	9.C	10.C
11.A	12.A	13.B	14.A	15.C

The First LAP
Language Activity Pages
pp. 16–17

A: 1.C 2.A 3.D; **B:** 1.A 2.A 3.A 4.B; **C:** 1.B 2.B 3.A; **D:** 1. Answers will vary. 2. Answers will vary.

Unit 3
Drafting
pp. 18–21

1.A	2.B	3.B	4.A

Unit 4
Drafting
pp. 22–25

1.A	2.B	3.A	4.B

The Second LAP
Language Activity Pages
pp. 26–27

A: 1.B 2.C 3.C; **B:** 1.B; **C:** 1.C; **D:** 1. Answers will vary. 2. Answers will vary.

Unit 5
Revising
pp. 28–31

1.C	2.B	3.B	4.C	5.B
6.B	7.C	8.B		

Unit 6
Revising
pp. 32–35

1.C	2.A	3.C	4.A	5.C
6.B	7.A	8.C	9.C	

Unit 7
Revising
pp. 36–37

1.B	2.A	3.B	4.B	5.A

Unit 8
Revising
pp. 38–43

1.A	2.A	3.A	4.A	5.A
6.B	7.B	8.B	9.A	10.A

Unit 9
Revising
pp. 44–47

1.B	2.B	3.A	4.B	5.A
6.B	7.A	8.A	9.A	10.B
11.B	12.A	13.B	14.B	15.A
16.B	17.C	18.A	19.A	20.B
21.C	22.C	23.C	24.A	25.B
26.B	27.C	28.B		

The Third LAP
Language Activity Pages
pp. 48–49

A: 1.B 2.D; **B:** 1.B 2.D 3.C 4.A; **C:** 1. Yes 2. Yes 3. No; **D:** 1. Answers will vary. 2. Answers will vary.

Unit 10
Editing/Proofreading
pp. 50–53

1.B	2.C	3.A	4.C	5.A
6.C	7.C	8.B	9.B	10.A
11.B	12.C	13.B	14.C	15.B
16.A	17.C	18.B	19.A	20.B
21.A	22.B	23.C	24.B	25.C

Unit 11
Proofreading Marks
pp. 54–57

1.A	2.B	3.C	4.A	5.C
6.B	7.B	8.B	9.C	10.B
11.A	12.C			

Unit 12
Publishing
pp. 58–61

1.B	2.A	3.A	4.B	5.C
6.D	7.F	8.A	9.B	10.E
11.D	12.F	13.A	14.B	15.C
16.E				

The Last LAP
Language Activity Pages
pp. 62–63

A: 1.C 2.D; **B:** Check student work for correct proofreading marks. 1. the *l* in *leakey* should be underlined three times 2. a close-up symbol should be between *be* and *fore* 3. the *l* in *london* should be underlined three times, a comma and a caret symbol should be between *london* and *england*, the *e* in *england* should be underlined three times 4. *then* should have a delete symbol drawn through it, *than* and a caret symbol should be set after *then* 5. a lowercase slash symbol should be drawn through the *p* in *Paintings* 6. the *s* in *stoneAge* should be underlined three times, the space symbol and a caret symbol should be between the *e* and *A* in *stoneAge* **C:** Check student work for correct proofreading marks. New words to be inserted are, in order: *huge, Earth, millions, reptiles, tough, aggressive, jaws, sharp, gentle;* **D:** 1. Answers will vary. 2. Answers will vary.

Unit 1
Getting Ideas
pp. 6–9

1.A	2.D	3.D	4.C	5.D
6.B	7.A	8.C	9.C	10.D
11.A	12.A	13.C	14.B	15.A
16.C	17.A	18.B	19.B	20.C

Unit 2
Planning
pp. 10–15

1.B	2.A	3.C	4.A	5.A
6.B	7.C	8.A	9.C	10.C
11.B	12.A	13.B	14.C	15.B
16.B	17.A	18.A	19.B	20.C
21.B	22.B	23.A	24.C	25.B
26.A	27.C	28.A	29.A	30.B
31.B	32.C			

Unit 3
Drafting
pp. 16–19

1.A	2.B	3.B	4.A	5.B

Unit 4
Drafting
pp. 20–23

1.A	2.B	3.B	4.A	5.B

The First LAP
Language Activity Pages
pp. 24–25

A: 1.F 2.T 3.F 4.T 5.F 6.T 7.T 8.F 9.T 10.F 11.F 12.T;
B: 1.E 2.A 3.C 4.D 5.B;
C: 1.B 2.A 3.B 4.A 5.A;
D: 1. Answers will vary.
2. Answers will vary.

Unit 5
Revising
pp. 26–31

1.C	2.C	3.A	4.C	5.B
6.A	7.A	8.C	9.B	10.B
11.C	12.C	13.A	14.A	15.B
16.C	17.A	18.B	19.B	20.A
21.C	22.A	23.B	24.B	25.C

Unit 6
Revising
pp. 32–35

1.A	2.B	3.B	4.A	5.A
6.A	7.B	8.B	9.A	10.A

The Second LAP
Language Activity Pages
pp. 36–37

A: 1.F 2.T 3.T 4.F 5.T 6.T 7.F 8.F 9.F 10.T; **B:** 1.D 2.F 3.A 4.E 5.C 6.B; **C:** 1.B 2.F 3.H 4.M; **D:** 1. Answers will vary. 2. Answers will vary.

Unit 7
Revising
pp. 38–41

1.C	2.B	3.A	4.C	5.B
6.B	7.C	8.C	9.A	10.B
11.A	12.C	13.B	14.C	

Unit 8
Revising
pp. 42–45

1.A	2.C	3.A	4.A	5.C
6.B	7.B	8.A	9.A	10.A
11.B	12.A	13.B	14.B	15.A
16.B	17.B	18.A	19.B	20.A
21.A	22.A			

Unit 9
Revising
pp. 46–49

1.C	2.B	3.B	4.A	5.C
6.A	7.C	8.A	9.A	10.B
11.B	12.A	13.A	14.B	15.A
16.A				

The Third LAP
Language Activity Pages
pp. 50–51

A: 1.F 2.F 3.F 4.T 5.T 6.T 7.F 8.T 9.F 10.T;
B: 1. friendly 2. instruments 3. strums 4. beats 5. padded 6. music; **C:** 1.A 2.D 3.H 4.K;
D: 1. Answers will vary.
2. Answers will vary.

Unit 10
Editing/Proofreading
pp. 52–55

1.B	2.C	3.C	4.A	5.C
6.C	7.A	8.C	9.C	10.B
11.A	12.A	13.C	14.B	15.C
16.C	17.A	18.B	19.B	20.C
21.C	22.C	23.B	24.C	25.A
26.B	27.A	28.C		

Unit 11
Editing/Proofreading
pp. 56–59

1.A	2.B	3.C	4.C	5.B
6.A	7.B	8.C	9.A	10.B
11.C	12.C	13.A	14.B	15.A
16.A	17.C	18.A	19.B	20.C

Unit 12
Publishing
pp. 60–61

1.C	2.G	3.D	4.A	5.H
6.B	7.E	8.F	9.D	10.H
11.A	12.B	13.C	14.F	15.G
16.E	17.I	18.K	19.J	20.L

The Last LAP
Language Activity Pages
pp. 62–63

A: 1.T 2.F 3.F 4.T 5.F 6.T 7.T 8.F 9.T 10.T; **B:** 1.B 2.B 3.A 4.A 5.A 6.B 7.A 8.A;
C: 1.A 2.C 3.E 4.I 5.K 6.O;
D: 1. Answers will vary.
2. Answers will vary.

Unit 1
Getting Ideas
pp. 6–9

1.A	2.B	3.C	4.D	5.B
6.C	7.A	8.B	9.C	10.D
11.A	12.C	13.B	14.C	15.C
16.A	17.C	18.B	19.A	20.C
21.B	22.C	23.A	24.B	

Unit 2
Planning
pp. 10–15

1.C	2.A	3.B	4.A	5.C
6.A	7.B	8.A	9.C	10.C
11.B	12.C	13.B	14.A	15.B
16.A	17.A	18.C	19.B	20.A
21.C	22.B	23.B	24.A	25.C
26.C	27.A	28.B	29.C	30.A
31.C	32.A			

Unit 3
Drafting
pp. 16–19

1.B	2.A	3.A	4.B

Unit 4
Drafting
pp. 20–23

1.B	2.B	3.A

The First LAP
Language Activity Pages
pp. 24–25

A: 1.C 2.B 3.A 4.C 5.A;
B: 1.C 2.D 3.E 4.B 5.A;
C: 1.B 2.B 3.B 4.A;
D: 1. Answers will vary.
2. Answers will vary.

Unit 5
Revising
pp. 26–31

1.A	2.B	3.B	4.A	5.C
6.B	7.A	8.C	9.A	10.B
11.A	12.B	13.C	14.B	15.B
16.C	17.A	18.A	19.C	20.A

Unit 6
Revising
pp. 32–35

1.B	2.A	3.B	4.B	5.B
6.A	7.A	8.A	9.B	10.A

The Second LAP
Language Activity Pages
pp. 36–37

A: 1.F 2.F 3.F 4.F 5.F 6.F
7.T 8.F; **B:** 1.F 2.G 3.C 4.B
5.E 6.A 7.D; **C:** 1.C 2.E 3.G;
D: 1. Answers will vary.
2. Answers will vary.

Unit 7
Revising
pp. 38–41

1.B	2.C	3.A	4.C	5.B
6.A	7.B	8.A	9.C	10.C
11.B	12.A	13.A	14.C	

Unit 8
Revising
pp. 42–45

1.B	2.B	3.A	4.C	5.C
6.A	7.C	8.B	9.A	10.C
11.C	12.A	13.B	14.C	15.B
16.C	17.B	18.B	19.B	20.C
21.A	22.B	23.A	24.C	

Unit 9
Revising
pp. 46–49

1.C	2.A	3.B	4.C	5.B
6.A	7.C	8.B	9.C	10.B
11.C	12.B	13.A	14.C	

The Third LAP
Language Activity Pages
pp. 50–51

A: 1.B 2.C 3.A 4.C; **B:** 1.B
2.A 3.E 4.D 5.C; **C:** 1.B 2.D
3.G 4.J; **D:** 1. Answers will
vary. 2. Answers will vary.

Unit 10
Editing/Proofreading
pp. 52–55

1.B	2.C	3.A	4.B	5.A
6.C	7.B	8.C	9.A	10.A
11.A	12.A	13.A	14.B	15.C
16.B	17.B	18.C	19.A	20.C
21.B	22.C			

Unit 11
Editing/Proofreading
pp. 56–59

1.B	2.C	3.B	4.A	5.C
6.C	7.B	8.B	9.A	10.C

Unit 12
Publishing
pp. 60–61

1.C	2.G	3.H	4.A	5.B
6.E	7.F	8.D	9.C	10.F
11.G	12.B	13.D	14.H	15.E
16.A				

The Last LAP
Language Activity Pages
pp. 62–63

A: 1.F 2.F 3.T 4.F 5.F 6.F
7.T 8.T; **B:** 1.A 2.B 3.A 4.B
5.A 6.B 7.A 8.A 9.B 10.B;
C: 1. Yes 2. Yes 3. When the
president of the United States,
Woodrow Wilson, learned of
Douglass's historic discovery,
he designated the area a
national monument. 4. Yes
5. Over time, as layers of gravel
and sand were deposited, the
bones of dinosaurs hardened
into fossils within the rock
layers. 6. The remains of
eleven species of dinosaurs
have been found in the quarry.
7. One of those species is the
plant-eating saurapod, the
largest of all animals ever to
walk Earth. 8. Scientists at the
National Park Service have
spent many years carefully
chipping away rock fragments
from one wall of the quarry to
reveal a rock layer that
includes more than 1,500
dinosaur bones. **D:** 1. Answers
will vary. 2. Answers will vary.

Unit 1
Getting Ideas
pp. 6–9

1.B　2.D　3.C　4.C　5.A
6.B　7.A　8.D　9.C　10.D
11.A　12.B　13.D　14.B　15.B
16.C　17.A　18.C　19.C　20.B
21.A　22.D

Unit 2
Planning
pp. 10–11

1.C　2.B　3.A　4.C　5.C
6.A

Unit 3
Planning
pp. 12–17

1.A　2.C　3.C　4.B　5.C
6.A　7.B　8.B　9.A　10.C
11.B　12.C　13.C　14.A　15.C
16.A　17.A　18.B　19.C　20.A
21.B　22.A　23.C　24.B　25.B
26.C　27.A　28.A

The First LAP
Language Activity Pages
pp. 18–19

A: 1.A　2.A　3.B　4.B　5.C;
B: 1.C　2.E　3.D　4.B　5.A;
C: 1.A　2.C; **D:** 1. Answers will vary. 2. Answers will vary.

Unit 4
Drafting
pp. 20–21

1.A　2.A

Unit 5
Drafting
pp. 22–25

1.A　2.B

Unit 6
Revising
pp. 26–31

1.C　2.B　3.B　4.C　5.A
6.A　7.C　8.B　9.A　10.B
11.B　12.C　13.B　14.A　15.B
16.B

The Second LAP
Language Activity Pages
pp. 32–33

A: 1.T　2.F　3.T　4.T　5.F　6.F;
B: 1. The State of Georgia
2. State Symbols of Georgia
3.-6. (can be in any order):
Tree: Live Oak, Flower: Cherokee Rose, Song: "Georgia on My Mind", Bird: Brown Thrasher; **C:** 1.C　2.D　3.G　4.I　5.K; **D:** 1. Answers will vary. 2. Answers will vary.

Unit 7
Revising
pp. 34–37

1.C　2.B　3.A　4.B　5.A

Unit 8
Revising
pp. 38–41

1.B　2.C　3.A　4.C　5.B
6.B　7.C　8.A　9.B　10.A

Unit 9
Revising
pp. 42–47

1.B　2.C　3.B　4.A　5.C
6.A　7.A　8.C　9.B　10.B
11.C　12.B　13.B　14.B　15.C
16.A　17.C　18.B

The Third LAP
Language Activity Pages
pp. 48–49

A: 1.B　2.C　3.C　4.A;
B: 1. clatter 2. a flashlight and a map 3. bursting with
4. eluded 5. pitch-black; **C:** 1.B
2.E　3.G　4.L; **D:** 1. Answers will vary. 2. Answers will vary.

Unit 10
Editing and Proofreading
pp. 50–53

1.C　2.B　3.B　4.A　5.C
6.C　7.B　8.C　9.B　10.C
11.B　12.C　13.A　14.A　15.B
16.C　17.C　18.A

Unit 11
Editing and Proofreading
pp. 54–59

1.B　2.A　3.C　4.B　5.C
6.A　7.B　8.C　9.C　10.A
11.B　12.A　13.C　14.B

Unit 12
Publishing
pp. 60–61

1.C　2.G　3.E　4.A　5.B
6.H　7.F　8.D　9.C　10.F
11.G　12.B　13.D　14.H　15.E
16.A

The Last LAP
Language Activity Pages
pp. 62–63

A: 1.F　2.F　3.T　4.F　5.T　6.T
7.F　8.T; **B:** 1.A　2.A　3.B　4.A
5.B　6.A　7.B　8.A　9.A　10.A;
C: 1. Yes 2. He bought the Louisiana Territory, which stretched along the Mississippi River from the border of Canada and Mexico and doubled the size of the United States. 3. Jefferson strongly encouraged American expansion westward. 4. One of the ways he did this was by authorizing Meriwether Lewis and William Clark to undertake a large-scale exploration of the new territory. 5. Yes 6. The expedition took Lewis and Clark more than two years to complete. 7. However, they successfully led a group of men from Missouri to the Pacific and back again, traveling about 8,000 miles through dangerous territories by canoe, by horseback, and on foot. 8. Yes 9. Upon their return to Washington, the two explorers were greeted as heroes. 10. Yes; **D:** 1. Answers will vary. 2. Answers will vary.

Unit 1

Getting Ideas
pp. 6–9

1.C 2.D 3.A 4.D 5.C
6.A 7.D 8.C 9.D 10.C
11.A 12.C 13.C 14.D 15.A
16.B 17.B 18.A 19.D 20.A
21.C 22.C

Unit 2

Planning
pp. 10–15

1.B 2.C 3.B 4.A 5.C
6.A 7.B 8.C 9.C 10.A
11.C 12.A 13.B 14.D 15.B
16.A 17.C 18.B 19.A 20.C

The First LAP

Language Activity Pages
pp. 16–17

A: 1.T 2.F 3.T 4.F 5.T;
B: 1.B 2.A 3.B 4.A; **C:** 1.B
2.A 3.A; **D:** 1. Answers will
vary. 2. Answers will vary.

Unit 3

Drafting
pp. 18–23

1.B 2.A 3.A 4.A

Unit 4

Revising
pp. 24–29

1.B 2.A 3.C 4.B 5.C
6.C 7.A 8.B 9.C 10.A
11.B 12.A 13.C 14.A 15.A

Unit 5

Revising
pp. 30–33

1.B 2.A 3.C 4.B 5.A
6.B 7.B 8.A

The Second LAP

Language Activity Pages
pp. 34–35

A: 1.T 2.T 3.F 4.F 5.F 6.T;
B: E, D, C, A, B; **C:** 1.D 2.F
3.H 4.J; **D:** 1. Answers will
vary. 2. Answers will vary.

Unit 6

Revising
pp. 36–39

1.C 2.B 3.A 4.A

Unit 7

Revising
pp. 40–41

1.B 2.B

Unit 8

Revising
pp. 42–45

1.A 2.B 3.A 4.A 5.C
6.A 7.B 8.C 9.C 10.A
11.B 12.A

Unit 9

Revising
pp. 46–49

1.B 2.C 3.A 4.A 5.B
6.C 7.A 8.B 9.C 10.B
11.B 12.C 13.A 14.C 15.B

The Third LAP

Language Activity Pages
pp. 50–51

A: 1.C 2.A 3.B 4.A;
B: 1. caught a glimpse of
2. bitter orange skin 3. rumble
4. beamed 5. honking; **C:** 1.B
2.D 3.G 4.J; **D:** 1. Answers will
vary. 2. Answers will vary.

Unit 10

Editing and Proofreading
pp. 52–55

1.C 2.B 3.B 4.C 5.A
6.C 7.A 8.C 9.B 10.B
11.B 12.B 13.C 14.B 15.A
16.A 17.C 18.B 19.B 20.A

Unit 11

Editing and Proofreading
pp. 56–59

1.C 2.C 3.B 4.A 5.C
6.B 7.B 8.C

Unit 12

Publishing
pp. 60–61

1.C 2.F 3.G 4.B 5.D
6.H 7.E 8.A 9.C 10.J
11.I 12.A 13.H 14.E 15.F
16.D 17.B 18.G

The Last LAP

Language Activity Pages
pp. 62–63

A: 1.F 2.T 3.T 4.F 5.T 6.F;
B: 1.B 2.A 3.A 4.B 5.A 6.B
7.A 8.A; **C:** 1. B/For five years,
General Benedict Arnold
served heroically as a
commander of Patriot troops.
2. D/At the same time, he was
vain and arrogant, and he often
maneuvered his way into
military situations so that he
could seize the glory of a
victory before another general
did. 3. F/Perhaps all of these
factors partly explain why such
an accomplished military
leader would betray his
compatriots for 20,000 pounds
in silver, worth roughly two
million dollars today.
4. H/Arnold never explained
his motivation for his
treasonous actions.
D: 1. Answers will vary.
2. Answers will vary.

Unit 1
Parts of a Book
pp. 6–9

1.C	2.A	3.B	4.A	5.A
6.C	7.B	8.B	9.A	10.C

Unit 2
Using Books
pp. 10–15

1.B	2.A	3.C	4.A	5.C
6.B	7.A	8.B	9.C	10.A
11.C	12.A	13.C	14.C	15.B
16.C	17.C	18.B	19.C	20.B
21.A	22.C	23.A	24.A	

The First LAP
Language Activity Pages
pp. 16–17

A: 1. author 2. title
3. illustrator 4. chapters;
B: 1.B 2.D 3.C 4.A;
C: *Harvey Goes to School,*
Jane Cooke, Stan Smith;
D: 1. Answers will vary.
2. Answers will vary.

Unit 3
Using a Table of Contents: Chapters
pp. 18–23

1.C	2.B	3.A	4.A	5.C
6.C	7.A	8.C	9.C	10.A
11.A	12.B	13.A	14.C	15.A
16.B	17.C	18.B	19.A	20.C
21.C	22.A	23.B	24.C	

Unit 4
Using a Table of Contents: Page Numbers
pp. 24–29

1.C	2.A	3.B	4.A	5.C
6.B	7.A	8.C	9.B	10.C
11.A	12.B	13.C	14.A	15.C
16.B	17.C	18.A	19.B	20.A
21.C	22.A	23.C	24.A	25.B

The Second LAP
Language Activity Pages
pp. 30–31

A: 1. table of contents
2. chapter 3. page number;
B: 1. 4 2. 13 3. 26 4. 50
5. 67; **C:** 1. three 2. page 50
3. Soups 4. No 5. Yes 6. page
31; **D:** 1. Answers will vary.
2. Answers will vary.

Unit 5
Using an Encyclopedia
pp. 32–33

1.B	2.B	3.A	4.C	5.A
6.C	7.C	8.A	9.A	10.B

Unit 6
Using an Encyclopedia
pp. 34–37

1.B	2.C	3.A	4.B	5.B
6.A	7.A	8.C	9.B	10.C
11.A	12.A	13.B	14.C	15.B
16.A	17.B	18.C	19.A	20.A
21.B	22.B	23.C	24.B	25.B
26.C	27.A	28.A		

Unit 7
Reading a Chart
pp. 38–41

1.A	2.B	3.B	4.B	5.A
6.A	7.B	8.B	9.A	10.A
11.B	12.B	13.A	14.B	15.B
16.B	17.A	18.B	19.A	20.B

The Third LAP
Language Activity Pages
pp. 42–43

A: 1. set 2. volume 3. Letters
4. last 5. Charts; **B:** 1.D 2.B
3.E 4.A 5.C; **C:** 1. two
2. three 3. Miss Hine 4. 8:30
A.M.; **D:** 1. Answers will vary.
2. Answers will vary.

Unit 8
Taking a Survey
pp. 44–49

1.B	2.A	3.A	4.A	5.B
6.C	7.C	8.A	9.B	10.A
11.C	12.B	13.B	14.B	15.C
16.C	17.B	18.B	19.C	20.A
21.C	22.B	23.B	24.B	25.B
26.A	27.C	28.C	29.A	30.B

Unit 9
Finding Information
pp. 50–55

1.C	2.A	3.B	4.B	5.C
6.A	7.B	8.C	9.A	10.C
11.B	12.A	13.A	14.B	15.B
16.C				

Unit 10
Taking Notes
pp. 56–61

1.B	2.C	3.A	4.B	5.A
6.C	7.B	8.C	9.A	10.B
11.B	12.C	13.B	14.C	

The Last LAP
Language Activity Pages
pp. 62–63

A: 1. sentences 2. Notes
3. Surveys 4. chart; **B:** 1.C 2.A
3.D 4.E 5.B; **C:** 1. Things in
Your Room 2. two 3. three
4. two 5. More people have a
desk. **D:** 1. Answers will vary.
2. Answers will vary.

Unit 1
Using a Library
pp. 6–9

1.B 2.A 3.C 4.A 5.C
6.B 7.C 8.B 9.B 10.C
11.A 12.C 13.B 14.A 15.B
16.A

Unit 2
Using a Table of Contents
pp. 10–13

1.C 2.C 3.C 4.D 5.A
6.D 7.C 8.A 9.B 10.C
11.A 12.C 13.B 14.C

The First LAP
Language Activity Pages
pp. 14–15

A: 1.C 2.A 3.B 4.D;
B: 1. page 9 2. page 3
3. page 5; **C:** 1.B 2.D 3.C
4.A; **D:** 1. Answers will vary.
2. Answers will vary.

Unit 3
Using an Encyclopedia
pp. 16–17

1.C 2.D 3.B 4.D 5.C
6.C

Unit 4
Key Word Searching
pp. 18–21

1.C 2.B 3.C 4.C 5.A
6.B 7.B 8.C 9.A 10.B
11.A 12.B 13.A 14.B 15.A
16.A 17.A 18.A

Unit 5
Evaluating a Web Site
pp. 22–25

1.A 2.B 3.A 4.B 5.B
6.A 7.A 8.A 9.A 10.B
11.A 12.B 13.A 14.A 15.B
16.A 17.A 18.B 19.A 20.A

The Second LAP
Language Activity Pages
pp. 26–27

A: 1.C 2.C; **B:** 1.A 2.B; **C:** 1.B
2.B 3.A; **D:** 1. Answers will
vary. 2. Answers will vary.

Unit 6
Reading a Chart
pp. 28–31

1.B 2.C 3.C 4.B 5.B
6.A 7.C 8.C 9.B 10.A

Unit 7
Taking a Survey
pp. 32–35

1.B 2.A 3.C 4.D 5.A
6.C 7.B 8.D 9.B 10.A
11.B 12.D 13.A 14.C 15.B
16.D

Unit 8
Reading a Diagram
pp. 36–39

1.C 2.B 3.B 4.B 5.C
6.A 7.C 8.B 9.C 10.A
11.C 12.A 13.B 14.A 15.C

The Third LAP
Language Activity Pages
pp. 40–41

A: 1.B 2.A; **B:** 1.C 2.A; **C:** 1.B
2.A; **D:** 1. Answers will vary.
2. Answers will vary.

Unit 9
Getting Ideas
pp. 42–45

1.A 2.B 3.B 4.B 5.A
6.B 7.B 8.A 9.A 10.B
11.B 12.A 13.B 14.B 15.A
16.A 17.A 18.A 19.A 20.B

Unit 10
Asking Questions
pp. 46–49

1.B 2.B 3.A 4.B 5.A
6.B 7.B 8.B 9.A 10.B
11.B 12.A 13.B 14.B 15.A

Unit 11
Making a Research Statement
pp. 50–51

1.B 2.B 3.A 4.B 5.B
6.A 7.A 8.A 9.B 10.A

Unit 12
Finding Information
pp. 52–55

1.A 2.B 3.B 4.A 5.A
6.A 7.B 8.A 9.A 10.A
11.A 12.A 13.B 14.A

Unit 13
Taking Notes
pp. 56–61

1.B 2.B 3.B 4.A 5.C
6.B 7.C 8.A 9.C 10.B

The Last LAP
Language Activity Pages
pp. 62–63

A: 1.A 2.C 3.A; **B:** 1.B 2.A;
C: 1.A 2.B 3.B; **D:** 1. Answers
will vary. 2. Answers will vary.

Unit 1
Using a Library
pp. 6–9

1.C 2.C 3.B 4.A 5.C
6.A 7.B 8.B 9.A 10.C
11.B 12.A 13.C 14.A 15.B
16.B 17.C 18.B 19.C 20.A
21.A 22.B

Unit 2
Using a Table of Contents
pp. 10–11

1.B 2.A 3.A 4.C 5.A
6.B 7.C 8.A

Unit 3
Using an Index
pp. 12–13

1.A 2.C 3.A 4.C 5.B
6.B 7.C 8.A 9.B 10.B

The First LAP
Language Activity Pages
pp. 14–15

A: 1.B 2.B 3.A; **B:** 1.B 2.A
3.C; **C:** 1.A 2.C 3.D 4.B;
D: 1. Answers will vary.
2. Answers will vary.

Unit 4
Using an Encyclopedia
pp. 16–17

1.D 2.A 3.B 4.C 5.D
6.D 7.B 8.A

Unit 5
Key Word Searching
pp. 18–21

1.C 2.A 3.C 4.C 5.A
6.B 7.C 8.A 9.B 10.C
11.C 12.B 13.B 14.A 15.A
16.A 17.A 18.B 19.A 20.B
21.A 22.B 23.A 24.A

Unit 6
Evaluating a Web Site
pp. 22–25

1.A 2.A 3.B 4.A 5.B
6.B 7.A 8.A 9.A 10.B
11.B 12.A 13.B 14.B 15.B
16.B 17.A 18.B 19.A 20.B
21.A 22.B 23.A 24.A 25.A
26.A

The Second LAP
Language Activity Pages
pp. 26–27

A: 1.C 2.A 3.B; **B:** 1.A 2.B
3.B; **C:** 1.A 2.B 3.A;
D: 1. Answers will vary.
2. Answers will vary.

Unit 7
Reading a Chart
pp. 28–31

1.A 2.B 3.C 4.B 5.D
6.A 7.B 8.A 9.B 10.D
11.B 12.A 13.D 14.C 15.B
16.D 17.C 18.C

Unit 8
Taking a Survey
pp. 32–35

1.D 2.C 3.A 4.B 5.B
6.A 7.B 8.A 9.A 10.B
11.C 12.B 13.A 14.C 15.B
16.A

Unit 9
Reading a Diagram
pp. 36–39

1.C 2.A 3.D 4.A 5.B
6.C 7.D 8.D 9.C 10.D
11.A 12.D 13.A 14.C 15.D
16.B 17.B 18.D

The Third LAP
Language Activity Pages
pp. 40–41

A: 1.A 2.B 3.A; **B:** 1.A 2.C;
C: 1.A 2.B; **D:** 1. Answers will
vary. 2. Answers will vary.

Unit 10
Getting Ideas
pp. 42–45

1.A 2.B 3.C 4.B 5.C
6.A 7.C 8.A 9.B 10.C
11.A 12.C 13.B 14.C 15.C
16.A 17.B 18.B 19.A 20.B

Unit 11
Asking Questions
pp. 46–49

1.A 2.B 3.B 4.A 5.A
6.B 7.B 8.A 9.A 10.A
11.B 12.A 13.B 14.A 15.B
16.B 17.A 18.B 19.A 20.A
21.B 22.A 23.A 24.B 25.A
26.A 27.B 28.A 29.B 30.B

Unit 12
Making a Research Statement
pp. 50–53

1.B 2.C 3.A 4.B 5.A
6.B 7.C 8.C 9.A 10.B
11.B 12.B 13.A 14.C 15.A
16.C 17.B 18.A 19.C 20.B

Unit 13
Finding Information
pp. 54–57

1.A 2.C 3.B 4.C 5.B
6.C 7.B 8.B 9.A 10.B
11.A 12.B 13.A 14.C 15.A
16.A 17.C 18.C

Unit 14
Evaluating Information
pp. 58–61

1.C 2.B 3.C 4.A 5.B
6.C 7.A 8.B 9.B 10.A
11.C 12.C

The Last LAP
Language Activity Pages
pp. 62–63

A: 1.C 2.B 3.C; **B:** 1.B 2.A;
C: 1.A 2.B 3.A 4.B 5.A;
D: 1. Answers will vary.
2. Answers will vary.

Unit 1
Using a Table of Contents
pp. 6–7

1.B 2.C 3.C 4.C 5.A
6.C 7.D 8.A

Unit 2
Using an Index
pp. 8–9

1.D 2.C 3.D 4.A 5.B
6.A 7.C 8.D 9.B 10.A

Unit 3
Finding Magazine and Newspaper Articles
pp. 10–13

1.C 2.A 3.A 4.B 5.C
6.B 7.D 8.C 9.A 10.B
11.C 12.D 13.C 14.B 15.A
16.A 17.B 18.D 19.B 20.B
21.A 22.C 23.C 24.B 25.D
26.B 27.C 28.B

The First LAP
Language Activity Pages
pp. 14–15

A: 1.C 2.A 3.B; **B:** 1.B 2.C
3.A; **C:** 1.B 2.B; **D:** 1. Answers
will vary. 2. Answers will vary.

Unit 4
Key Word Searching
pp. 16–19

1.A 2.A 3.C 4.B 5.C
6.A 7.C 8.B 9.A 10.A
11.B 12.B 13.A 14.B 15.A
16.A 17.B 18.A 19.A 20.B
21.B 22.A 23.B 24.A 25.B
26.B

Unit 5
Evaluating a Web Site
pp. 20–23

1.C 2.A 3.B 4.C 5.B
6.A 7.B 8.C 9.C 10.A
11.B 12.C 13.C 14.A 15.C
16.C

The Second LAP
Language Activity Pages
pp. 24–25

A: 1.C 2.C 3.B; **B:** 1.A 2.B;
C: 1.B 2.A; **D:** 1. Answers will
vary. 2. Answers will vary.

Unit 6
Getting Ideas
pp. 26–27

1.D 2.C 3.D 4.B 5.C
6.C 7.D 8.C 9.C 10.B

Unit 7
Asking Questions
pp. 28–29

1.D 2.B 3.C 4.A 5.C
6.D 7.C 8.A 9.A 10.C

Unit 8
Making a Research Statement
pp. 30–33

1.B 2.C 3.A 4.B 5.B
6.A 7.C 8.A 9.A 10.B
11.B 12.C 13.C 14.C 15.A
16.C 17.B 18.C 19.B 20.B
21.C 22.A 23.C 24.A 25.B
26.C

Unit 9
Finding Information
pp. 34–35

1.A 2.B 3.C 4.C 5.A
6.A 7.B 8.C 9.A 10.A
11.A 12.B 13.B 14.A 15.C
16.B

Unit 10
Comparing Information across Sources
pp. 36–39

1.B 2.A 3.C 4.B 5.C
6.A

The Third LAP
Language Activity Pages
pp. 40–41

A: 1.C 2.A 3.A; **B:** 1.C 2.B;
C: 1.C 2.A 3.A; **D:** 1. Answers
will vary. 2. Answers will vary.

Unit 11
Evaluating Information
pp. 42–45

1.C 2.B 3.C 4.A 5.B
6.C 7.B 8.B 9.A 10.B
11.A 12.C 13.C 14.A 15.C
16.B

Unit 12
Taking Notes
pp. 46–47

1.B 2.A 3.B 4.D

Unit 13
Summarizing
pp. 48–51

1.A 2.B 3.C 4.A 5.C
6.B 7.C 8.A

Unit 14
Writing an Outline
pp. 52–55

1.C 2.D 3.B 4.C 5.D
6.A 7.C 8.D 9.B 10.B
11.C 12.D 13.A 14.B

Unit 15
Writing Paragraphs
pp. 56–59

1.C 2.A 3.B 4.B 5.C
6.A 7.B 8.B

Unit 16
Writing a Bibliography
pp. 60–61

1.D 2.B 3.C 4.B

The Last LAP
Language Activity Pages
pp. 62–63

A: 1.C 2.A 3.B 4.A; **B:** B;
C: C; **D:** 1. Answers will vary.
2. Answers will vary.

Unit 1
Using a Table of Contents and an Index
pp. 6–7

1.C	2.D	3.D	4.B	5.C
6.D	7.B	8.A	9.B	10.C

Unit 2
Using an Encyclopedia
pp. 8–9

1.D	2.A	3.B	4.C	5.D
6.D	7.B	8.B	9.A	10.C

Unit 3
Finding Magazine and Newspaper Articles
pp. 10–13

1.D	2.C	3.C	4.B	5.A
6.C	7.C	8.B	9.C	10.A
11.C	12.D	13.A	14.A	15.B

The First LAP
Language Activity Pages
pp. 14–15

A: 1.C 2.C 3.A; **B:** 1.C 2.A;
C: A; **D:** 1. Answers will vary.
2. Answers will vary.

Unit 4
Key Word Searching
pp. 16–17

1.A	2.A	3.B	4.C	5.A
6.B	7.A	8.D	9.B	10.C

Unit 5
Evaluating a Web Site
pp. 18–19

1.A	2.B	3.B	4.A	5.A
6.A	7.A	8.B	9.A	10.A
11.A	12.A	13.B	14.A	15.A

Unit 6
Reading Graphs and Charts
pp. 20–23

1.D	2.B	3.C	4.A	5.C
6.B	7.C	8.D	9.D	10.B
11.B	12.C	13.A	14.B	15.C
16.A				

The Second LAP
Language Activity Pages
pp. 24–25

A: 1.B 2.C 3.A; **B:** 1.B 2.B 3.A
4.A; **C:** 1.B 2.A; **D:** 1. Answers
will vary. 2. Answers will vary.

Unit 7
Getting Ideas and Narrowing Your Topic
pp. 26–27

1.A	2.D	3.D	4.B	5.C
6.B	7.A	8.D		

Unit 8
Formulating Questions
pp. 28–29

1.A	2.C	3.B	4.A	5.D
6.B	7.D	8.D	9.A	10.C

Unit 9
Making a Research Statement
pp. 30–31

1.C	2.A	3.C	4.B	5.A
6.C	7.B	8.C	9.C	10.C
11.B	12.B			

Unit 10
Identifying Sources
pp. 32–33

1.B	2.B	3.A	4.C	5.A
6.B	7.A	8.B	9.A	10.B

Unit 11
Comparing Information across Sources
pp. 34–37

1.A	2.B	3.C	4.C	5.C
6.B				

The Third LAP
Language Activity Pages
pp. 38–39

A: 1.C 2.A 3.C; **B:** 1.A 2.A;
C: 1.A 2.A 3.A; **D:** 1. Answers
will vary. 2. Answers will vary.

Unit 12
Taking Notes
pp. 40–43

1.B	2.A	3.C	4.B	5.D
6.C				

Unit 13
Summarizing
pp. 44–45

1.A	2.C	3.A	4.C	5.B

Unit 14
Writing an Outline
pp. 46–47

1.D	2.A	3.B	4.C	5.B
6.A				

Unit 15
Writing Introductory Paragraphs
pp. 48–51

1.A	2.B	3.B	4.A	5.C
6.A	7.B	8.A	9.B	10.B
11.B	12.A	13.A	14.C	

Unit 16
Writing Supporting Paragraphs
pp. 52–53

1.A	2.B	3.A	4.C	5.A
6.A	7.A	8.C		

Unit 17
Writing Concluding Paragraphs
pp. 54–57

1.A	2.A	3.A	4.B	5.A
6.A	7.B	8.B	9.A	10.B
11.B	12.A	13.B	14.B	

Unit 18
Writing a Bibliography
pp. 58–61

1.B	2.B	3.D	4.B	5.D
6.C	7.C	8.A	9.B	10.A

The Last LAP
Language Activity Pages
pp. 62–63

A: 1.C 2.A 3.B 4.C; **B:** 1.B;
C: B; **D:** 1. Answers will vary.
2. Answers will vary.

Unit 1
Getting Ideas and Narrowing a Topic
pp. 6–7

1.D	2.C	3.D	4.B	5.C
6.A	7.C	8.B	9.B	10.D

Unit 2
Formulating Questions
pp. 8–9

1.B	2.C	3.D	4.B	5.D
6.B	7.A	8.C	9.D	10.D
11.C	12.D			

Unit 3
Making a Research Statement
pp. 10–11

1.B	2.C	3.A	4.C	5.A
6.A	7.A	8.B	9.C	10.A
11.C	12.B			

Unit 4
Finding Information
pp. 12–13

1.B	2.A	3.A	4.C	5.A
6.B	7.C	8.C	9.A	10.A
11.B	12.A			

The First LAP
Language Activity Pages
pp. 14–15

A: 1.A 2.B 3.B; **B:** 1.B 2.C
3.C; **C:** 1.B 2.A 3.B;
D: 1. Answers will vary.
2. Answers will vary.

Unit 5
Using a Table of Contents and an Index
pp. 16–17

1.C	2.A	3.B	4.C	5.C
6.D	7.A	8.B	9.B	10.A

Unit 6
Finding Newspaper and Magazine Articles
pp. 18–21

1.D	2.C	3.B	4.B	5.A
6.C	7.A	8.D	9.B	10.D
11.B	12.B	13.C	14.A	15.B
16.D	17.C	18.B		

Unit 7
Key Word Searching
pp. 22–23

1.C	2.A	3.B	4.C	5.C
6.C	7.A	8.B	9.C	10.A
11.B	12.A	13.C	14.B	

Unit 8
Evaluating Web Sites
pp. 24–25

1.A	2.A	3.B	4.B	5.A
6.B	7.B	8.A	9.B	10.A
11.B	12.B	13.B	14.A	15.B
16.B	17.B	18.B		

The Second LAP
Language Activity Pages
pp. 26–27

A: 1.B 2.C 3.A; **B:** 1.A 2.B
3.A 4.B 5.A 6.A; **C:** 1.B 2.C;
D: 1. Answers will vary.
2. Answers will vary.

Unit 9
Reading Graphs and Charts
pp. 28–31

1.B	2.C	3.D	4.B	5.D
6.B	7.D	8.B	9.C	10.B
11.C	12.B	13.C	14.A	15.D
16.B				

Unit 10
Comparing Information across Sources
pp. 32–35

1.B	2.C	3.A	4.C	5.A
6.B	7.A	8.C		

Unit 11
Taking Notes
pp. 36–39

1.A	2.B	3.C	4.A	5.A
6.C	7.D	8.A		

Unit 12
Summarizing
pp. 40–41

1.B	2.C	3.C	4.A

Unit 13
Writing an Outline
pp. 42–45

1.C	2.A	3.C	4.B	5.D
6.B	7.A	8.D	9.B	10.C
11.D	12.B	13.A	14.C	

The Third LAP
Language Activity Pages
pp. 46–47

A: 1.C 2.A 3.A 4.A; **B:** 1.A;
C: C; **D:** 1. Answers will vary.
2. Answers will vary.

Unit 14
Writing Introductory Paragraphs
pp. 48–49

1.B	2.B	3.A	4.A	5.B
6.A				

Unit 15
Writing Supporting Paragraphs
pp. 50–51

1.B	2.A	3.B	4.A	5.C
6.B	7.A	8.B	9.C	10.C

Unit 16
In-Text Citations
pp. 52–55

1.B	2.C	3.A	4.B	5.A
6.B	7.A	8.B	9.C	10.B
11.A	12.B	13.C	14.A	15.B
16.B	17.C	18.A		

Unit 17
Writing Concluding Paragraphs
pp. 56–57

1.A	2.B	3.B	4.A	5.B
6.B				

Unit 18
Writing a Bibliography
pp. 58–61

1.C	2.B	3.A	4.D	5.B
6.D	7.A	8.A	9.B	10.D
11.D	12.B	13.B	14.D	15.C

The Last LAP
Language Activity Pages
pp. 62–63

A: 1.A 2.C 3.C; **B:** 1.C 2.B;
C: C; **D:** 1. Answers will vary.
2. Answers will vary.

Unit 1
Getting Ideas and Narrowing a Topic
pp. 6–7

1.D 2.B 3.A 4.C 5.B
6.C 7.A 8.D 9.C 10.D
11.B 12.A

Unit 2
Formulating Questions
pp. 8–9

1.A 2.B 3.C 4.D 5.D
6.C 7.D 8.A 9.D 10.B
11.A 12.C

Unit 3
Making a Research Statement
pp. 10–11

1.C 2.A 3.B 4.A 5.C
6.A 7.B 8.C 9.A 10.A
11.C 12.B

Unit 4
Finding Information
pp. 12–13

1.B 2.A 3.C 4.A 5.C
6.B 7.B 8.B 9.B 10.B
11.A 12.B 13.C 14.B 15.B
16.A 17.B 18.A

The First LAP
Language Activity Pages
pp. 14–15

A: 1.B 2.A 3.B; **B:** 1.B 2.A
3.D; **C:** 1.B 2.A 3.C;
D: 1. Answers will vary.
2. Answers will vary.

Unit 5
Using an Atlas
pp. 16–19

1.B 2.C 3.C 4.A 5.D
6.C 7.D 8.C 9.C 10.D
11.B 12.A 13.B 14.B

Unit 6
Finding Newspaper and Magazine Articles
pp. 20–23

1.B 2.D 3.D 4.C 5.C
6.A 7.A 8.C 9.D 10.B
11.D 12.A 13.C 14.D 15.C
16.B

Unit 7
Key Word Searching
pp. 24–25

1.A 2.B 3.A 4.C 5.B
6.A 7.C 8.B 9.B 10.A
11.B 12.B

Unit 8
Evaluating Web Sites
pp. 26–29

1.A 2.B 3.A 4.A 5.B
6.B 7.A 8.B 9.A 10.B
11.A 12.B 13.A 14.A 15.B
16.B 17.A 18.A 19.A 20.B
21.A 22.B 23.B 24.A 25.B
26.A 27.A 28.A

Unit 9
Reading Graphs and Charts
pp. 30–33

1.D 2.C 3.A 4.C 5.B
6.A 7.D 8.C 9.A 10.B
11.C 12.B 13.C 14.D 15.B
16.C 17.D 18.A

The Second LAP
Language Activity Pages
pp. 34–35

A: 1.B 2.C 3.C 4.D; **B:** 1.D
2.C 3.A 4.B 5.E; **C:** 1.C 2.A;
D: 1. Answers will vary.
2. Answers will vary.

Unit 10
Comparing Sources
pp. 36–39

1.C 2.A 3.B 4.C 5.B
6.C 7.A 8.B

Unit 11
Taking Notes
pp. 40–41

1.B 2.C 3.D 4.D

Unit 12
Summarizing
pp. 42–43

1.A 2.B 3.B 4.A

Unit 13
Writing an Outline
pp. 44–47

1.B 2.D 3.A 4.C 5.B
6.B 7.C 8.B 9.D 10.C
11.A 12.D 13.B 14.A

The Third LAP
Language Activity Pages
pp. 48–49

A: 1. taking notes 2. summary
3. paraphrase 4. outline;
B: B. environmental substances;
B,3. pesticides; C,2. X-rays;
II. treatment; **C:** 1.C 2.B;
D: 1. Answers will vary.
2. Answers will vary.

Unit 14
Writing Introductory Paragraphs
pp. 50–51

1.B 2.C 3.B 4.A 5.B

Unit 15
Writing Supporting Paragraphs
pp. 52–53

1.A 2.C 3.B 4.A 5.B
6.C 7.B 8.A

Unit 16
In-Text Citations
pp. 54–57

1.B 2.A 3.C 4.B 5.C
6.A 7.B 8.A 9.B 10.A
11.B 12.C 13.A 14.C 15.B
16.C

Unit 17
Writing Concluding Paragraphs
pp. 58–59

1.A 2.A 3.B 4.A 5.B
6.A

Unit 18
Writing a Bibliography
pp. 60–61

1.D 2.B 3.A 4.D 5.B

The Last LAP
Language Activity Pages
pp. 62–63

A: 1.C 2.A 3.E 4.B 5.D;
B: 1.A 2.A; **C:** 1.B 2.A;
D: 1. Answers will vary.
2. Answers will vary.

Unit 1
Getting Ideas and Narrowing Your Topic
pp. 6–7

1.D   2.B   3.B   4.A   5.B
6.D   7.B   8.C   9.A   10.D
11.A   12.B

Unit 2
Formulating Questions
pp. 8–9

1.A   2.D   3.A   4.B   5.D
6.B   7.C   8.C   9.D   10.D
11.A   12.B

Unit 3
Making a Research Statement
pp. 10–11

1.B   2.A   3.C   4.B   5.A
6.C   7.B   8.A   9.C   10.B
11.A   12.B

Unit 4
Finding Information
pp. 12–13

1.B   2.B   3.A   4.C   5.A
6.B   7.C   8.B   9.A   10.A
11.A   12.C   13.B   14.A   15.A
16.C   17.B   18.B

The First LAP
Language Activity Pages
pp. 14–15

A: 1.B   2.A   3.C; **B:** 1.B   2.C
3.A   4.B; **C:** 1.B   2.A   3.B;
D: 1. Answers will vary.
2. Answers will vary.

Unit 5
Using an Atlas
pp. 16–19

1.B   2.A   3.C   4.B   5.C
6.B   7.D   8.A   9.C   10.C
11.C   12.D   13.B   14.B   15.C

Unit 6
Finding Newspaper and Magazine Articles
pp. 20–23

1.C   2.A   3.B   4.D   5.C
6.A   7.C   8.B   9.A   10.D
11.C   12.B   13.C   14.C

Unit 7
Key Word Searching
pp. 24–25

1.C   2.A   3.C   4.A   5.C
6.B   7.A   8.C   9.B   10.A
11.B   12.B

Unit 8
Evaluating Web Sites
pp. 26–29

1.B   2.A   3.B   4.A   5.B
6.B   7.B   8.A   9.A   10.B
11.A   12.B   13.A   14.B   15.B
16.A   17.B   18.A   19.B   20.B
21.A   22.B   23.B   24.A   25.B
26.A   27.B   28.A   29.A   30.A

Unit 9
Reading Graphs and Charts
pp. 30–33

1.B   2.A   3.D   4.C   5.B
6.D   7.A   8.D   9.A   10.D
11.D   12.A   13.D   14.B   15.D
16.B

The Second LAP
Language Activity Pages
pp. 34–35

A: 1.D   2.C   3.C   4.B; **B:** 1.C
2.B   3.A   4.E   5.D; **C:** 1.C   2.A;
D: 1. Answers will vary.
2. Answers will vary.

Unit 10
Comparing Sources
pp. 36–39

1.C   2.B   3.C   4.A   5.B
6.A   7.A   8.A

Unit 11
Taking Notes
pp. 40–41

1.C   2.D   3.A   4.B

Unit 12
Summarizing
pp. 42–43

1.A   2.B   3.A   4.A

Unit 13
Writing an Outline
pp. 44–47

1.B   2.D   3.A   4.C   5.B
6.A   7.B   8.D   9.C   10.C
11.B   12.D   13.A   14.A

The Third LAP
Language Activity Pages
pp. 48–49

A: 1.A   2.A   3.C; **B:** A, 1, a. for all skiers; A, 2, b. go down hill and use ramp; go as fast as possible; B, 1. downhill; B, 2, a. shorter course than downhill; **C:** 1.B   2.C;
D: 1. Answers will vary.
2. Answers will vary.

Unit 14
Writing Introductory Paragraphs
pp. 50–51

1.C   2.A   3.C   4.C   5.A

Unit 15
Writing Supporting Paragraphs
pp. 52–53

1.A   2.B   3.C   4.C   5.A
6.C   7.A   8.B

Unit 16
In-Text Citations
pp. 54–57

1.B   2.A   3.B   4.C   5.A
6.C   7.A   8.A   9.B   10.C
11.B   12.A   13.B   14.B   15.B
16.C

Unit 17
Writing Concluding Paragraphs
pp. 58–59

1.A   2.B   3.A   4.B   5.B
6.A

Unit 18
Writing a Bibliography
pp. 60–61

1.B   2.A   3.B   4.C   5.B

The Last LAP
Language Activity Pages
pp. 62–63

A: 1.B   2.C   3.A; **B:** 1.A   2.A;
C: 1.B   2.B; **D:** 1. Answers will vary.   2. Answers will vary.

Specific Skill Series
for Language Arts

ANSWER KEYS

for
Placement Tests

Form X

Primary
pp. 6–17

1.B	2.A	3.B	4.B	5.A
6.A	7.A	8.B	9.A	10.A
11.A	12.B	13.B	14.B	15.B
16.C	17.B	18.C	19.C	20.A
21.B	22.A	23.C	24.C	25.A
26.C	27.C	28.B	29.A	30.A
31.B	32.B	33.B	34.B	35.A
36.B	37.A	38.D	39.C	40.B
41.C	42.B	43.C	44.C	45.A
46.B	47.A	48.C	49.C	50.A
51.B	52.C	53.A	54.A	55.B
56.C	57.C	58.B	59.C	60.C
61.B	62.B	63.A	64.C	65.B
66.A	67.B	68.C	69.A	70.B
71.B	72.A	73.A	74.B	75.B

Form X

Intermediate
pp. 18–29

1.A	2.D	3.C	4.C	5.A
6.B	7.B	8.D	9.A	10.D
11.B	12.C	13.C	14.D	15.A
16.B	17.A	18.B	19.A	20.B
21.B	22.B	23.C	24.B	25.B
26.C	27.A	28.B	29.C	30.A
31.B	32.B	33.A	34.B	35.B
36.A	37.A	38.B	39.A	40.A
41.B	42.A	43.A	44.B	45.A
46.B	47.B	48.B	49.A	50.C
51.C	52.B	53.D	54.C	55.B
56.D	57.A	58.B	59.C	60.A
61.A	62.B	63.A	64.A	65.A
66.B	67.B	68.A	69.A	70.C
71.D	72.A	73.B	74.C	75.B
76.C	77.C	78.B	79.D	80.C
81.A	82.B	83.B	84.B	85.A
86.A	87.B	88.B	89.A	90.A
91.B	92.A	93.B	94.A	95.A
96.B	97.A	98.D	99.D	100.B
101.B	102.C	103.C	104.C	105.A

Form X

Advanced
pp. 30–37

1.C	2.A	3.B	4.A	5.A
6.C	7.A	8.B	9.B	10.A
11.B	12.B	13.B	14.A	15.B
16.A	17.A	18.B	19.B	20.A
21.A	22.B	23.B	24.A	25.A
26.B	27.B	28.A	29.A	30.A
31.A	32.A	33.B	34.C	35.C
36.A	37.C	38.A	39.A	40.B
41.B	42.B	43.A	44.A	45.A
46.B	47.B	48.A	49.B	50.B
51.B	52.B	53.A	54.B	55.B
56.B	57.B	58.A	59.A	60.B
61.A	62.B	63.A	64.B	65.A
66.B	67.B	68.A	69.C	70.C
71.B	72.A	73.B	74.A	75.B
76.D	77.D	78.B		

Form Y

Primary
pp. 40–51

1.B	2.A	3.B	4.A	5.B
6.B	7.A	8.A	9.B	10.A
11.B	12.A	13.A	14.A	15.A
16.B	17.B	18.A	19.C	20.B
21.C	22.A	23.A	24.B	25.A
26.B	27.B	28.B	29.A	30.B
31.A	32.B	33.A	34.A	35.B
36.B	37.B	38.C	39.A	40.B
41.B	42.D	43.A	44.C	45.B
46.B	47.A	48.A	49.A	50.B
51.A	52.B	53.B	54.B	55.A
56.C	57.B	58.A	59.A	60.A
61.C	62.C	63.B	64.C	65.D
66.C	67.C	68.A	69.B	70.A
71.C	72.D	73.B	74.C	

Form Y

Intermediate
pp. 52–63

1.A	2.A	3.A	4.A	5.B
6.A	7.A	8.B	9.B	10.A
11.B	12.C	13.D	14.C	15.A
16.D	17.B	18.A	19.B	20.A
21.A	22.B	23.B	24.A	25.A
26.B	27.C	28.B	29.A	30.B
31.B	32.D	33.C	34.C	35.B
36.A	37.A	38.C	39.C	40.B
41.A	42.B	43.A	44.B	45.A
46.B	47.B	48.A	49.B	50.A
51.B	52.A	53.B	54.B	55.A
56.B	57.B	58.A	59.B	60.A
61.B	62.A	63.C	64.C	65.A
66.B	67.B	68.A	69.C	70.C
71.A	72.D	73.D	74.A	75.C
76.B	77.D	78.A	79.B	80.A
81.B	82.C	83.B	84.A	85.B
86.A	87.B	88.B	89.A	90.B
91.A	92.A	93.B	94.A	95.A
96.B	97.A	98.B	99.C	100.C
101.D	102.A	103.B	104.A	105.B
106.A				

Form Y

Advanced
pp. 64–71

1.A	2.C	3.C	4.B	5.E
6.C	7.E	8.A	9.B	10.A
11.C	12.B	13.B	14.A	15.C
16.B	17.B	18.A	19.B	20.B
21.B	22.A	23.A	24.A	25.B
26.A	27.B	28.A	29.A	30.A
31.B	32.B	33.A	34.B	35.A
36.B	37.A	38.B	39.A	40.A
41.A	42.B	43.B	44.A	45.B
46.A	47.A	48.B	49.B	50.A
51.B	52.A	53.A	54.B	55.B
56.A	57.C	58.A	59.A	60.A
61.C	62.B	63.B	64.B	65.A
66.A				

Form X

Primary
pp. 6–17

1.A	2.B	3.A	4.A	5.B
6.B	7.A	8.B	9.B	10.A
11.B	12.B	13.A	14.B	15.B
16.B	17.A	18.B	19.A	20.B
21.A	22.A	23.A	24.B	25.A
26.A	27.B	28.A	29.A	30.A
31.B	32.B	33.A	34.B	35.B
36.A	37.B	38.A	39.A	40.A
41.B	42.A	43.B	44.B	45.C
46.C	47.C	48.B	49.B	50.B
51.A	52.A	53.B	54.B	55.A
56.B	57.A	58.A	59.B	60.B
61.A	62.B	63.A	64.B	65.B
66.B	67.A	68.B	69.C	70.B
71.C	72.A	73.B	74.B	75.A
76.B	77.A	78.A		

Form X

Intermediate
pp. 18–29

1.A	2.B	3.A	4.A	5.A
6.B	7.A	8.B	9.A	10.A
11.B	12.A	13.C	14.C	15.C
16.A	17.B	18.A	19.B	20.A
21.B	22.B	23.B	24.A	25.B
26.B	27.A	28.B	29.A	30.A
31.B	32.B	33.B	34.B	35.B
36.B	37.C	38.B	39.A	40.A
41.C	42.A	43.B	44.A	45.B
46.A	47.B	48.A	49.B	50.B
51.A	52.A	53.B	54.C	55.A
56.A	57.B	58.C	59.B	60.A
61.C	62.B	63.B	64.A	65.B
66.A	67.A	68.B	69.A	70.B
71.B	72.B	73.A	74.B	75.A
76.B	77.A	78.B	79.A	80.B
81.B	82.A	83.A	84.B	85.A
86.B	87.B	88.A	89.B	90.A
91.B	92.B	93.A	94.A	95.B
96.A	97.B	98.A	99.A	100.B
101.B	102.A	103.B	104.A	105.B
106.A	107.A	108.B	109.A	110.B
111.A	112.B	113.B	114.B	115.B
116.B				

Form X

Advanced
pp. 30–37

1.B	2.A	3.C	4.A	5.A
6.C	7.B	8.A	9.B	10.B
11.C	12.A	13.B	14.A	15.C
16.A	17.B	18.C	19.C	20.A
21.B	22.C	23.C	24.A	25.A
26.C	27.B	28.A	29.B	30.A
31.A	32.B	33.A	34.B	35.A
36.B	37.B	38.A	39.A	40.A
41.A	42.B	43.A	44.A	45.B
46.B	47.B	48.B	49.A	50.A
51.C	52.A	53.B	54.B	55.A
56.A	57.B	58.A	59.B	60.A
61.B	62.B	63.B	64.B	65.B
66.C	67.A	68.B	69.C	70.A
71.C	72.C			

Form Y

Primary
pp. 40–51

1.A	2.A	3.B	4.A	5.B
6.B	7.B	8.A	9.B	10.A
11.B	12.B	13.A	14.B	15.B
16.A	17.A	18.A	19.A	20.B
21.B	22.A	23.B	24.A	25.A
26.B	27.A	28.B	29.A	30.B
31.A	32.B	33.B	34.A	35.A
36.B	37.A	38.B	39.A	40.B
41.A	42.A	43.B	44.A	45.A
46.B	47.A	48.B	49.A	50.B
51.B	52.A	53.A	54.B	55.A
56.A	57.B	58.A	59.B	60.B
61.B	62.A	63.A	64.B	65.B
66.A	67.B	68.A	69.B	70.B
71.A	72.B	73.A	74.B	75.B
76.A	77.B	78.B	79.A	80.A
81.B	82.A	83.A	84.B	85.B
86.A				

Form Y

Intermediate
pp. 52–63

1.C	2.C	3.B	4.A	5.C
6.B	7.A	8.C	9.B	10.A
11.B	12.A	13.A	14.B	15.B
16.B	17.A	18.B	19.C	20.A
21.B	22.A	23.A	24.B	25.C
26.B	27.B	28.B	29.A	30.B
31.B	32.A	33.B	34.B	35.B
36.B	37.B	38.A	39.B	40.B
41.A	42.A	43.B	44.A	45.B
46.A	47.B	48.A	49.B	50.B
51.B	52.A	53.B	54.A	55.A
56.B	57.A	58.B	59.A	60.C
61.A	62.C	63.C	64.B	65.B
66.A	67.A	68.B	69.A	70.B
71.B	72.B	73.A	74.B	75.B
76.A	77.A	78.B	79.B	80.A
81.A	82.A	83.B	84.B	85.B
86.A	87.A	88.B	89.B	90.B
91.B	92.A	93.B	94.A	95.B
96.B	97.B	98.A	99.B	100.B
101.A	102.A	103.A	104.B	105.B
106.A	107.A	108.A	109.B	110.B
111.B	112.B	113.A	114.B	

Form Y

Advanced
pp. 64–71

1.B	2.A	3.B	4.C	5.B
6.A	7.A	8.B	9.B	10.A
11.B	12.C	13.C	14.A	15.C
16.B	17.A	18.B	19.A	20.C
21.A	22.B	23.C	24.A	25.A
26.B	27.A	28.A	29.B	30.B
31.A	32.A	33.B	34.A	35.B
36.B	37.A	38.A	39.B	40.C
41.A	42.B	43.C	44.A	45.B
46.B	47.B	48.C	49.C	50.A
51.B	52.C	53.A	54.A	55.B
56.A	57.A	58.A	59.A	60.A
61.B	62.B	63.B	64.A	65.B
66.B	67.B	68.B	69.B	70.A
71.B	72.B			

Form X

Primary
pp. 6–17

1.C	2.A	3.B	4.C	5.B
6.A	7.B	8.B	9.B	10.A
11.B	12.A	13.B	14.B	15.B
16.B	17.A	18.A	19.C	20.B
21.B	22.A	23.B	24.A	25.A
26.A	27.B	28.B	29.A	30.B
31.A	32.B	33.A	34.B	35.B
36.C	37.B	38.A	39.C	40.C
41.C	42.B	43.B	44.D	45.C
46.A	47.A	48.B	49.A	50.C
51.D	52.C	53.B	54.C	55.A
56.C	57.A	58.B	59.B	60.A
61.C	62.B			

Form X

Intermediate
pp. 18–29

1.B	2.A	3.B	4.C	5.D
6.A	7.A	8.C	9.B	10.D
11.C	12.B	13.A	14.B	15.B
16.C	17.C	18.B	19.A	20.B
21.A	22.A	23.A	24.B	25.A
26.B	27.B	28.A	29.B	30.A
31.C	32.A	33.D	34.C	35.C
36.B	37.A	38.C	39.D	40.B
41.B	42.B	43.A	44.A	45.C
46.C	47.B	48.A	49.C	50.A
51.C	52.B	53.A	54.C	55.B
56.C	57.A	58.A	59.B	60.B
61.C	62.A	63.A	64.B	65.C
66.D	67.C	68.C	69.A	70.B
71.A	72.D	73.A	74.B	75.C
76.C	77.C	78.A	79.B	80.C
81.A	82.B	83.B	84.A	85.C
86.A	87.A	88.C	89.C	90.C

Form X

Advanced
pp. 30–37

1.A	2.A	3.C	4.C	5.C
6.A	7.B	8.B	9.C	10.C
11.A	12.A	13.C	14.B	15.C
16.B	17.B	18.B	19.C	20.C
21.A	22.B	23.D	24.B	25.B
26.C	27.D	28.B	29.C	30.C
31.B	32.B	33.B	34.A	35.D
36.C	37.A	38.C	39.C	40.A
41.C	42.A	43.B	44.A	45.C
46.C	47.B	48.C	49.C	50.A
51.B	52.B	53.A	54.A	55.C
56.C	57.C	58.A	59.C	60.B

Form Y

Primary
pp. 40–51

1.B	2.A	3.C	4.B	5.A
6.B	7.A	8.B	9.A	10.A
11.A	12.B	13.A	14.B	15.B
16.A	17.B	18.B	19.A	20.C
21.B	22.B	23.B	24.B	25.A
26.A	27.B	28.A	29.B	30.B
31.A	32.B	33.B	34.A	35.A
36.B	37.B	38.A	39.C	40.C
41.B	42.B	43.B	44.C	45.B
46.A	47.A	48.B	49.A	50.C
51.A	52.D	53.A	54.B	55.C
56.A	57.B	58.C	59.C	60.B

Form Y

Intermediate
pp. 52–63

1.B	2.C	3.C	4.D	5.C
6.C	7.C	8.A	9.C	10.A
11.D	12.B	13.C	14.A	15.C
16.B	17.A	18.B	19.A	20.B
21.A	22.B	23.B	24.B	25.A
26.B	27.A	28.B	29.A	30.B
31.C	32.D	33.B	34.A	35.D
36.C	37.A	38.C	39.C	40.B
41.C	42.A	43.B	44.B	45.A
46.C	47.B	48.A	49.B	50.C
51.C	52.C	53.B	54.C	55.C
56.A	57.A	58.C	59.B	60.C
61.D	62.B	63.A	64.A	65.D
66.C	67.B	68.D	69.B	70.A
71.C	72.A	73.C	74.C	75.B
76.C	77.A	78.B	79.B	80.C
81.A	82.A	83.B	84.B	85.B
86.C	87.A	88.B		

Form Y

Advanced
pp. 64–71

1.C	2.B	3.C	4.D	5.C
6.B	7.D	8.D	9.C	10.C
11.B	12.C	13.A	14.A	15.B
16.C	17.C	18.A	19.B	20.B
21.A	22.D	23.B	24.A	25.D
26.A	27.D	28.A	29.A	30.C
31.D	32.D	33.A	34.B	35.A
36.A	37.C	38.A	39.C	40.A
41.A	42.C	43.B	44.A	45.C
46.B	47.A	48.C	49.C	50.B
51.A	52.B			

Form X

Primary
pp. 6–17

1.B	2.A	3.C	4.B	5.A
6.A	7.A	8.B	9.B	10.A
11.B	12.E	13.C	14.D	15.B
16.A	17.B	18.B	19.A	20.A
21.B	22.B	23.B	24.C	25.A
26.B	27.C	28.A	29.A	30.B
31.A	32.A	33.B	34.B	35.B
36.A	37.C	38.A	39.B	40.C
41.A	42.B	43.A	44.B	45.A
46.B	47.A	48.C	49.B	50.B
51.A	52.C	53.B	54.C	55.A
56.B	57.A	58.C	59.C	60.B
61.B	62.A	63.B	64.C	65.A
66.C	67.A	68.B	69.A	70.C
71.A	72.B	73.C	74.B	75.B
76.B				

Form X

Intermediate
pp. 18–29

1.C	2.A	3.B	4.C	5.A
6.D	7.A	8.C	9.B	10.C
11.A	12.C	13.D	14.B	15.B
16.D	17.C	18.D	19.A	20.B
21.A	22.B	23.A	24.A	25.B
26.B	27.A	28.A	29.B	30.B
31.A	32.A	33.B	34.A	35.A
36.A	37.C	38.B	39.D	40.B
41.A	42.D	43.C	44.B	45.D
46.A	47.B	48.B	49.B	50.B
51.A	52.A	53.B	54.A	55.A
56.B	57.A	58.A	59.B	60.A
61.B	62.B	63.B	64.A	65.B
66.B	67.B	68.A	69.B	70.A
71.B	72.B	73.A	74.B	75.B
76.A	77.B	78.B	79.C	80.B
81.B	82.D	83.A	84.C	85.A
86.D	87.A	88.B	89.C	90.D
91.B	92.A	93.A	94.B	95.B
96.A	97.B	98.B	99.A	100.A
101.A	102.B	103.A	104.A	105.B
106.B	107.A	108.B	109.B	110.B
111.A	112.A	113.B	114.A	115.A
116.C	117.B	118.D	119.A	120.B
121.A	122.B	123.A	124.B	125.B
126.A				

Form X

Advanced
pp. 30–37

1.A	2.A	3.A	4.A	5.B
6.B	7.B	8.B	9.B	10.A
11.B	12.C	13.C	14.B	15.B
16.A	17.C	18.A	19.C	20.B
21.A	22.B	23.A	24.B	25.B
26.A	27.B	28.B	29.C	30.A
31.B	32.B	33.B	34.A	35.A
36.B	37.B	38.B	39.A	40.A
41.B	42.B	43.A	44.B	45.A
46.A	47.B	48.B	49.B	50.A
51.A	52.B	53.A	54.C	55.B
56.A	57.C	58.B	59.A	60.C
61.C	62.A	63.C	64.B	65.A
66.A	67.B	68.B	69.A	70.B
71.B	72.A	73.B	74.A	75.A
76.B	77.B	78.A	79.A	80.A
81.A	82.B	83.B	84.A	85.B
86.A	87.C	88.B		

Form Y

Primary
pp. 40–51

1.A	2.C	3.B	4.B	5.A
6.B	7.A	8.A	9.B	10.B
11.A	12.B	13.E	14.B	15.D
16.C	17.A	18.B	19.A	20.B
21.B	22.B	23.A	24.C	25.B
26.B	27.A	28.A	29.B	30.C
31.A	32.A	33.B	34.A	35.B
36.A	37.B	38.C	39.B	40.A
41.B	42.C	43.A	44.A	45.B
46.A	47.A	48.B	49.A	50.B
51.A	52.C	53.C	54.B	55.B
56.A	57.C	58.A	59.B	60.A
61.C	62.B	63.B	64.A	65.C
66.B	67.A	68.A	69.C	70.B
71.A	72.B	73.C	74.A	75.B
76.A	77.A	78.C	79.B	80.A
81.A	82.C	83.B	84.C	

Form Y

Intermediate
pp. 52–63

1.B	2.C	3.B	4.D	5.D
6.A	7.A	8.C	9.A	10.C
11.B	12.D	13.B	14.A	15.C
16.A	17.A	18.B	19.B	20.B
21.A	22.B	23.A	24.B	25.B
26.A	27.B	28.A	29.B	30.A
31.A	32.B	33.A	34.C	35.B
36.D	37.B	38.A	39.D	40.D
41.B	42.B	43.A	44.B	45.B
46.B	47.A	48.A	49.B	50.A
51.B	52.C	53.A	54.D	55.B
56.B	57.C	58.C	59.B	60.D
61.B	62.B	63.B	64.A	65.A
66.B	67.B	68.A	69.D	70.B
71.C	72.A	73.C	74.D	75.A
76.C	77.C	78.B	79.A	80.B
81.B	82.C	83.A	84.C	85.C
86.B	87.B	88.A	89.C	90.B
91.A	92.B	93.A	94.A	95.A
96.B	97.B	98.B	99.A	100.B
101.A	102.C	103.A	104.A	105.B
106.A	107.B	108.C	109.A	110.C
111.C	112.D			

Form Y

Advanced
pp. 64–71

1.B	2.C	3.C	4.B	5.A
6.C	7.C	8.C	9.B	10.B
11.C	12.C	13.B	14.A	15.C
16.C	17.A	18.C	19.B	20.C
21.A	22.B	23.A	24.B	25.B
26.A	27.A	28.B	29.A	30.B
31.A	32.A	33.A	34.C	35.B
36.B	37.C	38.A	39.C	40.C
41.A	42.C	43.B	44.C	45.B
46.B	47.A	48.B	49.B	50.B
51.A	52.A	53.A	54.C	55.B
56.A	57.C	58.C	59.A	60.B
61.A	62.B	63.B	64.B	65.A
66.B	67.A	68.B	69.B	70.B
71.B	72.A	73.A	74.A	75.B
76.B	77.B	78.A	79.B	80.B

Form X

Primary
pp. 6–17

1.C	2.B	3.C	4.A	5.C
6.E	7.A	8.B	9.F	10.D
11.A	12.E	13.B	14.C	15.D
16.D	17.C	18.A	19.B	20.A
21.A	22.B	23.B	24.A	25.B
26.B	27.A	28.B	29.A	30.A
31.A	32.B	33.B	34.B	35.A
36.A	37.B	38.A	39.B	40.A
41.B	42.A	43.A	44.A	45.B
46.C	47.B	48.C	49.A	50.B
51.A	52.A	53.B	54.B	55.A
56.A	57.A	58.C	59.B	60.A
61.C	62.B	63.A	64.A	65.B
66.B	67.A	68.A	69.B	70.A

Form X

Intermediate
pp. 18–29

1.A	2.A	3.B	4.A	5.A
6.B	7.B	8.A	9.B	10.A
11.B	12.A	13.A	14.B	15.A
16.A	17.B	18.A	19.A	20.B
21.A	22.A	23.B	24.B	25.A
26.B	27.A	28.A	29.A	30.B
31.A	32.C	33.A	34.C	35.B
36.B	37.B	38.D	39.B	40.A
41.C	42.D	43.A	44.B	45.A
46.B	47.B	48.A	49.B	50.B
51.B	52.B	53.A	54.B	55.B
56.A	57.A	58.B	59.B	60.A
61.B	62.B	63.A	64.B	65.B
66.B	67.A	68.A	69.B	70.B
71.A	72.B	73.A	74.A	75.B
76.A	77.A	78.B	79.B	80.B
81.B	82.A	83.B	84.A	85.B
86.A	87.A	88.A	89.C	90.C
91.C	92.A	93.C	94.C	95.C
96.B	97.A	98.B	99.A	100.C

Form X

Advanced
pp. 30–37

1.C	2.A	3.A	4.B	5.A
6.C	7.B	8.C	9.A	10.B
11.B	12.A	13.B	14.B	15.A
16.A	17.A	18.B	19.A	20.C
21.A	22.D	23.B	24.C	25.A
26.B	27.D	28.C	29.A	30.C
31.B	32.A	33.B	34.C	35.B
36.A	37.A	38.A	39.A	40.B
41.D	42.B	43.D	44.A	45.B
46.A	47.B	48.D	49.B	50.C
51.B	52.A	53.B	54.B	55.B
56.A	57.A	58.A	59.B	60.B
61.B	62.A	63.A	64.A	65.B
66.B	67.A	68.A	69.B	70.A
71.B	72.B	73.B	74.B	75.A

Form Y

Primary
pp. 40–51

1.B	2.C	3.A	4.B	5.D
6.A	7.C	8.F	9.E	10.B
11.B	12.D	13.C	14.A	15.E
16.C	17.B	18.D	19.A	20.B
21.B	22.B	23.A	24.B	25.B
26.B	27.A	28.B	29.B	30.A
31.A	32.B	33.B	34.B	35.A
36.A	37.A	38.B	39.A	40.A
41.B	42.A	43.B	44.A	45.B
46.B	47.B	48.A	49.C	50.B
51.A	52.C	53.A	54.B	55.C
56.B	57.A	58.B	59.A	60.A
61.C	62.B	63.C	64.A	65.B
66.C	67.A	68.B	69.A	70.A
71.A	72.B			

Form Y

Intermediate
pp. 52–63

1.A	2.B	3.B	4.A	5.A
6.B	7.B	8.A	9.A	10.B
11.A	12.A	13.A	14.A	15.B
16.B	17.B	18.A	19.A	20.B
21.A	22.A	23.B	24.A	25.A
26.B	27.C	28.B	29.A	30.B
31.C	32.A	33.C	34.A	35.B
36.C	37.A	38.B	39.B	40.A
41.C	42.C	43.B	44.B	45.A
46.B	47.A	48.B	49.B	50.B
51.B	52.A	53.A	54.B	55.A
56.B	57.A	58.A	59.B	60.A
61.B	62.A	63.A	64.B	65.A
66.A	67.B	68.B	69.B	70.A
71.B	72.A	73.A	74.B	75.A
76.A	77.A	78.B	79.A	80.B
81.B	82.A	83.B	84.A	85.A
86.A	87.A	88.A	89.A	90.B
91.A	92.B	93.C	94.A	95.B
96.A	97.C	98.A	99.B	100.C

Form Y

Advanced
pp. 64–71

1.A	2.A	3.B	4.B	5.A
6.A	7.B	8.A	9.B	10.B
11.A	12.A	13.B	14.A	15.B
16.A	17.B	18.A	19.B	20.A
21.A	22.A	23.A	24.B	25.A
26.C	27.A	28.B	29.B	30.A
31.C	32.A	33.B	34.A	35.B
36.A	37.A	38.A	39.B	40.B
41.A	42.C	43.C	44.B	45.A
46.B	47.C	48.B	49.A	50.B
51.A	52.B	53.A	54.B	55.B
56.A	57.A	58.B	59.A	60.A
61.B	62.A	63.B	64.B	65.A
66.A	67.A	68.B	69.A	70.B
71.A	72.B	73.B	74.A	

Form X

Primary
pp. 6–17

1.C	2.H	3.A	4.D	5.G
6.F	7.E	8.B	9.B	10.B
11.A	12.A	13.C	14.B	15.A
16.C	17.A	18.B	19.B	20.B
21.B	22.A	23.A	24.B	25.B
26.A	27.B	28.A	29.A	30.B
31.B	32.C	33.C	34.B	35.A
36.B	37.B	38.A	39.C	40.C
41.A	42.C	43.A	44.B	45.B
46.A	47.B	48.C	49.A	50.A
51.D	52.B	53.C	54.D	55.A
56.B	57.A	58.C	59.D	60.A
61.D	62.B	63.B	64.D	65.B
66.D	67.A	68.B	69.C	70.A
71.B	72.D	73.B	74.A	75.C
76.B	77.B	78.A	79.A	80.B
81.A	82.B	83.A	84.B	85.A

Form X

Intermediate
pp. 18–29

1.B	2.A	3.B	4.C	5.A
6.A	7.B	8.A	9.A	10.C
11.B	12.A	13.A	14.B	15.A
16.B	17.A	18.A	19.B	20.A
21.B	22.A	23.B	24.C	25.A
26.B	27.A	28.B	29.C	30.B
31.A	32.C	33.A	34.B	35.A
36.A	37.B	38.B	39.A	40.A
41.A	42.A	43.A	44.B	45.C
46.B	47.A	48.C	49.C	50.B
51.B	52.C	53.A	54.C	55.B
56.A	57.B	58.C	59.A	60.C
61.A	62.B	63.C	64.B	65.B
66.B	67.A	68.B	69.B	70.A

Form X

Advanced
pp. 30–37

1.B	2.B	3.C	4.B	5.A
6.B	7.A	8.A	9.B	10.B
11.A	12.A	13.B	14.C	15.A
16.C	17.A	18.A	19.A	20.B
21.B	22.B	23.B	24.A	25.A
26.A	27.C	28.C	29.A	30.A
31.B	32.A	33.A	34.B	35.B
36.B	37.B	38.A	39.A	40.A
41.B	42.B	43.C	44.A	45.B

Form Y

Primary
pp. 40–51

1.D	2.A	3.G	4.C	5.B
6.E	7.F	8.H	9.A	10.B
11.A	12.A	13.B	14.C	15.B
16.A	17.C	18.C	19.B	20.A
21.C	22.A	23.B	24.B	25.A
26.B	27.A	28.A	29.B	30.A
31.B	32.B	33.A	34.C	35.B
36.A	37.A	38.B	39.C	40.A
41.A	42.B	43.A	44.B	45.A
46.A	47.B	48.A	49.A	50.A
51.C	52.D	53.C	54.B	55.D
56.B	57.A	58.C	59.D	60.D
61.B	62.A	63.C	64.D	65.B
66.C	67.A	68.B	69.C	70.B
71.D	72.A	73.D	74.C	75.B
76.C	77.B	78.B	79.B	80.A
81.A	82.B	83.A	84.A	85.B
86.B	87.A	88.A		

Form Y

Intermediate
pp. 52–63

1.D	2.C	3.B	4.D	5.A
6.C	7.B	8.A	9.D	10.B
11.A	12.C	13.B	14.C	15.A
16.B	17.B	18.B	19.A	20.A
21.B	22.B	23.A	24.A	25.C
26.B	27.A	28.B	29.C	30.A
31.C	32.C	33.B	34.B	35.B
36.B	37.B	38.B	39.A	40.B
41.B	42.A	43.B	44.B	45.A
46.A	47.A	48.C	49.A	50.B
51.B	52.A	53.C	54.B	55.C
56.B	57.A	58.B	59.C	60.B
61.A	62.C	63.B	64.B	65.B
66.A	67.B	68.B		

Form Y

Advanced
pp. 64–71

1.A	2.A	3.A	4.B	5.A
6.A	7.B	8.B	9.B	10.A
11.C	12.B	13.C	14.A	15.B
16.B	17.B	18.A	19.B	20.A
21.B	22.B	23.B	24.A	25.A
26.A	27.B	28.B	29.A	30.A
31.B	32.C	33.A	34.B	35.A
36.A	37.B	38.A	39.A	40.B
41.B	42.B	43.B	44.A	45.A
46.B				

Form X

Primary
pp. 6–17

1.A	2.A	3.B	4.B	5.C
6.A	7.C	8.B	9.A	10.D
11.C	12.A	13.B	14.C	15.C
16.B	17.C	18.B	19.D	20.C
21.B	22.B	23.A	24.A	25.B
26.B	27.A	28.A	29.C	30.C
31.B	32.C	33.A	34.B	35.A
36.A	37.B	38.B	39.A	40.B

Form X

Intermediate
pp. 18–29

1.B	2.A	3.A	4.C	5.A
6.C	7.A	8.B	9.A	10.A
11.B	12.A	13.C	14.D	15.A
16.B	17.B	18.B	19.B	20.B
21.A	22.C	23.B	24.A	25.A
26.C	27.B	28.B	29.D	30.A
31.B	32.C	33.B	34.C	35.A
36.B	37.C	38.A	39.A	40.C
41.A	42.B			

Form X

Advanced
pp. 30–37

1.B	2.A	3.A	4.B	5.B
6.E	7.D	8.C	9.B	10.C
11.A	12.A	13.A	14.A	15.C
16.B	17.B	18.B	19.B	20.B
21.A	22.D	23.C	24.C	25.B

Form Y

Primary
pp. 40–51

1.A	2.B	3.B	4.C	5.A
6.B	7.C	8.A	9.B	10.D
11.C	12.A	13.A	14.B	15.C
16.B	17.B	18.C	19.D	20.B
21.B	22.A	23.A	24.C	25.A
26.A	27.C	28.A	29.A	30.B
31.A	32.A	33.B	34.B	35.B
36.A	37.A	38.B		

Form Y

Intermediate
pp. 52–63

1.B	2.A	3.B	4.A	5.B
6.C	7.B	8.C	9.A	10.A
11.C	12.A	13.B	14.D	15.C
16.C	17.A	18.A	19.A	20.B
21.B	22.C	23.C	24.A	25.B
26.C	27.A	28.C	29.D	30.C
31.A	32.D	33.C	34.A	35.B
36.B	37.C	38.B	39.B	40.A
41.C	42.A	43.B	44.B	

Form Y

Advanced
pp. 64–71

1.B	2.B	3.A	4.C	5.A
6.C	7.E	8.C	9.A	10.B
11.A	12.C	13.B	14.C	15.B
16.A	17.A	18.B	19.B	20.A
21.B	22.A	23.C	24.B	25.A

Form X

Primary
pp. 6–17

1.A	2.B	3.B	4.A	5.B
6.B	7.A	8.A	9.B	10.A
11.B	12.A	13.B	14.A	15.B
16.B	17.B	18.A	19.B	20.A
21.A	22.B	23.B	24.B	25.A
26.C	27.A	28.B	29.A	30.B
31.A	32.B	33.B	34.A	35.C
36.B				

Form X

Intermediate
pp. 18–29

1.C	2.C	3.C	4.C	5.B
6.C	7.B	8.B	9.C	10.B
11.A	12.C	13.B	14.A	15.A
16.B	17.C	18.C	19.A	20.C
21.C	22.A	23.B	24.C	25.B
26.A	27.B	28.C	29.A	30.A
31.B	32.A	33.B	34.C	35.C
36.A	37.C	38.B	39.A	40.A
41.A	42.A	43.B	44.C	

Form X

Advanced
pp. 30–37

1.B	2.B	3.A	4.C	5.B
6.C	7.C	8.A	9.A	10.B
11.C	12.B	13.C	14.A	15.B
16.C	17.A	18.A	19.B	20.C

Form Y

Primary
pp. 40–51

1.A	2.A	3.B	4.A	5.A
6.A	7.B	8.A	9.B	10.A
11.A	12.A	13.A	14.B	15.A
16.A	17.B	18.A	19.B	20.B
21.B	22.B	23.A	24.A	25.B
26.A	27.C	28.C	29.B	30.A
31.B	32.B	33.A	34.B	35.B

Form Y

Intermediate
pp. 52–63

1.A	2.A	3.B	4.C	5.B
6.A	7.C	8.C	9.B	10.A
11.B	12.C	13.B	14.A	15.A
16.B	17.C	18.A	19.C	20.B
21.C	22.B	23.A	24.A	25.C
26.A	27.B	28.C	29.B	30.C
31.B	32.B	33.C	34.A	35.B
36.C	37.B	38.C	39.B	40.B
41.C	42.A	43.C	44.B	

Form Y

Advanced
pp. 64–71

1.A	2.B	3.A	4.C	5.B
6.B	7.A	8.C	9.C	10.C
11.B	12.A	13.B	14.A	15.C
16.A	17.A	18.C	19.A	20.C
21.B	22.B			

▰▰▰ Form X ▰▰▰
Primary
pp. 6–17

1.B	2.C	3.A	4.C	5.C
6.C	7.A	8.A	9.B	10.C
11.A	12.B	13.B	14.C	15.A
16.C	17.D	18.A	19.D	20.A
21.B	22.A	23.B	24.A	25.A
26.B	27.A	28.B	29.D	30.B
31.A	32.B	33.B	34.B	35.D
36.A	37.B	38.C	39.B	40.B
41.A	42.C	43.A	44.A	45.B
46.A	47.B	48.A	49.C	50.A
51.B	52.C			

▰▰▰ Form X ▰▰▰
Intermediate
pp. 18–29

1.C	2.B	3.A	4.A	5.B
6.D	7.B	8.B	9.A	10.C
11.A	12.A	13.B	14.B	15.A
16.B	17.C	18.B	19.C	20.B
21.D	22.A	23.B	24.C	25.C
26.A	27.C	28.B	29.A	30.B
31.A	32.B	33.B	34.B	35.B
36.A	37.B	38.B	39.C	40.D
41.B	42.D	43.B	44.C	45.A
46.C	47.A	48.B	49.C	50.A
51.B	52.A	53.B	54.A	55.B

▰▰▰ Form X ▰▰▰
Advanced
pp. 30–37

1.B	2.D	3.D	4.C	5.C
6.A	7.A	8.B	9.A	10.B
11.A	12.B	13.A	14.B	15.A
16.B	17.A	18.B	19.D	20.B
21.C	22.A	23.D	24.A	25.B
26.B	27.A	28.C	29.B	30.A
31.C	32.B	33.A	34.C	35.B
36.A	37.B	38.C	39.C	40.A

▰▰▰ Form Y ▰▰▰
Primary
pp. 40–51

1.A	2.C	3.C	4.B	5.B
6.C	7.B	8.A	9.A	10.B
11.A	12.C	13.A	14.B	15.C
16.A	17.B	18.C	19.A	20.B
21.B	22.A	23.A	24.A	25.A
26.C	27.B	28.D	29.A	30.B
31.B	32.A	33.B	34.B	35.D
36.D	37.B	38.A	39.C	40.B
41.A	42.C	43.C	44.A	45.A
46.C	47.C	48.B	49.A	50.C

▰▰▰ Form Y ▰▰▰
Intermediate
pp. 52–63

1.A	2.C	3.C	4.B	5.D
6.B	7.C	8.C	9.C	10.A
11.C	12.B	13.C	14.B	15.C
16.C	17.A	18.C	19.C	20.A
21.D	22.D	23.B	24.B	25.A
26.C	27.B	28.C	29.C	30.C
31.B	32.B	33.A	34.C	35.B
36.A	37.B	38.B	39.A	40.C
41.D	42.D	43.C	44.D	45.A
46.A	47.B	48.C	49.A	50.C
51.B	52.C	53.B	54.A	55.B
56.C	57.A	58.B	59.B	60.C

▰▰▰ Form Y ▰▰▰
Advanced
pp. 64–71

1.C	2.D	3.B	4.D	5.A
6.C	7.D	8.C	9.B	10.A
11.B	12.B	13.A	14.B	15.A
16.A	17.A	18.A	19.B	20.C
21.B	22.B	23.C	24.C	25.D
26.D	27.A	28.A	29.B	30.A
31.C	32.B	33.A	34.B	35.A
36.A	37.B	38.A	39.B	40.A
41.B	42.B	43.A	44.B	45.B

Specific Skill Series
for Language Arts

Student Worksheets and Student Record Sheets

Name_____ Level _____

Date _____ Unit _____

- ❑ Grammar
- ❑ Spelling
- ❑ Paragraphs
- ❑ Usage
- ❑ Vocabulary
- ❑ Writing Process
- ❑ Mechanics
- ❑ Sentences
- ❑ Research

1._____	16._____	31._____	46._____
2._____	17._____	32._____	47._____
3._____	18._____	33._____	48._____
4._____	19._____	34._____	49._____
5._____	20._____	35._____	50._____
6._____	21._____	36._____	51._____
7._____	22._____	37._____	52._____
8._____	23._____	38._____	53._____
9._____	24._____	39._____	54._____
10._____	25._____	40._____	55._____
11._____	26._____	41._____	56._____
12._____	27._____	42._____	57._____
13._____	28._____	43._____	58._____
14._____	29._____	44._____	59._____
15._____	30._____	45._____	60._____

Use the back of this worksheet if you need more space.

LAPs _____

_____

_____

Name_____ Level _____

Date _____ Unit _____

❑ Grammar   ❑ Usage   ❑ Mechanics
❑ Spelling   ❑ Vocabulary   ❑ Sentences
❑ Paragraphs   ❑ Writing Process   ❑ Research

1._____	16._____	31._____	46._____	61._____	76._____
2._____	17._____	32._____	47._____	62._____	77._____
3._____	18._____	33._____	48._____	63._____	78._____
4._____	19._____	34._____	49._____	64._____	79._____
5._____	20._____	35._____	50._____	65._____	80._____
6._____	21._____	36._____	51._____	66._____	81._____
7._____	22._____	37._____	52._____	67._____	82._____
8._____	23._____	38._____	53._____	68._____	83._____
9._____	24._____	39._____	54._____	69._____	84._____
10._____	25._____	40._____	55._____	70._____	85._____
11._____	26._____	41._____	56._____	71._____	86._____
12._____	27._____	42._____	57._____	72._____	87._____
13._____	28._____	43._____	58._____	73._____	88._____
14._____	29._____	44._____	59._____	74._____	89._____
15._____	30._____	45._____	60._____	75._____	90._____

Use the back of this worksheet if you need more space.

LAPs _____

_____

_____

_____

_____

Specific Skill Series Student Record Sheet

Name _____

Unit	Grammar		Usage		Mechanics		Spelling		Vocabulary	
	Date Completed	Score	Date Completed	Score	Date Completed	Score	Date Completed	Score	Date Completed	Score
1										
2										
3										
4										
5										
6										
7										
8										
9										
10										
11										
12										
13										
14										
15										
16										
17										
18										
19										
20										
21										

Specific Skill Series Student Record Sheet

Name _____

Unit	Sentences		Paragraphs		Writing Process		Research	
	Date Completed	Score	Date Completed	Score	Date Completed	Score	Date Completed	Score
1								
2								
3								
4								
5								
6								
7								
8								
9								
10								
11								
12								
13								
14								
15								
16								
17								
18